IN THE STRUGGLE

In the Struggle

Scholars and the Fight against Industrial
Agribusiness in California

Daniel J. O'Connell and Scott J. Peters

NEW VILLAGE PRESS • NEW YORK

Published in the United States by New Village Press
bookorders@newvillagepress.net
www.newvillagepress.org
New Village Press is a public-benefit, nonprofit publisher
Distributed by NYU Press

Library of Congress Cataloging-in-Publication Data
Names: O'Connell, Daniel J. (Executive director of Central Valley Partnership) author. | Peters, Scott J. (Scott Joseph), author.
Title: In the struggle : politically engaged scholarship in the San Joaquin Valley of California / Daniel J. O'Connell and Scott J. Peters.
Description: First edition. | New York : New Village Press, [2021] | Includes bibliographical references and index. | Summary: "From the early twentieth century and across generations to the present, In the Struggle brings together the stories of eight politically engaged scholars, documenting their opposition to industrial-scale agribusiness in California. As the narrative unfolds, their previously censored and suppressed research, together with personal accounts of intimidation and subterfuge, is introduced into the public arena for the first time. In the Struggle lays out historic, subterranean confrontations over water rights, labor organizing, and the corruption of democratic principles and public institutions. As California's rural economy increasingly consolidates into the hands of land barons and corporations, the scholars' work shifts from analyzing problems and formulating research methods to organizing resistance and building community power. Throughout their engagement, they face intense political blowback as powerful economic interests work to pollute and undermine scientific inquiry and the civic purposes of public universities. The findings and the pressure put upon the work of these scholars-Paul Taylor, Ernesto Galarza, and Isao Fujimoto among them-are a damning indictment of the greed and corruption that flourish under industrial-scale agriculture. After almost a century of empirical evidence and published research, a definitive finding becomes clear: land consolidation and economic monopoly are fundamentally detrimental to democracy and the well-being of rural societies"— Provided by publisher.
Identifiers: LCCN 2020051065 (print) | LCCN 2020051066 (ebook) | ISBN 9781613321225 (paperback) | ISBN 9781613321232 (hardback) | ISBN 9781613321249 (ebook)
Subjects: LCSH: Agricultural industries—California—San Joaquin Valley. | Water rights—California—San Joaquin Valley. | Labor unions—Organizing—California—San Joaquin Valley.
Classification: LCC HD9000.9.U6 C56 2021 (print) | LCC HD9000.9.U6 (ebook) | DDC 338.109794/8—dc23
LC record available at https://lccn.loc.gov/2020051065
LC ebook record available at https://lccn.loc.gov/2020051066
Publication Date: July 2021
First Edition

Cover photo: Ernesto Galarza. Courtesy of Occidental College Special Collections and College Archives, People Files, Ernesto Galarza.

CONTENTS

This book aims to be useful, like a guidebook, as it maps a battlefield arcing across four generations of organizing and research.

Its stories and findings lay out a history of engagement with scholars positioned as political actors on fields of struggle. Across time, they inform and teach. They show us how to fight—and what's worth fighting for.

In solidarity and succession, they collaborated and learned together, deploying knowledge into theaters of action. Each picking up the work of their predecessors, their lessons course together—tributaries to a deepening river flowing into our present moment of possibility. Compiled here, this collective journey is a roadmap that lays out tactics of organizing and refines theories of engagement.

Today, as battles continue, we benefit from their shared lessons and experience. Use them in preparation, as Paul Taylor advised, to "study your targets."

Follow lines of inquiry until you have answers, apply new findings, and advance.

Remember, contests over truth are wars of attrition.

Introduction

In August of 2011, I completed my doctoral dissertation at Cornell University. The study emerged from a decade-long search for more effective ways to make political change as a scholar.

Primarily a narrative history, the dissertation analyzed the work of social scientists who questioned the effects of industrial agriculture on rural society in California's Central Valley over the last century. It took years to bring the story into focus, and then more to flesh it out.

In December of 2011, a few months after completing my degree, I emailed Scott Peters (previously chair of my dissertation committee) from Belgium where I was visiting family.

Scott,

I have been meaning to send you an email, and after a week settling in over here am finally getting around to it.

It has been a period of transition at work. I have left Sequoia Riverlands Trust to start at American Farmland Trust as their representative in the San Joaquin Valley.

The new job will likely give me latitude to write. I will not be in a set office, and I plan on taking ethnographic research notes while working (hoping that I can use the material later). The position is ideal for publishing our coming work.

Regarding our book—I have been giving it much thought. The going has been slow, due in some measure to my personality, which painstakingly enters into projects slowly and then builds more and more momentum. This has been frustrating to say the least!

Recently, I gave the dissertation to an old Tulare farmer (Ray Melikian, a WWII fighter pilot, and father-in-law to another friend and farmer). His feedback was: "Every farmer should read this book." I have been soliciting feedback from others as well.

Before I left, I gave my first presentation (mostly on Taylor, Gold-schmidt, and the Arvin-Dinuba study) to a valley audience—the Unitarian Universalist Fellowship asked me to give it as a "sermon." They were also interested and enthusiastic.

Recently in Montreal, I gave a similar presentation at Goldschmidt's AAA [American Anthropological Association] memorial seminar hosted by Paul Durrenberger and Kendall Thu. Again, the reaction of the audience seemed good. (Kendall and Paul have since asked if I would contribute a chapter to a book they want to put together on Goldschmidt).

I will let you know how progress goes and try to get something to you by the New Year.

Have a wonderful Christmas!

Daniel

Years earlier, Scott had been the first to encourage my application to Cornell and offered funding for a research assistantship. From the start, he continually secured the space from which I grew.

We slowly invested in each other's increasingly aligned projects: his work within the national system of land-grant colleges and universities to strengthen the system's public purposes and democratic values; and my own search to find a more powerful role for scholars' work in the world.

Upon completing my degree, our collaboration continued. I had known early on that my doctoral research (already structured in narrative) needed to be made even more accessible, translated away from the academy for everyday use.

My dissertation was an artifact of credentialed knowledge, a weapon to be wielded in certain circumstances, but its findings were always meant to be applied back into actual campaigns. A book was the easiest way to convey its lessons.

Our hope is that succeeding generations within and beyond the academy will join and extend the work.

* * *

We designed this book as a mosaic narrative told by the people who lived its history. Piece by piece, each of its scholars contributes to a quilted storyline that becomes defined as we step back to see it as a whole. Distinctly, over time and from differing perspectives, an overarching story becomes clear through their testimonies.

The scholars' findings and the pressure put upon their work are a damning indictment of the greed and corruption that flourish under California's system of industrial agriculture. After almost a century of empirical evidence and published research, a definitive finding becomes clear: economic monopoly and land consolidation are fundamentally detrimental to agrarian democracy and the well-being of rural societies. In establishing this truth, we also witness what was previously unseen, off stage and behind the curtain: powerful agribusiness interests in the state actively undermined, threatened, and attacked critically-oriented inquiry into and research on California's dominant agricultural system.

Eight narrators guide us through their research, teachings, and experiences in the following chapters—Walter Goldschmidt, Paul Taylor, Ernesto Galarza, Dean MacCannell, Don Villarejo, Isao Fujimoto, Trudy Wischemann, and Janaki Jagannath. Their chapters are compiled from their published papers, books, oral histories, interviews, and correspondence. We have assembled this bricolage of stories into a distilled account of their hard-won lessons, with each chapter a distinctive saga of its own, embedded in a larger drama linking them all together. Almost a century of sustained research and activism is condensed here, not only in statistical datasets or empirical measures, but through accounts of intimidation and subterfuge. The story of their trials illuminates the significance and validity of their findings.

We begin in Chapter 1 with Walter Goldschmidt, who was in his 90s when I had the opportunity to first visit him. The focus of the chapter is the Arvin-Dinuba case study, which Goldschmidt conducted for the United States government in 1944 to determine the implications for implementing the Reclamation Act of 1902 in California's San Joaquin Valley. The law mandated that water infrastructure projects, including the building of dams and canals, support small family-owned farms rather than large landholdings owned by land barons and corporations. Though pressured and intimidated while conducting his study, Goldschmidt's research was completed and clearly illustrated the negative effects of industrial-scale agriculture on community well-being. It was censored immediately, and a follow-up study was suppressed, forcing him to defend his findings. These were eventually compiled and published in his book, *As You Sow: Three Studies in the Social Consequences of Agribusiness.*[1] The story of this early research is our entryway to understanding the unabated corruption associated with the large-scale agribusiness in the valley.

While Goldschmidt and his Arvin-Dinuba study are now relatively well-known, fewer people are aware of Paul Taylor. As I burrowed into *As You Sow*'s history, it became apparent that Taylor's work not only guided Goldschmidt, but all of the scholars I chronicled in my doctoral study. Moreover, he influenced the politics of agriculture in the United States. He was instrumental in bringing federal aid to Dust Bowl refugees, and initiated far-reaching research into farm labor, including some of the first academic studies focused on the plight of immigrant Mexican farmworkers. He held uncompromised commitments in support of the family farm and against industrial agribusiness. Chronologically, then, we step back in Chapter 2, which opens with Taylor leading a battalion of Marines at Belleau Wood in the First World War. This scene from the battlefront foreshadowed the intensity of the contest he soon waded into as he confronted California's empire of industrial agriculture at the height of its influence. He was intimately joined in this cause—fighting for agrarian democracy—by his wife and partner, the photographer Dorothea Lange.

If there is one outlier in our early history of politically engaged scholarship in the valley (comprised as it is of already unconventional personalities), it is Ernesto Galarza. At the same time, he may be the model for work still before us. Even as a young child he was already working as a farmworker, and therefore uniquely positioned by first-hand experiences that calloused his bearing with added fortitude, tenacity, and toughness. Galarza held no misconceptions of the system's fairness, nor doubts of his opponent's strengths. Methodically, he spent years in preparation for battle. After graduate training at both Stanford and Columbia universities, Galarza did not take a position as a professor. Instead, he worked as an organizer and researcher with a farm labor union. From that position, he leveraged his academic training and combined it with his intimate knowledge of Mexican culture and farmworkers' lived experience. Openly, he named his objective: to overturn the power structure of California, which he began by attacking its agribusiness foundations. In Chapter 3, we witness these battles. Advances were made, but with sacrifice. Most strategic was the dismantling of the Bracero program of federally imported farm labor from Mexico, an accomplishment that contributed to the early successes of the United Farm Workers union.

After Chapter 3, our narrative jumps forward into the next generation of scholars. Whereas Goldschmidt, Taylor, and Galarza endured McCarthy-era harassment in a reactionary political environment, the next group of scholars arrived as the 1960s social movements convulsed college campuses and society at large. Two of them, Isao Fujimoto and Dean MacCannell, were among the first rural sociologists hired by the University of California. Both came from Cornell's Rural Sociology Department, which seeded UC Davis's new department of Applied Behavioral Studies—a haven of student activism on campus. A third scholar, Don Villarejo, chose a separate course of action, aligned with Fujimoto and MacCannell but independent from their institutional constraints. Knowing the history of stonewalling that had occurred in California's universities, he built a non-profit organization into a research institute. The resulting California Institute for Rural Studies, often allied with labor unions, utilized "research for action" as a method to mobilize rural communities.

In Chapter 4, we hear Dean MacCannell's testimony as he "retests" what has widely become known as the Goldschmidt hypothesis. Having been suppressed for three decades, the retest finally proceeded under MacCannell, who used regression statistics as his primary method. This research was set within yet another politically charged historical moment when community groups and scholars were pushing to implement reclamation law as the final segments of the Central Valley Project—the region's gargantuan water infrastructure development of dams and canals—was built out on the west side of the valley. Like those before him, MacCannell again experienced the intensity of agribusiness influence on his scientific research and findings. Threats and intimidation were constants as powerful stakeholders from the valley pressured MacCannell and the UC Davis administration. Regardless of the pressure, he conducted multiple studies. All of them substantiated Goldschmidt's original findings from the 1940s. Even with conclusive findings in hand, however, no significant progress was made to mitigate the negative effects of industrial agriculture nor in halting the strengthening political power of corporate agribusiness.

Aware of past political limitations imposed on research into California's agricultural system and rural society by the university and government, Don Villarejo positioned his innovative work literally on the edge of institutions. The California Institute of Rural Studies (CIRS), which he helped initiate and then lead, was physically located only a few blocks from the UC Davis campus. In many respects, CIRS became the state's rural sociology department. Perhaps because of the need to raise its own funds, and the independence this afforded, CIRS also evolved into a nimble and flexible institution for research and engagement as it allied with labor unions and immigrant communities in the valley. In Chapter 5, Villarejo interrogates industrialized agriculture, naming culprits and dispelling myths, through action research.

In many respects, my own evolution as a scholar began with Isao Fujimoto. And I am but one of many students who continue to work in the spirit of his life and values. Raised on the Yakima Indian reservation, and interred with his Japanese family during World War II, Isao became the father of movements as an influential instructor over fifty years at the University of California at Davis. His "war stories" not only illustrate the politics of the valley, but also the prejudice that confronted many scholars from immigrant backgrounds or racialized communities who entered universities in the 70s and 80s as professors. A close personal friend and mentor, Chapter 6 shows Isao's influence, even on this book, through our correspondence and his counsel while I conducted my doctoral study.

Moving into the present day, we bring forward the voices of two women to conclude the narrative. The discrimination women faced (and continue to confront) in higher education during the twentieth century inordinately weighted the early history of valley research toward men. We close the book with the profiles of Trudy Wischemann and Janaki Jagannath, who enhance the narrative as the enormous contributions of women come into focus as they increasingly lead movements toward justice, equity, and empowerment in the region today.

Trudy Wischemann personally knew or worked with five of the six scholars from my original study. Unlike these scholars, however, she is the only one who moved to the region to dedicate her life to being a rural advocate. In Chapter 7, she speaks from her Republican upbringing and brings in religion as a framework for engagement. Importantly, she names "the river" as a metaphor for the history of politically engaged scholarship that she has witnessed and participated in firsthand. She takes on differing roles—as a journalist, musician, and preacher—beyond a position narrowly defined as "scholar."

As an emerging scholar, Janaki Jagannath concludes the book in Chapter 8 by speaking from her experience as a community legal worker assisting farmworkers. She represents a diverse emerging movement founded upon intersectional organizing. Not anchored to previous objectives, today's activists, organizers, and scholars are charting their own path by joining global movements for environmental justice, food sovereignty, and agroecology. Janaki is our entryway to the coming uprising.

* * *

As we move forward through the book, each chapter profiles a particular scholar's life and work, largely told through their own voice. The chapters are not meant to be complete biographies, nor is the book a comprehensive history of politically engaged scholarship in the region. We recognize the need for many additional books to illuminate more actors and chapters, expanding the story.

The scholars in this book tell their stories from numerous positions—within farmworker strikes, in legislative testimony, at academic lectures. They give personal testimony of battles fought against formidable opponents as they describe being "baptized by fire," "engaging in struggle," and "going into battle." Once engaged, they fought to advance specific values and principles, often in solidarity with some of the most oppressed communities in our country—farmworkers and farm families recently arrived from distant lands toiling on modern-day plantations. Through their voices, we bring forward and document how publicly funded research into these conditions was pressured, censored, and suppressed at public universities and within the federal government. In doing so, we join these scholars in their work, and its cause.

A broad indictment arises as the narrative unfolds. The scholars' research findings clearly and definitively reveal the negative effects of agribusiness consolidation at the expense of farm laborers, family farms, and society at large. Through their research, industrial agriculture is empirically proven to cause inequality and deprivation, through monopolistic ownership of natural resources, manipulative control of public investment and private capital, and the design of an economy that benefits a handful over the many. While statistics establish facts, the truth and validity of the findings are even more damningly illustrated when paired with the previously untold stories of intimidation, bribery, vindictive litigation, and threats against these scholars' professional positions and personal lives.

The book's scenes play out in multiple settings. Foremost among them are the agricultural fields of California's San Joaquin Valley, sites of historic discrimination, strife, and violence. The Valley is one of the most racially segregated and economically polarized places in the United States. While it is the world's most agriculturally productive region, paradoxically, it also has the highest levels of poverty, pollution, and hunger in the United States.

Hidden under this narrative of despair are the diverse and resilient people of the region. Statistics may document inequity and injustice, but they often fail to capture the nuance and power welling up within particular acts of resistance and opportunity. Movements, aligned with past struggles, are underway today and are breaking through historic structures of oppression.

The stories in this book are like seeds planted in rich alluvial soil on the last days of winter. Voicing them keeps them alive.

May they bloom and fruit abundantly.

* * *

Stories situate our lives and carry truths.

Many are echoes of the past, almost silent, but still resonate within social memory, waiting to be awakened. They offer hope, encouragement, and prophetic wisdom, particularly at times like these when our lives are convulsed by historic crises worsened with corrupt leadership. More troubling, particularly for scholars, is an expanding mistrust of how to articulate shared truths.

The loss of memory robs us of our ability to understand and act—of knowing who we are, where we stand, and what we stand for. As Isao Fujimoto reminds us: *"It is said that if we are going to make any sense of what we are doing, we have to know what story we are in."*

Knowing our stories enables us to imagine and write our future, and to effectively accomplish the work before us.

These stories guide our way forward.

1

Baptism by Fire

WALTER GOLDSCHMIDT

My fieldwork began in the summer of 2006.

Still in the midst of my campus-based coursework, I wanted to have an early look at the southern San Joaquin Valley. A pass-through to feel the ground, establish relationships, and define the questions I wanted to answer.

I was awarded a small dissertation research grant from Cornell's Education Department. It was enough to rent a car and buy food for a month, but not enough for accommodations. I planned to camp out on a farm.

At my desk in the graduate student warren on the fourth floor of Kennedy Hall, I prepared for the visit, reaching out through a network of allies, scholars and organizations. Amid a mental survey of "who to meet," it randomly occurred to me—when had Walter Goldschmidt died? I googled his name. No date.

A rush of excitement, and possibility. Another search of UCLA's anthropology department, then an email address. I paused, amazed that I may have the opportunity to meet him in person.

Moments later, on June 5, 2006, I email him:

Professor Goldschmidt,
I am currently a doctoral student at Cornell in the Education Department. This summer I will be visiting the southern San Joaquin Valley to look into doing ethnographic work regarding issues of inequality and power, specifically relating to water and land.

I have read about you and your work quite often. Isao Fujimoto and others at UC Davis talked of you while I did research toward a master's degree there. Also, here at Cornell, you are mentioned often, sometimes just the word "Goldschmidt" is used to make a point regarding issues of scale in agriculture.

I would be honored to have an opportunity to talk with you about your work, and even the work of Paul Taylor, regarding the Central Valley. (I was a Peace Corps volunteer in Africa and may find your work there interesting as well, though I am not as familiar with it.) Also, I would like any advice you might have on researching in the Valley.

I hope we have an opportunity to meet. I fly into the Bay Area on July 3rd and leave from Southern California on July 31st. Most of the time I will be in Visalia staying at the Visalia Friends (Quaker) Meetinghouse.
Sincerely,
Daniel O'Connell

An hour later, a reply:

Dear Daniel,
I will be glad to meet with you and am delighted that somebody is looking into what is happening. I expect to be here all summer and if you let me know in advance, we can plan a meal together.
Warmest regards,
Walter.

The next day, I emailed some available dates and we scheduled a meeting for July 28th.

Meeting Goldschmidt

After a month in the valley, the drive to Goldschmidt's home was one of contrasts. Passing through Bakersfield in late summer, a dense haze obscured the surrounding mountains.

Just days earlier, I crossed the bottom of Lake Tulare imagining the Serengeti-scale wilderness once present on the landscape. The largest lake west of the Mississippi was gone. Today, an expanse laid out in precise grids of endlessly cultivated, laser-leveled fields worked by house-sized tractors and abused farmworkers. I contemplated such a complete up-ending of an ecosystem, economy, and balance of life, as I climbed the Grapevine heading south to Los Angeles.

Goldschmidt's home was in Brentwood Hills near Bel Air. I drove up the hillside streets, rising above the city. At this first visit, I refrained from taking extensive notes, preferring to get to know him as a person rather than a research subject. After the meeting, however, I jotted the following entry into my fieldnotes:

7/28/06—OBSERVATIONAL NOTES: BRENTWOOD HILLS, LOS ANGELES CA, WALTER GOLDSCHMIDT'S HOUSE (978 NORMAN PLACE)

I arrived a half an hour early at 3:30pm. I had an early start just in case there was traffic. I exited the 405 at Sunset, up Bundy into the hills. I began to realize that Goldschmidt wasn't a poor professor.

The gate was open at the end of a long driveway. The house was quiet in the way an unpeopled house is, weeks of stillness settled into the landscape. Up the garden stairs to the main house. All the doors wide open.

The front door was open too. I called a greeting . . . heard the shower running and decided to wait outside. Walked down to the study. Sat in the garden. Peaceful. A Buddhist-themed study was over the garage next to the swimming pool. The pool was designed to look like a pond, set in brick between the study and the house. The property on a hillside. Waterfalls fell through the gardens feeding a koi pond and swimming pool.

Back at the house, Goldschmidt finished his shower. "Caught me with my pants down," he said. He had on only a pair of shorts, waddling out from the bathroom. Later he would refer to himself as "cherubic" at 93 years old. It was a fairly accurate description. He walked slowly, but he was sharp mentally. Later he mentioned a time when Isao Fujimoto, Dean MacCannell, and Trudy Wischemann were working on putting an article together for the journal *Science*.

After talking in the living room, he asked if I wanted a beer. Our conversations ranged for the next seven hours. He said that he had fallen the night before. He had turned out the light. Evening had come quickly, it was dark and he had to take a piss—"now." He set off for the toilet. "I don't know if the misstep or piss occurred first, but I fell and pissed." We had a long laugh over it. He said he had hoped some television show had filmed his blooper.

It was hot. He asked if I wanted to take a swim. I asked if he minded if I had another beer. "Of course not, and bring one for me." He was unsteady as he walked. It would have been highly precarious if he tried to get into the pool on his own. I helped him in, taking both his hands to get him into the water. I suggested hand rails. He swam back and forth in the small pool. The water was cool. Leaves and pine needles fell into it from the overhanging trees. A waterfall fell into the pool from the shallow end. We talked about Africa.

Later we sat on the deck that surrounded his study. The deck had been painted black the day before, but it was dry. He said that the garden and study were designed by a Japanese guy. He and his wife used to have parties in the garden. Earlier he had asked if I would help him move some things in the study. He had me lay out some carpets on the floor and bring up a small table from the garage.

In the study, there was a large pile of papers with a note saying "for Dan" on top. I hadn't noticed them previously, though he had mentioned that he had some papers for me. Now I realized that he was giving me his files on the Central Valley. They were straightforward, uncluttered by extraneous information (as Dorothea Lange had advised him as a young man)—published articles, a number of correspondences (many with Trudy), newspaper articles, transcripts . . . .

Later in the evening he would mention how research was a process. His work had followed on Taylor, Taylor had followed on John R. Commons. Since he had finished, Isao, Dean MacCannell and others had continued it, particularly Trudy. He was inviting and encouraging. This giving of files (which Chuck Geisler at Cornell also did by loaning his to me) is a special honor an academic opens to a fellow scholar. There is a high degree of trust, camaraderie, respect, and mentoring in the act. It is a passing on of your work and yourself.

We changed into dry clothes. Amy, his Filipino cook who comes on Tuesdays and Fridays (hence the Friday invitation), had arrived. They went back and forth like an old married couple throughout the evening. Later, we barbequed steak. I helped prepare the charcoal in a long metal cylinder with mesh holding the briquettes and newspaper beneath to fire them. Old school.

Sunset through the large trees. We sat in the yard above the pool. Goldschmidt asked if I wanted a whiskey. He had a bottle of Jim Beam.

Up the hill, just above us, was the Getty museum. His backyard fence was the museum's perimeter. "I used to walk the dog up there," pointing up the hill to the museum.

It was a visit filled with drinking, laughter, stories, and remembrances. A mix of many traits: he was charming, refreshingly vulgar, and intellectually challenging, but more than anything a welcoming host. I felt accepted.

There were a few times that I could not help but jot down quotes. After I asked about what Dorothea Lange was like, he told of when she had taken him out to photograph the asparagus harvest. She had also given him advice:

- "Don't fill your files with needless information—she didn't take a picture if it wasn't right."
- "Make taking a picture a non-event. Forget that the camera is there."

Since then I have pondered how her advice related to research: maintain a patient focus on your object over time and treat the research process as everyday work.

Goldschmidt had his opinions (*"There is too much emphasis on competition and conflict, not enough on cooperation"*) and eloquence (*"The community is the echo chamber of the soul"*).

Well into evening, armful of paper in hand, I said good night.

After this first month in the valley and visit with Goldschmidt, I still had not settled on a set of research questions to investigate. I wanted the valley to speak them back to me. What was pertinent *now* for both the local people and academic community? What remained unexplored or needed to be clarified?

Slowly, I was wading into the water—or was I being pulled in. In later years, I realized that in gifting his files to me there came an implicit expectation to continue the work. In any case, I kept a correspondence with him over the direction of my dissertation.

On August 8, 2006, after a series of emails, Goldschmidt wrote to me:

Dear Dan,

Your email of Aug 3 just surfaced in the kitchen midden that covers my desk and I thought it needed a reply. You have a lot of ideas running through your head, any one of which would be good, I am sure. But you need to find a focus and plan your research around it—something specific and clear to you which then you could find a means of tackling in a finite span of time. First of all, forget about what I did more than sixty years ago and don't expect anyone to have heard of it. (They could hardly be expected to remember it!)

Of the suggestions in your letter, I think the more important and politically volatile is to uncover institutional restraints and road-blocks to efforts at local improvement. A comparison might be interesting, but that would be hard to do if you are trying to work along with the group. You must read the studies made on water districts by the guy who was at Claremont and whose name I am blocking on. Ask Trudy; he was one of her heroes.[1] You have to think through the process: what kinds of measures aside from participant observation you are going to use, how you will relate to the community; if it is largely Spanish-speaking, is your Spanish up to the task?

When you have these ducks in a row let me see if I can knock them over.

Good luck,

Walter

His advice to seek the "politically volatile" in identifying "institutional restraints" resonated with me, though I was still determining a precise focus for my study.

That winter, back in Ithaca, I went over Goldschmidt's files. They illustrated that he had never stopped caring about his initial, controversial study in the valley. The letters and correspondence he had saved also pointed my way into understanding how a lineage of scholars collaborated over time.

My fieldnote from that evening read:

1/3/07—REFLECTIVE OBSERVATION

Last night I finished a cursory review of Goldschmidt's papers. I have had them since the summer but let them sit for a while—ruminate and build. Now returning to California, and perhaps meeting with him again, I went over them.

MacCannell stands out in the academic documents. There is an interesting jousting match with Refugio Rochin during an extended court proceeding. They include transcripts of the academic scholars reporting under oath—being examined and cross-examined by lawyers.

Trudy Wischemann sent Goldschmidt numerous letters that illustrate her negotiating higher education. They show a very different perspective as she "feels" her way to and through the problems seen in the Central Valley.

Isao Fujimoto has a couple of pieces in the papers, but isn't represented much in an academic sense. But I know that he had a tremendous impact on the academic community, particularly the students, at Davis.

MacCannell early on recognizes Isao in a preface to some papers and reports, but since Isao was not publishing his findings in academic journals, it is highly difficult to cite his work formally, in a way that the academy and higher education can acknowledge.

Following this entry, I catalogued all of the papers that Goldschmidt had given me. I began to consider the legacy of scholarship in the region in earnest.

Goldschmidt was eager to pass on the story. I sensed how much he did not want it to be forgotten. His famous case study of Arvin and Dinuba was not ready to fade away because its relevance had never waned.

As You Sow

Walter Goldschmidt's *As You Sow* is a landmark work in the field of rural sociology.

The book is relentless, progressing like a long march, pacing off innumerable steps that lead to its conclusions. The empirical evidence stacks and links together, revealing that industrialized agriculture is corrosive to the civic and economic life of rural communities.

From its inception, the study that comprises the core of the book was controversial. No other single piece of research in the valley was as virulently contested over a longer period of time. Powerful interests relentlessly weighed in to hinder, obscure, censor, and suppress its findings.

In retrospect, after almost eighty years, we are now able to look back and assess what happened to the study. Today, Goldschmidt's implicit biblical forewarning—"as you sow, so you shall reap"—has shown itself to be prescient, particularly given the Valley's paradox of extraordinary agricultural production and wealth generation amidst extreme poverty and destitution.

Figure 1.1. Walter Goldschmidt, as a Ph.D. student at UC Berkeley in the 1940s. Courtesy of Mark Goldschmidt.

Goldschmidt studied under Paul Taylor as a graduate student at UC Berkeley, and from 1940 to 1946, he was employed as a staff researcher with USDA's Bureau of Agricultural Economics (BAE).

On May 14, 1940, writing from the Midwest, he mailed an update to Taylor on his then-current work with the BAE:

Dear Paul:

I spent Saturday with Hanson, the Coordinator for the Southern Great Plains area and spent Monday afternoon with Bonnen and Magee. I wish that you and Dorothea could have been present, as a lot of interesting facts were brought out.

Hanson is with us 100 per cent. He understands the problems and sees the solution as we do. He wants me to return to Ark. to take part in a week's school, covering problems of the Great Plains. He will have the local planning committees in from all over the area and wants me to "give 'em the works."

Both Bonnen and Magee were new to the concepts which I presented but they rose to them in a most gratifying way. They are anxious to cooperate in some studies which I proposed and would like very much to have a good Casa Grande demonstration in the High Plains area.

Bonnen was quite worked up over a modern "enclosure movement" which he believes is disemploying men in many sections, faster than the tractor ... [by] putting land back into pasture, letting the tenants go, and then returning cattle on the land. This goes on in connection with consolidation of farms. In one case which he cited, 18 farms, each formerly supporting a family, are now in one large holding under a single-family management, with cattle replacing cotton. He is very much concerned about this situation. Rural schools are being closed down and towns affected by this forced exodus of former tenants. The land owner can make more net money out of cattle than one of tenants. The common saying is "I just can't keep on supporting those tenants."

Grapes of Wrath has made Texas and Okl. very conscious of the migrant problem. Hanson says that the thinking of the local planning committees has expanded astonishingly recently. He feels that they are about ready to follow the ideas which I express in my book. He says that in two or three years the ideas are apt to be a part of their everyday thinking.

I'll be in Little Rock tomorrow and in Washington on Sunday.

Sincerely yours,

Walter[2]

More an organizer than researcher in this early correspondence, Goldschmidt lays out references to the "enclosure movement" and the "consolidation of farms," associating them with the erosion of a democratic ideal. The defense of democracy necessitated contesting economic monopolies that excluded most people from accessing land.

A few months after he wrote this letter, Goldschmidt began his dissertation research. He conducted a holistic study of the small San Joaquin Valley community of Wasco, California. It took eight months to complete. His methods were influenced by Robert and Helen Lynd's research of shifting social and economic dynamics in a small town in the Midwest (published as *Middletown: A Study in Modern American Culture* in 1929 and *Middletown in Transition: A Study in Cultural Conflicts* in 1937). His dissertation work directly informed the design of the Arvin-Dinuba study that he began in the spring of 1944 as a staff researcher with the BAE—research that was purposefully constructed to answer the most controversial questions around reclamation policy in the Central Valley of California.

Here is Goldschmidt explaining his research in the Valley during his March 1, 1972, testimony to the Subcommittee on Monopoly of the Select Committee on Small Business in the United States Senate:

> I am an anthropologist; while still a graduate student I became interested in the possibility of using the techniques and the theories of anthropology for the study of modern American community.
>
> I was supported in my dissertation by a fund made available by M. L. Wilson, then Director of the Extension Service, to the Bureau of Agricultural Economics, U.S.D.A. My study of Wasco, a town in the San Joaquin Valley, was completed in 1941. It served as the dissertation that was required for the Ph.D. degree which I received in 1942 from the University of California, Berkeley, by which time I was on the regular staff of the BAE. This study of Wasco showed that the industrialized farming that characterizes San Joaquin Valley resulted in an urbanized rural life . . .
>
> Shortly after the completion of this study, I was seconded to a task force engaged in research on the Central Valley Project under the general direction of Dr. Marion Clawson, funding for which was provided by the Department of Interior. The Central Valley Project Studies consisted of a collaborative effort to provide answers to a number of basic policy questions resulting from the engineering plans then underway. One of these dealt with the problems attendant upon the so-called acreage limitation law and the implications for the application of that law to lands supplied by waters developed under the giant reclamation project in California. This question read, in part, as follows: What effects will this project have on agricultural economy and rural life in the Central Valley?[3]

The "acreage limitation law" Goldschmidt refers to here is officially called the National Reclamation Act of 1902 (P.L. 57–161, 32 Stat. 388, sometimes called "the Newland Act"). A key provision of the Act was a 160-acre limitation on the supply of inexpensive water to farmers, who also had to be residents. (Farmers with farms larger than 160 acres had access to water, but they had to pay full market price for all water used beyond 160 acres.) Both the acreage limitation and the residency requirement were meant to enshrine in national policy a democratic standard that explicitly supports small, family-scale agriculture as a foundation for an equitable rural society. The Central Valley Project (CVP) that Goldschmidt refers to, which was originally devised in 1933, was (and still is) a water management and development project that includes the construction of dams, canals, and reservoirs. (See Chapter 3 for an extended discussion of the CVP and the Reclamation Act.)

As Goldschmidt noted above, a key policy question he was asked to take up as part of the BAE's Central Valley Project Studies had to do with effects proposed CVP engineering plans might have on economic and cultural life in the Central Valley.[4] To answer this and other related questions, Goldschmidt conducted a case study that compared two towns—Arvin and Dinuba—of similar composition, economic productivity, and demographic size within the same geographic region. The primary difference was that Dinuba was predominantly surrounded by small family farms while Arvin was enveloped by mostly large-scale producers. Goldschmidt understood that the BAE's questions were "amenable to direct empirical investigation" and a research design could be "formulated on strict scientific principles of controlled comparison."[5]

> In each of the two communities we examined public records, interviewed community leaders, and ordinary citizens, and took a questionnaire from a scientifically constructed random sample of the population. This questionnaire was designed to give us the following information: (1) household composition, occupation, nature of farm enterprise (for farm operators) and the like; (2) social participation in community affairs; (3) economic status and participation; and (4) level of living. In addition to the information that I and my team assembled in the field, we had accurate information provided by others on the following items: (1) the limits of the community as determined by a team of rural sociologists, (2) the size of farms by two measures obtained from the records of the Agricultural Adjustment Agency by economists equipped to analyze such data, (3) the total value of agricultural products from the previous year obtained in the same manner and from the same source, and (4) the value of retail sales by major categories of business enterprise obtained from the state sales tax records.[6]

Underlying a straightforward research design was the looming task of implementing and enforcing the acreage limitation and residency requirements of the 1902 Reclamation Act. They were clearly meant to apply to the Central Valley Project, as they already were applied to other areas in the western United States.[7] All farmers with farms larger than the 160-acre limit who signed contracts to receive federal water were obligated to follow the law. As the project's planning and construction began, so too did the awareness (and anxiety in some quarters) arise of enforcing its mandated requirements. The region, under the law, was poised to literally bloom, but not just in crop production. An expansive, voluntary land reform was to follow the water deliveries, promising to more equitably redistribute land across the valley.

What Goldschmidt was not prepared for was the reaction he received when he conducted the study:

> I could regale this Committee beyond its endurance with stories about this public pressure—as for instance our small team (myself and two enumerators, one of whom was my wife) listened to ourselves being vilified on the radio each noon, as we ate our lunch in Dinuba's pleasant little park, by the newscasters sponsored by the Associated Farmers of California.
>
> This regular entertainment was brought to a close only after I took advantage of an equal time provision and answered his charges on radio time paid for by the Associated Farmers themselves. The columnist, Sokolsky, devoted a column to us at least once, the commentator Fulton Lewis, Jr. devoted a half-hour broadcast to us, while the urban presses of San Francisco and Los Angeles (hardly disinterested parties to the issue themselves) made repeated attacks and the conservative agriculture press carried on a constant barrage of complaint about what they called our "dirty rug questionnaire." This was the visible part of the pressure.
>
> You do not have to take my word for this. Twenty years after the study was made, an agricultural historian gave the incident a full, heavily footnoted treatment, which was published in the California Historical Society Quarterly, and which sets forth rather fully the efforts to discredit the work.[8]

Even while doing his fieldwork, Goldschmidt found the results "overwhelming," noting that they "are apparent to the casual visitor and become greater and greater as more information is made available."[9] He determined that the scale of agricultural businesses in Arvin skewed the occupancy structure resulting in the predominance of wage labor.

This led to "direct effects upon the social conditions in the community," including poor housing, poverty, the existence of "slum conditions," and limited capacity to address these problems on a community level.[10]

A highly transitory labor pool with few resources and little time to participate in local civic life resulted from the seasonality of agricultural production and economic consolidation. Arvin's few wealthy large landowners, among them the DiGiorgio Fruit Corporation, were oriented to urban centers away from the rural towns where they owned the land, manipulated resources, and controlled labor. These land baron's lack of residency and outward orientation were found to be a cause of "social poverty."[11]

Here is Goldschmidt continuing with his congressional testimony, drawing from his research findings, which conclusively answered the BAE's research questions:

> The differences between the communities were impressive; they were set forth in my assembly of findings and should perhaps be placed in record here: The small farm community supported 62 separate business establishments, to but 35 in the large-farm community; a ratio in favor of the small-farm community of nearly 2:1.
>
> 1. The volume of retail sales in the small-farm community during the 12 month period analyzed was $4,383,000 as against only $2,535,000 in the large-farm community. Retail trade in the small-farm community was greater by 61 percent.
> 2. The expenditure for household supplies and building equipment was over three times as great in the small-farm community as it was in the large-farm community.
>
> The investigation disclosed other vast differences in the economic and social life of the two communities, and affords strong support for the belief that small farms provide the basis for a richer community life, and a greater sum of those values for which America stands, than do industrialized farms of the usual type.
>
> It was found that—
>
> 1. The small farm supports in the local community a larger number of people per dollar volume of agricultural production than an area devoted to larger-scale enterprises, a difference in its favor of about 20 percent.

2. Notwithstanding their greater numbers, people in the small-farm community have a better average standard of living than those living in the community of large-scale farms.

3. Over half of the breadwinners in the small farm community are independently employed businessmen, persons in white-collar employment, or farmers, in the large-farm community the proportion is less than one-fifth.

4. Less than one-third of the breadwinners in the small-farm community are agricultural wage laborers (characteristically landless, and with low and insecure income) while the proportion of persons in this position reaches the astonishing figure of nearly two-thirds of all persons gainfully employed in large-farm community.

5. Physical facilities for community living—paved streets, sidewalks, garbage disposal, sewage disposal, and other public services—are far greater in the small-farm community; indeed, in the industrial farm community some of these facilities are entirely wanting.

6. Schools are more plentiful and offer broader services in the small-farm community, which is provided with four elementary schools and one high school; the large-farm community has but a single elementary school.

7. The small-farm community is provided with three parks for recreation; the large-farm community has a single playground, loaned by a corporation.

8. The small-farm town has more than twice the number of organizations for civic improvement and social recreation than its large-farm counterpart.

9. Provision for public recreation centers, Boy Scout troops, and similar facilities for enriching the lives of the inhabitants is proportionate in the two communities in the same general way, favoring the small-farm community.

10. The small-farm community supports two newspapers, each with many times the news space carried in the single paper of the industrialized-farm community.

11. Churches bear the ratio of 2:1 between the communities, with the greater number of churches and churchgoers in the small-farm community.

12. Facilities for making decisions on community welfare through local popular elections are available to people in the small-farm community; in the large-farm community such decisions are in the hands of officials of the county.[12]

In these comparisons, Goldschmidt quantified economic and civic conditions of the two towns, then associated the findings to their "strong support for . . . those values for which America stands." But what are those values, and what did the findings mean for realizing them in the region?

The question boils down to this: What economic structure is most conducive to and appropriate for a democracy? The presence of economic inequality in Arvin negatively affected the social and civic life in that community. Its retail economy was dependent on the purchasing power of migrant farmworkers who lacked sufficient resources to sustain a vibrant small business sector. Consumers simply did not have the money to spend in local stores.

Capital in local economies is like blood flowing in a body—it needs to repeatedly circulate. The farmers in Dinuba were small business enterprises themselves. They were entrepreneurial. They spent money and made purchases in town, while in Arvin the farmers took their profits to more distant urban centers. Money hemorrhaged out of Arvin's economy.

Anemic economic growth undermined community development where corporate farming dominated. In these industrial agriculture systems, there was no multiplier effect from small farmers purchasing goods and services within their rural towns. Without a middle class, civic institutions and political structures atrophied.

Goldschmidt described a "continuative effect" where the lack of civic structures, such as a diversity of churches and adequate schooling, reinforced a problematical perception of communities like Arvin. People with the means to choose avoided these communities because they were not seen as secure or thriving places to live and raise a family.

The Goldschmidt hypothesis clearly linked these damaging effects to large-scale farming. A key finding from *As You Sow* was:

Large-scale farm operation is immediately seen to take an important part in the creation of the conditions found in Arvin. Its direct causative effect is to create a community made up [of] a few persons of high economic position, and a mass of individuals whose economic status and whose security and stability are low, and who are economically dependent directly on the few. In the framework of American culture, more particularly that of industrialized farming, this immediately creates a situation where community participation and leadership, economic well-being, and business activities are relatively impoverished.[13]

Goldschmidt found that communities like Arvin resembled "company towns."[14] Other scholars documented similar trends in research they conducted on economic concentration in small manufacturing communities. Cities with bases of small businesses provided foundations for a sounder, more balanced economic life than ones dominated by corporate monopoly.[15]

Following the original study, subsequent research confirmed Goldschmidt's original conclusions. In 1942, Paul Wallace Gates' examination of land policy in the western United States found that large landholders retarded the development of community institutions including libraries and churches.[16] By 1977, the Small Farm Viability Project revisited Arvin and Dinuba to conduct a re-test of the original study and reconfirmed the original findings.[17] Numerous other studies and academic papers have since validated, supported, or substantiated Goldschmidt's conclusions. William Heffernan later summarized that "all relevant research to date suggests that a corporate type of agriculture results in a reduction in the quality of life for at least some people, especially the hired workers in rural communities."[18]

The logic and significance of what is now referred to as "the Goldschmidt hypothesis" resonated beyond academic circles. Wendell Berry made almost identical observations as Goldschmidt:

In rural communities dominated by very large firms, the settlement and housing patterns reflect the increasingly transient nature of the labor force. The symbol of the large corporate farm becomes the trailer house. Community institutions suffer from lack of leadership, and from the lack of a sense of commitment on the part of the labor force to long-run community welfare. Those institutions that survive take on a dependent character reflecting the paternalistic role of the dominant firms. Income levels may stabilize, but at the expense of a

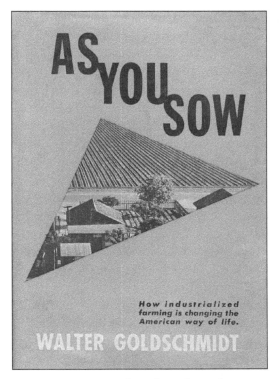

Figure 1.2. *As You Sow*, first edition dust jacket, 1947.
Courtesy of Mark Goldschmidt.

decline in local capacity for risk-taking, decision-making, and investment of family labor in farms and local businesses.[19]

The Arvin-Dinuba findings were clear: an economy skewed to benefit
corporate agriculture with its consolidated landholdings had profoundly
negative outcomes for the rural residents living in nearby towns and
communities.[20]

. . . So You Shall Reap

Goldschmidt's Arvin-Dinuba study was fiercely attacked, primarily
because it reinforced the significance of the 1902 Reclamation Act's acreage limitation and residency requirements.

An April 1947 *Business Week* article found the Arvin-Dinuba study to be "one of the heaviest pieces of artillery that they have added to their arsenal in years," noting it would be used "as a weapon to keep the big farmers thirsty."[21] Paul Taylor later recognized that for "friends of the family-size farm" the study was useful "as a weapon of resistance."[22]

Goldschmidt's study, once completed, was forwarded up the BAE's chain of command. It is at this moment that the dominant institutional position of the United States government becomes clearer, because the findings were met with resistance. At higher levels within the federal bureaucracy, the research was criticized as "subjective." Eventually, the Secretary of Agriculture, Clinton Anderson, in support of the BAE's new chief O. V. Wells, simply refused to release the final study.

At the same time, agribusiness efforts to undermine and overturn the reclamation law's acreage limitation restrictions were expanded in Congress. In 1944, Californian Congressman Elliott submitted a buried amendment to exempt the Central Valley Project from the acreage provision in an Omnibus Rivers and Harbor bill. While the measure quietly passed the House of Representatives, controversy exploded by the time it reached the Senate. Three Senate subcommittees eventually held hearings on the law.

Arguments from the hearings were later condensed in a BAE report on the history of the Central Valley Project.[23] Those in favor held that the reclamation law was not applicable or would be unenforceable under California's agricultural system. Those opposed drew from the law's longstanding political positions and philosophical principles. One of these arguments succinctly frames the issue:

> The original and primary purpose of acreage limitation in reclamation law is to promote sound communities of independent farmers who will make homes on the land. Those who framed the law believed that protection of smaller working farmers from land monopoly and land speculation would assure better community institutions, more stable business, better or more stable school conditions for children, and a more democratic rural society.[24]

It was a statement supported by the BAE's own findings from Goldschmidt's recently completed research. The Elliott amendment was thwarted—the first of many attempts to undermine the law's application in California.

While agribusiness mobilized, the community at large was generally unaware of the reclamation law. In this vacuum, government bureaucracies were easily influenced by powerful private interests, which undermined implementation. In this context, Goldschmidt's planned second-phase of BAE research—a broader analysis of 25 towns in the region—was essential to confirm, validate, and broadcast the BAE's Arvin-Dinuba research findings.

The planned 25-town study promised to scientifically inform the public policy debate around reclamation policy, and further justify the importance of implementing the law.

Using the differentials between Arvin and Dinuba, we intended to develop something like an index of community quality. This index (or the several items analyzed separately) would be based upon the salient differences found between Arvin and Dinuba, but consisting of items that could readily be obtained either from published sources, by direct inquiry, or by direct observation. We had in mind such things as: The number of churches, civic organizations, and extra-curricular school clubs such as Boy Scouts; acreage in public parks; number and kind of retail outlets locally available; the existence of such important local enterprises as newspapers and banks; the number of teachers residing in the community and their average length of tenure.

Once we formulated such an index it would be possible to plot the values obtained against the farm size of each of the 25 communities in the San Joaquin Valley, as listed on table 1 of our report. I believe you can readily see that this would have been a powerful tool for the study of the relationship that I, as a public servant, had been asked to establish. It would, incidentally, have had another effect: de-emphasis of attention to the two towns as such. (I have always felt that it was a matter of some unfairness that so much emphasis was placed upon the town as an individual social entity; I certainly had neither the desire nor the intent to cast aspersions upon the citizenry of a community.)[25]

Just as the original BAE findings were censored, however, the followup study was suppressed and disallowed.

Goldschmidt, speaking decades later, took away political lessons from his experience:

> I should say that we were never satisfied with the idea of making a comparison of two towns only and we had from the outset planned a second-phase of the study, but we were prevented from doing this.
>
> The story of why we were so prevented is perhaps more revealing of the problems derived from large-scale operations than would have been the results of such an endeavor and I must therefore review these events briefly. I was ordered by the bureau chief in Washington not to undertake the second phase of the study. He did so in response to a build-up of pressure from politically powerful circles.
>
> I am not indulging in these reminiscences merely to explain why the second phase was eliminated from our research; but rather to suggest that there are interests in this country—or that there were at the time—which did not want the evidence of the effect of corporate farming brought forward. They wanted to suppress the study, to defame it, to discredit it.
>
> It seems clear that efforts to suppress, discredit, and answer the study were inspired and fostered by those who did not want this data known. I believe that similar efforts will be made in respect to any endeavor to replicate the study, in California or elsewhere.
>
> It is for this reason that it is of the greatest importance, not only that the study be updated, expanded, and brought to bear on areas such as your own state of Wisconsin and elsewhere in the farming heartland, but that it be done with the sponsorship and support of this vital Committee of the United States Senate.[26]

Goldschmidt's lesson now extended beyond his research findings. The political response to his findings, and pressure exerted to censor and suppress scientific inquiry, demonstrated that large-scale agricultural interests were not only corrosive to rural life but also threatened scientific inquiry, democratic governance, and public process.

Goldschmidt was adamant about the need for further study:

> Let me return to the social consequences of the incursion of agribusiness into the rural landscape by reiterating the hope that you will find the means to reexamine this problem along the lines of my earlier study.

As your Committee is fully aware, the number of family-sized farms is rapidly dwindling throughout the United States and this change is taking place as a result of the incursion of large-scale corporations into the business of producing food and fiber. I am convinced that this development has been largely a product of policies of the United States Government—particularly policies with respect to agricultural support and with respect to farm labor.

Even if it is a product of "natural causes" this does not mean either that it is inevitable or that it is progressive. If, as my earlier investigation indicated for California, it is deleterious to community life, then certainly we should know this fact and undertake the formulation of policies which will stop the trend that has been taking place. It is important to determine whether, in fact, these deleterious effects are recurrent.

[. . .] The second phase, which I so regrettably was unable to prosecute, is also one that should most emphatically be pursued.[27]

In 1978, when *As You Sow* was republished, the reclamation controversies were again before Congress and the courts. Goldschmidt had drawn further conclusions in the intervening years that were now put down as a third part of the book, under the heading, "Agribusiness and Political Power." This section began:

The study of Arvin and Dinuba started a controversy across the breadth of the land when the study was being prosecuted and again after it appeared in print. This controversy is itself an expression of the effects of corporate farming on American life, and documenting its form and character will show how the machinery of propaganda is used to further corporate interests.[28]

Goldschmidt then describes in detail the political pressure put upon the study—naming names, specifying events, and citing primary source material. He concludes:

Wasco, Arvin and Dinuba tell us what industrialized agriculture does to the *local community* and how corporate agricultural operations exacerbate the disadvantages in this industrial system. The examination of the treatment of the Arvin-Dinuba study, however, tells us what this industrialized agriculture does to our *national life*.[29]

The foreboding "as you sow," an explicit warning, now took on a new menacing meaning: to ignore agribusiness and corporate farming's impact and influence endangers the integrity of democratic process and risks transgressions against promoting beneficial public policy.

In that same year, at the Rural Sociology Society (RSS) conference of 1978, thirty years after his original study, Goldschmidt joined a panel presentation with Phil Leveen, Jerry Moles, and Isao Fujimoto titled "California Agriculture and Rural Communities: Past, Present and Future." In his talk, he described the "sabotage" and "suppression" of the study, followed by political "attack" and "retaliation" against the Bureau of Agricultural Economics. Goldschmidt reported that the disbanding of the BAE resulted in "ending New Deal liberalism in agriculture once and for all and with it came the decline of investigation into the character of rural life."[30] Indeed, the Arvin-Dinuba study was identified as the "killing blow" for the BAE; it was a key factor in the Bureau's demise.[31]

By 1953, the BAE had been effectively dismantled, instigated by Californian Senator Sheridan Downey. After self-publishing *They Would Rule the Valley* in 1947, partly as a counterargument to Goldschmidt's findings, Downey added specific language to the Agricultural Appropriations Act for 1949 and subsequent legislation stating that "no part of funds herein appropriated or made available to the Bureau of Agricultural Economics under the heading 'Economic Investigation' shall be used for state or county planning, for conducting cultural surveys or for the maintenance of regional offices."[32]

What effect did this political history around the BAE's research on the Central Valley Project have for scholars and their work? How did it alter research approaches?

The political context of the valley not only influenced the federal government and public institutions, it also contorted and stressed assumptions around traditional social science. As powerful economic interests became objects of scientific inquiry, and their subterranean activities were exposed, agribusiness pushed back on the social scientists and their universities. This compelled the scholars to defend themselves, pulling them away from their ostensibly neutral positions and bringing them into the political fray.

If Goldschmidt's valley scholarship unmasked agribusiness, it also illustrated the social values and political character of social science that had been presented as objective.

There is one matter with respect to this study [Arvin-Dinuba] that must be brought into the foreground of our thought, because it is very important that we understand it. This is the matter of values . . .

The President's current all-out effort to analyze the causes of cancer operates on the assumption that cancer is bad and that therefore a cure for cancer is good. These are values that all of us accept. When an economist analyzes the profitability of an enterprise, he takes for granted that it is good to make a profit. Nothing the scientist does validates the assumption that cancer is bad and profits are good; what the scientist does is to determine the causes and conditions under which good or evil will prevail.

Now my research was made under similar conditions. It cannot prove that democratic, egalitarian communities with high levels of social participation and stability of population are good. This is a value that we share; it is a matter of commitment of faith, if you wish. What my research did was to assume the values to be real and to demonstrate the conditions in which they flourished or languished.

Now most social scientists have shied away from anything involved with values; they hold that they must remain value-neutral. It is a confusion I deplore, and it is one that has led, I think, to the dullness and irrelevance of much of sociological research. They forget that most science takes basic values for granted.

In the Arvin-Dinuba study we were examining the conditions that support or destroy these traditional values. It was then merely a matter of asking the right questions and following the basic tenets of scientific study to test this basic question against the realities as they existed.[33]

While personal values representing bias were corrosive to scientific findings, social values were integral to orienting inquiry. Values precede and frame research questions; they are not outcomes to be discovered.

Values, and the integrity to base research on foundational principles, also offer a defensive bulwark, a moral justification, and an occasional refuge from political pressure. Goldschmidt needed those, for, as Paul Taylor noted, as a result of his research he was "caught in the crossfire." Taylor called Goldschmidt's experience in this crossfire a "baptism by fire." It was a trial that extended beyond both of their lifetimes, without resolution.[34]

The treatment of the BAE research, the censorship of its findings, and the suppression of further scientific inquiry reveal the corrosive influence of corporate farming on our society. In turn, we can now hone and sharpen lessons for political engagement, activism, and scholarship that can be applied in the Central Valley and other geographies, locations, and communities.

Finally, examining and solving formidable social problems also help us to re-commit to our principles and sharpen our values. Here is Goldschmidt testifying before Congress in 1972 discussing the foundations of an agrarian democracy that he fought for:

> There are few who doubt that the nature of rural land tenure is intimately related to the character of the social order. Since the dawn of civilization, when intensive agriculture became the means by which man supplied his basic wants, the control of land has been a basic element in forming the character of society. By and large, where democratic conditions prevail, the man who tilled the soil was a free holder and in control of his enterprise. Where, on the other hand, the farming lands are owned and controlled in the urban centers, and the men engaged in production are merely peasants, serfs, or hired laborers, democratic institutions do not prevail.
>
> Those who framed our constitution and set the course of American history believed that this relationship was paramount. It lay behind Jeffersonian democracy; it lay behind the Homestead Act; and it lay behind the extension of the homestead principles in the development of irrigation under the Reclamation Act as formulated at the beginning of the century.[35]

The fight to uphold reclamation law was so ferocious because it was fundamental to the aim of securing the foundations of a democratic society. As the years passed, Goldschmidt witnessed the erosion of rural economies across the country. The resulting social costs and erosion of political principles that had begun in California's Central Valley now polluted the heartland of the United States.

This was illustrated in the newspaper clippings he kept in the files he had given to me at our first meeting. Just as Dorothea Lange had suggested to him as a young scholar, the files were uncluttered. Letters of correspondence, academic journal articles, research reports, a few pieces of journalism. Many newspaper articles were from the *Los Angeles Times* in 1985. The Midwestern farm crisis was front page news, and it was that crisis which he documented in his records. Many of the articles were from a year-long series titled, "Going, Gone: The Collapse of the Family Farm," and written by Larry Green, a staff writer at the paper.

The two front page articles on the Sunday, February 24th, 1985 issue stand out. One was headlined "Debts Could End Family Farm Era" and warned of "the greatest collapse of America's rural economy since the Great Depression." Worse still, the changes were a structural realignment that was going to fundamentally alter the landscape of the Midwestern United States.

The reporting in the article eerily follows Goldschmidt's arguments and findings:

> The loss of these family businesses has become an issue of social justice for urban and rural activists who see a revolutionary change in patterns of land ownership, resulting in the concentration of more and more farmland in the hands of fewer and fewer owners.
>
> "We are losing bits of our freedom when we lose the family farm," Des Moines Roman Catholic Bishop Maurice Dingman said in an interview. "We are losing our widespread ownership of property, and that can be dangerous . . . We go into Central America and tell them to break up those big landed estates, while in this country we have no structural policy saying we favor saving our family farms." . . .
>
> Main street businesses, agricultural lending institutions, rural churches, agribusiness and entire communities are feeling the pinch. Many will disappear along with the vanishing farmer.[36]

The 1980s Midwest farm crisis mirrored the more gradual transformation that had previously occurred in California's San Joaquin Valley.

Agribusiness consolidation threatened the basis of a democratic society.

Make People Angry

In December 2006, Goldschmidt emailed that he had undergone an operation and had been moved to an "assisted living" facility in Pasadena. It had been something with his brain, perhaps cerebral bleeding.

On June 29, 2007, I emailed him:

Professor Goldschmidt,
How have you been? I will be in southern California for a week, from July 2 to 9th to visit my family in Orange County. I was thinking of stopping by for a visit one morning or afternoon. Are you around and up for visiting?

I will be taking my qualifying exams in September, then moving west shortly thereafter. I will likely move to Visalia to conduct my research.

The other day I took a look at Paul Taylor's work that is catalogued in a special collection in Berkeley's Bancroft Library. Incredible correspondence . . . letters read like a who's who of the 1950s to the 1970s. I hope to get up there to take another look this year sometime.

Next week we will host the Facilitating Sustainable Agriculture Education conference here at Cornell. A group of about 7 graduate students (among them myself) and one post-doc pulled off the planning for this. Hopefully it may present itself as a potential alternative to Big Ag in the Land Grants and other universities.

Hope all is well.
Best,
Dan

Two days later, Goldschmidt replied:

Congratulations on the conference. Watch out behind you, for if you really get something going, it will end up in the corporations' pockets. I will be in all week; call me so we can set up a date, Walter.

On the morning of July 7, 2007, I drove up to Villa Gardens in Pasadena. As far as care facilities went, it was a quality place. Goldschmidt had a first-floor room, not far from the lobby and a short walk to the dining room. He squeezed a house-full of material into a one-bedroom apartment without clutter or crowding.

He had slowed and bowed a bit more. There were names he struggled to remember. Yet still he remained deeply invested in the valley at 94 years old.

I recorded our conversation and transcribed it into research notes.

Goldschmidt wanted to talk while he lay down in bed. I sat next to the bed while he spoke. Shades drawn, the room dark, he was tired.

"Heading into the valley . . . how would you go about research today?"

"Well, in the first place, it's been sixty years since I did that . . . it's so hard to know. No one thinks about communities the way we thought in those days. Or rather, the only people who think of community are the laborers. I haven't been in the valley. Last time, I was talking to anthropology students at Bakersfield State, and they had not heard of my study."

"If they were sociology students perhaps . . . ?" I offered.

"The first thing I would do, is try to get in touch with Wischemann."

"I know her, Trudy. She hangs out with the Quakers."

Goldschmidt continued, "She is a sentimental kind of person, but she knows the valley better than anyone else and you are asking practical questions on how to reach these people. Her religious identifications are pragmatic." He laughed: "They keep her in touch with the people . . . whatever maximizes that. She is a hero."

Turning to his research, I asked, "So you did the Wasco work first?"

"The Depression was giving way to the war; neither of them were friendly to traditional anthropology. I was looking for something to do my dissertation on. I had already written enough for two dissertations, but they were not submitted as being doctoral dissertations. I was trying to test ideas I had about the nature of society. I thought, 'What the hell, why don't I do a community study? I could use a town just as well as a tribe.' So my wife and I drove up and down the valley and picked the town of Wasco for a community study.

"Paul was very excited about it. I had gone to a seminar in Paul's home—he had a wonderful, big house—and got to know him through that. He was interested in anthropology. He was on the edge. He had married Dorothea Lange, the photographer."

"Why Wasco? You are considering looking at a community . . ."

"I wanted a community of a certain size and a certain independence from other communities and away from the highway. The 99 goes through the Central Valley. It is too much of an influence on community. My goal was to try to see how individuals were to advance their status, their family status, in a community.

"Did you pick Wasco because of the agricultural setting, because there were large farms . . . ?"

"No, as a matter of fact, the questions that animated my book emerged out of the Wasco research. Before that I did not know enough about it; I didn't have the experience. After I had had the experience, I realized that the growers had the capital . . . they had the land."

"So you finished up there . . ."

". . . I finished in Wasco, and it was just a month or two before we got into the war. My wife got pregnant in Wasco. She was working so god-damn hard, and she was three months pregnant before I got her to see a doctor. My son was born on November 11, and December 7 was the war. I guess we finished a month or two before that."

"So you were married, and she helped with the Wasco study?"

"She helped me . . . she did. Through all of it. She liked it."

The conversation shifted to his work with the Bureau of Agricultural Economics (BAE).

"The BAE had a regional office in Berkeley and the only social research agency in the whole Department of Agriculture. They even had a sociology sector. They called a meeting. They wanted a sociologist. As an undergraduate I took courses in economics, biology, and mostly in anthropology. No philosophy. No sociology. There was no [rural] sociology at Berkeley at the time."

"About '43, I guess it was, there came into being a new federal project called the 'Central Valley Project.' One of the biggest projects ever to have been done in the United States at the time, comparable in size and scope to the Tennessee Valley Authority. We set up an interdisciplinary, interagency research program. One of the problems was with the acreage limitation law. Do you know about the acreage limitation law?"

"The 1902 Reclamation Law."

"That is right."

". . . which Paul Taylor cared about. You once said that his needle was stuck on that at the end."

"He had gotten to be a little bit . . . I shouldn't have said it because Paul was a wonderful man. Absolutely devoted."

"It is a good thing to fight about."

"Damn right! As a matter of fact, I had a guilty conscience because of him when I left the fight. He was my conscience or else I would be waning now, rapidly waning."

I realized that Goldschmidt had never left the fight or its cause. Decades after Taylor's death, he seemed still with him in the struggle, refusing to let go, unwilling to give up. Had unfinished business—the fight—kept him alive these last years?

He spoke more of his research all those years ago.

"We were four weeks in Arvin, four weeks in Dinuba. We had driven down from Berkeley late afternoon in April. We arrived on a Sunday and we were tired. I hired a gal from Bakersfield named Beryl Strong. She was a good gal. She and my wife took the questionnaires. One of the first things I did was go to the manager of big DiGiorgio Farms. It was big, big. I wasn't going to trespass on their property. I am quite sure that the moment that I walked out of that DiGiorgio office, he immediately called the Associated Farmer's PR man in Fresno because the Argots mentioned that he was in town that week and he had my questionnaire.

"Word got out?"

"Yeah. I had also written a letter to all the graduates in the social sciences trying to get sources of information. I had gotten no answers. But one of those letters went to the daughter of the president who was an Associated Farmer. So everybody knew about the study. There was a radio program on every day about the weather, the price of potatoes or corn, and other things. The PR man spent a lot of time talking about Dr. Goldschmidt on the radio, and he could say the word 'doctor' just like it was 'bastard.' It didn't sound like it phonetically but had that connotation the way he said it."

"That was a fun welcome for you."

"Yeah, Bob Franklin, the PR man, got a copy of the questionnaire and started reading the questionnaire and talking about 'what Dr. Goldschmidt wanted to know.' He referred to it as a 'dirty rug questionnaire' because I asked about status of living questions."

Goldschmidt went on, "Then, I was called in to Berkeley and was told two things: (1) I was to finish what I was doing, and (2) I was to make a response on radio to Bob Franklin. No one had talked to him before. Also, I was not to do the second phase. That was crippling. Really. Somebody was fairly smart to see that the second phase was going to be the killer. I was ready to do regression curves to show how town inequality and farm size by acreage, by its productive value, were related to one another. All done by economists."

Back in the valley, Goldschmidt went to the radio station. "Franklin had a radio program and did public relations for the Associated Farmers. He may have had other jobs. I went in and sat down. I was in the waiting area and I see him coming. I get up and introduce myself to him. I didn't fit his image at all. No little bent over Jewish guy with a briefcase and spectacles. I was young, moderately good-looking, and looked like a fraternity boy. I mean we could have been playing tennis together just as well. We chatted, and he told me with great pride of the great tragedy of his life—the great tragedy was that he had arranged the burning of *The Grapes of Wrath*, it was all ready to go, and he was upstaged by Hitler, because he had planned it for the day that Hitler had marched on Poland. He didn't see the irony in that at all. I think the burning took place, but he didn't get any press for it, which is what the burning was for."

Switching topics, Goldschmidt then offered advice to me on how to do research, "You have to illustrate the obvious. I illustrated the obvious, too, but it was the obvious being denied. Anybody who looked at Arvin and Dinuba—Arvin was a piece of shit compared to Dinuba—but the point was that Arvin was not a poor town. The poorness was imposed by the system."

The conversation moved toward my research. I was still not sure of my research topic. I had suggested a few possibilities, including the idea of studying the history of social science scholarship in the valley.

"I am in education. I am interested in how researchers looked at this problem. Taylor, yourself, MacCannell, on down the line. As power and wealth have concentrated in this region, how have researchers looked at the problem methodologically and theoretically? How they tried to address it and worked with community in articulating the problem, for the community and for our society? All of you have gone about the problem in unique ways, and I think you were uniquely situated to the problems."

Goldschmidt commented, "You have moved around from one thing to another. You are going to end up living in a particular place because you are just one person and you don't have instant mobility. You may live in two places or something like that. I think you have to find your focus."

Then he asked, "Have you read Carey McWilliams?"

"I have it and plan to read it [his 1939 book, *Factories in the Field*]."

"He has done it as good as anybody. There is a new book out. Something written by two guys whose names I can never remember . . . the biggest agricultural producer in California . . ."

"*The King of California.*"

"Yeah, that's right."

"I read it. Boswell. It is interesting. They are journalists."

He contemplated favorably, "They are journalists. Carey was a journalist too."

He went back to discussing research, "That project is perfectly okay, so far as I am concerned. But it is nothing that I would be able to help you to resolve because that is following an intellectual history, and I don't know anything about doing research in that. Research is about trying to transform observations, which are incidents that you make in the field, into sets of finite organized data and establish a future proposition. That is the kind of thing I can help you on."

I asked, "How much should an anthropologist have identified their research question before they go in to do their research?"

"Well, I don't know. If you are going out to Ugabuga, you can't really know what you are going to find. When I came back from my fieldwork the first time I said 'I don't understand these people. I don't have any sense of how to put it together.' Then I went back, project in mind, which is the way you should do the research. I got it out of having been there. This is the same history that I had out of Arvin and Dinuba. It was second phase of what I had done."

I commented, "You are always moving on assumptions . . . What were the reasons that you choose the community? There are always different ways to view the world."

"I don't think you have to know going in but when you are doing something relating to social and political issues, and you know from the start you are doing it for those reasons, it helps. Wasco didn't solve any political issues though I was aware that there were political issues. The Okies were very much in mind and there were pitched battles. People were killed over unionization. Heads were certainly bashed in. The owners were breaking the unions. The Okies weren't well unionized, but the Communist Party had gotten enough of them to get them unionized. That is doing what communists would do, as everyone else doesn't. Well, they ended up with a very good active union with César Chávez. He didn't make that union, though. It is kind of godfather to the whole union movement."

Goldschmidt mentioned that the problems in California had been looked at since the founding of the state, back to the Spanish land grants. Then he tried to remember: "I am blocking on the name of the guy who studied water districts . . ."

"Goodall. Merrill Goodall."

"Yeah."

"Did you like his work?" I asked.

"Yes, I thought he was very good. I thought Merrill's problem was that he didn't take the extra step of making it propaganda amenable. He kept it on the academic side, whether he was shy or unsure of himself or that he was working for an institution that . . ." Goldschmidt began laughing.

I followed up, "So researchers, academics have a role in propagandizing, of putting their work out in a public arena."

"Well," he paused, doubting, "his research was so potentially inflammable. It ought to just make people get angry."

Regrettably, I did not continue to probe this line of questioning. Goldschmidt seemed to be saying that scholars were responsible for not only disseminating their findings but also picking the appropriate audience and mode of communication to affect, inform, or antagonize. It was a lesson that I noted for my own future work.

We had moved through some of the core stories and moved away from Goldschmidt's early work. Before leaving I had some incidental questions, picking up threads from our talk a year earlier. Wanting them on the record.

"Before I go, what was Dorothea Lange like?"

"She was kind of a flower child before they existed. A lot of mystic in her. She was modest. Very liberal and very sweet and very conscientious. I liked her very much. One time she had a hanging on the wall. A strange looking thing made out of wires and stuff. I thought, 'Where the hell had she gotten that dumb thing?' She said, 'I took it out of the fireplace.' It was some decorations that had gotten burned up. She thought it was beautiful. That was the kind of person she was. She was also one of the most famous photographers in the United States."

"Did you go out taking photos with her?"

"She took me out with her once. It was a very interesting experience. She had polio as a girl, so she had a gimpy walk. She wanted to get pictures of asparagus pickers in the delta area, in particular pictures that showed the relationship between the housing and the fields. She started pausing, then asked me to stop. She climbed out on top of the station wagon. She had me back up and position the car. Pretty soon, she came back to the car. I said, 'You didn't take any pictures?' She answered, 'They weren't any good.' And I said, 'It is the best you are going to get.' 'It doesn't matter. It's not any good. No use cluttering up your files with them.'

"Then we went around and came to where a group of pickers worked. It was early in the morning. This one guy was coming up with a trot that I can't imitate. It was a trot in which the legs were always bent. In one hand he had this knife where the blade ended in a fishtail. It was poked into the ground for the white part of the asparagus. He was poking the individual stalks and catching them in the other hand. When he had a handful, he put them down. He was singing. We parked at the end of the row. He hadn't seen her and just as he came at a distance that she wanted she said 'Hi.' He looked up and she clicked, did a little salute and got back in the car. I said, 'Aren't you even going to say thank you to these people?' She said, 'You have got to think of the camera as not even being there.' I have to say that I did not follow either of those good pieces of advice. Not that I thought that they were bad advice, but they don't work when you are doing ethnographic things."

Remembering my first meeting with Goldschmidt, he had earlier condensed these two stories and lessons of advice from Lange.

Looking at his bookshelf, packing my bag, I observed, "I see you have Carlos Castenada's stuff here. Did you take any heat for that? How was he viewed? He had a broad impact, yet I wonder how he was received in academic circles?"

"I helped him because his books are valuable."

"You helped him when he was at UCLA?"

"Well, I did one thing. I was on the editorial committee of the department. I was handed a manuscript. I talked to a number of my colleagues and a half a dozen were very positive about it. They were a mixed bag: the archeologist who he went out with when he first 'met' Don Juan; an anthropological student of mine that I had a high regard for; a linguist; a sociologist; and I think there was one other. I was charmed by it, but I could never get into it. He had been in my undergraduate class. I was also chairman of . . ."

Goldschmidt trailed off, remembering, then mentioned a dialogue with Castenada. "I called him in and asked him to show me his notes. He said, 'Okay, I will bring them in.' And the next time I saw him I said, 'You haven't brought the notes.' He said, 'Oh, I am sorry. I haven't gotten around to it. I will get them to you.' Of course, I never saw any because there aren't any. Or he never showed me there aren't any."

I suspected that Goldschmidt was chairman of Castenada's dissertation committee, but did not ask. He did, inevitably, write the foreword to the now famous book: *The Teachings of Don Juan: A Yaqui Way of Knowledge.*

"Was there really a Don Juan?"

"I doubt it. I think there was a model for it maybe."

"It is funny that something that doesn't have empirical backing resonated so much with the culture at the time."

"Yeah, it was exactly the right thing at the right time in the history of the United States youth."

Paul Taylor had once said the same thing about *As You Sow*.

In August 2009, Goldschmidt sent an email to his friends and colleagues with a link to a blog he has started.[37] He had hired an amanuensis to help him with writing and posts. I kept in contact that year.

On my last visit, he told me, "If you want to interview me again, you better do it now. I'm not going to last much longer." He was 96 years old. Rather than interview, I visited and we talked. He was increasingly difficult to understand, even when I was sitting next to him.

In our last conversation, he was concerned I was not moving forward with the study. Pushing me, impatient, he even suggested that I was afraid. I was emphatic, adamant, the work would be finished.

By this time, my research was defined, settled upon the unique praxis of scholars immersed in political battle against powerful adversaries in California. I had all the material needed to proceed.

Months before he died, I phoned him—I was writing the dissertation.

2

Study Your Targets

PAUL TAYLOR

Between storms, on a winter day in January of 2019, Scott and I make our pilgrimage to the Bancroft Library at UC Berkeley.

Driving up from Oakland, we park south of People's Park and walk up Telegraph Avenue onto campus. A remembrance of Mario Savio rises as we cross Sproul Plaza passing under South Gate.

We arrive to wait in the foyer with other assembled bookish visitors. A museum faces the archive's entrance. Historic photographs hang in its chamber. Russell Means glares across the room while Michael McClure, Bob Dylan, and Allen Ginsberg talk in the corner. Ironworkers confidently stand on rigging, and Harvey Milk dances on his election night. Frida Kahlo stands above Diego Rivera.

We store our bags and jackets in a locker. A staff person sits at the downstairs desk behind closed metal gates waiting to open. At 1:00 p.m. we file in and upstairs to the special collections. Boxes of letters, cartons of files, old reports, research notes jotted into small pads. The distilled remains of a life's work.

Unable to meet Taylor in person, we encounter him through his thoroughly archived papers which he painstakingly catalogued at the end of his life. Many previous scholars and activists have made similar visits to receive his counsel from across time.

The story opens, and we walk into it.

With the Marines at Chateau Thierry

In *Paul Schuster Taylor—California Social Scientist*, a three-volume oral history, Taylor included an appendix titled, "With the Marines at Chateau Thierry—Written in the Convalescent Hospital at Biarritz, France,

Sept. 22, 1918." It consists of a letter, excerpted here, that he wrote as a 23-year-old Marine Corps Lieutenant during World War I.

I'm going to try to do tonight what I couldn't bring myself to do before— tell you about my experiences during our last trip to the front. Of course, things are a bit vague because of necessary omissions to keep within the censorship. Also of course I can't say much about casualties, for that's a forbidden subject. Don't think that the things I say in regard to the conditions are in a spirit of complaint, for of course they aren't. Suppose that I adopt a diary form; it may help me to get the details in the right places.

June 6. The Colonel give us guides to take to our battalions. At Battalion Headquarters in a woods I find runners from my company which is in the front line. I get one of them to take me forward. We go across open fields and finally reach a farm (Triangle) about 150 yds. behind my company. The way beyond this is exposed to snipers and machine-gun fire. I send the runner back as there's no use going out while all is quiet in the middle of the day. A machine-gun Lieutenant is at the farm and gives me some bread, some honey the men found, and a cup of milk from one of the cows left by the refugees in their hurried flight. The machine-gun Lieutenant gets orders to prepare a Marine attack. I decide it's time to join my company, so I go out, partly crawling, and find my men in little rifle pits, dug in a hay field on the military crest (exposed slope) of the field.

The Boches start to shell us. Lieutenant Sellers comes in from our first platoon to report that his platoon is being gassed. A sniper shoots him on the way but he gets to the hole where the Captain and I are. Stretcher-bearers and the Hospital man take him to the dressing station at La Cense Farm. Later comes more shelling from the Boches. I look westward out of my hole and over in the valley opposite Bouresches I can see Marines attacking—running at top speed through a hail of machine gun bullets. I can see the bullets spray the dirt, but the Marines only keep on and never slacken; some stagger and fall. I use my field glasses and can see them try to crawl away from the bullets to the shelter of a slight fold in the ground. Most of them reach it; some never do. An interval,—and another wave rushes across that same bullet swept area. This time there are more streams of bullets spraying them. The Boches saw them and they are ready. They start across. Some get through; the rest falter—and then break for any shelter they can find. Human beings can't go through it. They throw away their packs, and thus lightened, work on by less storm-swept routes . . . During the evening we learn that the town was taken.

And so it goes for eight days, until Taylor's letter ends with a scene in Belleau Wood on June 14:

Night is falling. All we have had to eat is a small can of "monkey meat" (Argentine beef) to two men, and a box of hard bread (something like Uneedas) to three men. No water unless we had it in our canteens before. Most of us did as we knew how valuable it was. The shelling is steadily increasing in volume. The gas alarm has already been given in some places. The bombardment reaches a crescendo. Just then the order comes to me to take my platoon out of the woods. Through the barrage we must pass. I have every man hang onto the pack of the man ahead of him. It's pitch dark in the wood. There are no paths. They are throwing over big stuff, little stuff, gas shells, shrapnel, high explosive. The woods are torn to pieces. It is almost impossible to walk because of the fallen branches. If we are to get out I must see, so off comes the mask. I try to keep the mouthpiece in so as to breathe purely. I have to take it out to call to keep the platoon together and following. I stumble along over everything, fallen men, logs, etc. I try to note where the shells are thickest and pick the holes where there is the best chance of getting through. At last I find the Captain and get my men, most of them, out to where he is, but we are still in a bad place. I have my men lie on their stomachs, packs on their backs, to give maximum protection against shrapnel. We are still in the gas. It's a strong pungent odor. We are still being shelled terribly. Cries for aid and I can't aid. Only the hospital men can go about. They do wonderful work.

I get my men completely out of the woods once, but under orders take them back in. A long delay in the midst of the gas and bursting shells. The line of men is broken, the Captain gone, so I gather my men and take them back the only way I know. I find a doctor who cares for those who need attention and evacuates them. Pretty soon I begin to feel the effects of the gas. My eyes begin to smart and some other unpleasant (vomiting) symptoms assert themselves. I get into an ambulance and am carried to the field hospital. By that time I am completely blind and see no more to relate.

I've met two officers since, who saw the wood next day, and am more thankful than ever that so many of us are still alive. My eyes are as good as ever now.

It was terrible, but not so hard to endure then as it was all over—and even reliving it now, almost.

—Lt. P.S. Taylor 78th Company 6th Regiment Marines[1]

In an "Editorial note" dated July 1973 that Taylor included with his letter, he added:

During the Bouresches-Belleau Wood action Marine casualties, on a brigade strength of 7,200, were 5,711. They may have been more; my own gassing was not reported to my family until January 1919 because not earlier reported to the Marine Corps. My own estimate of the casualties of the 78th Marine Company during a single night was around 90 percent, overwhelmingly from gas, mostly "mustard" with some phosgene.[2]

The Battle of Belleau Wood was forever burned into Taylor's mind. It shaped his personality, and his approach to life. As he recalled, "in war you are up against it—you are up against the ultimate. You have responsibilities, and you do your best."[3]

He took his wartime experience and carried it throughout his life. It steeled his resolve on new battlefields, increasingly up against California's "power structure" of industrialized agriculture. As the fight intensified, he came to ally himself with rural folk on the ground who were also "up against it" in their own lives and battles.

Easy to underestimate, particularly for his adversaries, Taylor presented as a portly economics professor. His sedate, low-key demeanor camouflaged a tenacious and deliberate disposition more akin to a soldier than a scholar. He was, of course, both.

We weave this profile of his life and work together from his own words, his stories teaching many lessons.

Figure 2.1. Paul Taylor, Lieutenant 78th Company, 6th Regiment, United States Marine Corps, September 1918. Courtesy of the Oral History Center, The Bancroft Library, University of California, Berkeley.

The Application of Knowledge

Paul Taylor was born in 1895.

He grew up in Sioux City, Iowa, but his family roots were in Wisconsin. His upbringing was immersed within the rural life of Midwestern family farms. Eventually, he studied under renowned economist John

Commons at the University of Wisconsin, who, along with his students, "created the field of labor economics."[4]

> Commons' students just branched out and did all kinds of important things after they left the University! Students who were two and three years ahead of you would talk to you about the excitement of being a student of Commons. There was no question of "relevance" or "boredom" then. Heavens, no.
>
> Commons was always concerned with the application of knowledge. The question behind studying was always, "What do you do about those problems?" He took us out into the world.

Returning from war in Europe, what problems did Taylor take up? Trained briefly as a lawyer, he went on to become a social scientist. And after moving west, his Midwestern agrarian values began to grate upon the contradictions of California's "plantation agriculture."

> When I came back from France, I decided that I would give law a serious try. I went to summer school in 1919, taking all law, no economics. I had good professors, but the law didn't quite grip me.
>
> I asked advice of some of my older professor friends, and particularly of E. A. Ross, who was a leading sociologist of his generation. His response, when I put my question to him, was this: "Well, if you go into law, within a reasonable time you will probably be in one of the best legal firms of the country, perhaps in New York, and by the time you are in your forties, some case will come along on which you will work that will really grip your attention and your faculties and your interests. It will go to the United States Supreme Court. It will be an important case.
>
> "If you go into economics, from the time that you start, you can choose the subjects into which you wish to inquire, do your researching, make your studies. You can do that throughout your professional career."
>
> I remember that as the decisive point that clarified the issue in my mind. Right from the start I could work on what I thought was important. Shortly afterward, I came out to California.
>
> I wanted to do on agricultural labor something comparable to what Commons had done on industrial labor. I wanted to do it with both historical and contemporary emphasis on the west coast, because this

agricultural labor situation was so peculiar, so unique. I wanted to start something new, but I had no resources to pay salary and costs of field work.

California agriculture is not American agriculture at all in the Northern and Middle Western sense! This is plantation agriculture, more in the Southern than in the Northern tradition. The California land-water situation is totally different from the Middle West. It is a shock for a Middle Westerner to learn of it. I've been up against it, you might say, studying it and trying to change it, all of my life. My agricultural labor, and my water studies—that has meant exploring land and the water monopoly, and the power structure of California. Neither are Middle Western situations at all!

California agriculture is based upon the monopolization of the large Spanish land grants, not on the homestead land pattern. One way or another, these lands were all gobbled up by a few owners in the third quarter of the nineteenth century. First, they grabbed most of the land. Then, especially when they knew the water someday would come, they grabbed the rest of the land, *every acre of it* that they hadn't grabbed already! Speculation was on a gigantic scale!

From then on, they've been working to pump the money out of the Treasury to pay the costs of bringing the public's water to their private land, and so to reap the harvest that they've been after for a hundred years. This is the corporate takeover of land and water resources. Now they're working to permanently rivet their power over land and water.[5]

On the Ground in the Thirties

The Cotton Strike of 1933 shocked California.

Most mass uprisings shatter elites' presumption that they are both entitled and able to control economic systems. Cotton workers rose up to defend themselves, using the power of their collective voices and bodies to challenge growers.[6]

The cotton strike offers an early view into how Taylor operated in crisis as he took up his emerging role as a politically engaged scholar, expanding his position at the university into the agricultural fields and farm communities of California's Central Valley—and soon beyond to many regions of rural America.

The cotton strike in the early autumn of 1933 was the culmination of a whole succession of summer strikes that followed the harvesting of the crops. It was, and is, the most extensive strike in agriculture in the history of the United States. The picking of cotton was shut down very effectively from one end of the San Joaquin Valley to the other.

I was invited to go down into the Valley as an aide to [a fact-finding] commission [appointed in part by California's governor] by Monroe Deutsch, Provost of the University. I assume the reasons I was asked to go were (1) that my field was "labor economics," and (2) that I had recently been studying Mexican labor in agriculture. Also, I had visited the strike area only a week or two earlier, after the strike had broken out. I asked if I could take with me my graduate student, Clark Kerr, and the answer was yes.

I instructed Clark to keep close to the strikers and their spokesman, and to report to me on the temper of the strikers at least a couple of times a day; also to form his own estimate of about what terms it would take to settle the strike. The strikers were asking a dollar a hundred pounds for picking; the growers were offering 60¢ a hundred. I stayed close to the commissioners, the hearings, the growers, and the newspapermen at headquarters. That's the way we continued to divide our work until the end.

I drove Ira Cross [also on the fact-finding commission] home from Visalia in my car, and he asked me en route what I thought it would take to settle the strike. From my own and Clark's estimates, I replied, "Seventy-five cents a hundred." The commission, when it reconvened informally in San Francisco, proposed seventy-five cents a hundred, and that figure did in fact settle the strike.

Nobody to my knowledge was hostile to either my presence or to Clark Kerr's. We were both experienced in talking to people on all social and economic levels. So neither of us encountered any difficulty speaking to anyone—grower, laborer, official—or whatever. The situation was wide open.

The documentation which we put in, which was published later by the LaFollette Committee, I think shows, notably in the oral statements that were given to us and that we recorded in note form, that there was no trouble in talking with anyone. The lid was off. I have never known the Valley to be so open. The newspapers gave the fullest documentation to that social situation of any California strike that I know. People in the Valley were just taken aback, almost aghast, wondering what had hit them. The newspapers were the freest in reporting both the growers and the strikers of any time in my experience. That is one reason we wanted to document that particular strike, either orally or in print, as fully and freely as was possible then.

The strike impact was fresh, it was a "first." It caught everyone by surprise. Unions of farm workers were virtually unknown. Now there's more organized opposition to unionization. César Chávez faces highly organized opposition today. Yet he has not been able to conduct a strike on anything like the 1933 scale. His operations are more through use of the boycott. He has appealed to people in the markets outside of the producing area, rather than to people and their interests within the area.[7]

Taylor's last published book was *On the Ground in the Thirties*. The bulk of that book consists of Taylor's and Kerr's documentary history of the Cotton Strike of 1933, and its title directs us toward a particular kind of work: the work of scholars "on the ground," positioned within the problems they aim to solve.

The book's preface was written by Clark Kerr, who had been a doctoral student under Taylor and later went on to be the first chancellor of UC Berkeley in 1952, and in 1957, president of the University of California. Kerr recalled his professor and mentor:

Paul never gave me but two instructions: (1) to record what people said in their own words; and (2) to send him my notes as soon as possible. The reward was that he read these notes carefully and enjoyed them immensely.

I did not then fully realize to the extent I do now how rare a professor Paul really was. He has belonged to a very unusual breed of what might be called economic anthropologists with an interest in labor problems. These economic anthropologists made contact with reality, not through somebody else's statistics or through documents, but by talking with people and by thinking about what they heard. . . .

Scholars like Paul create the too few bridges to reality: bridges that cross those broad moats with the armchair theorists in their crenelated castles on one side and the everyday life of the market places on the other. . . . Paul was always out there finding out what was really happening while others played around with their theoretical models and ran their regression analyses. He leaves behind, not another model or two or a few statistical calculations, but, rather, some totally irreplaceable accounts of historical reality; of how it actually was when history was being made.[8]

Taylor's ethnographic methods were sharply questioned by some scholars in the field of economics. His response can be found in "Non-statistical Notes from the Field," a 1942 article Taylor published in *Land Policy Review*, where he critiques quantitative methods while insisting on an insurgent politically engaged economics.

> My method in the field is to observe, then to select. But some of my statistician friends demand numbers. When I tell them in detail what happened to a farm family I saw displaced in the Cotton Belt, they are likely to say, "What's that to us if you can't tell how many that has happened to?"
>
> Perhaps I can't, and I answer, "By the time you statisticians know the numbers, what I'm trying to tell you about in advance will be history, and you'll be too late. . . ."
>
> My statistician friends seem to love averages, and to be dissatisfied with my description if it doesn't strike them as "average" for the county, state, or perhaps the nation; if it isn't average it isn't typical, and it's only the typical that counts.
>
> Average of what? I ask myself. Typical of what? Aren't there many averages and many types? And if the average reveals, doesn't it by the same token conceal? Besides, maybe I'm not interested for the moment in averages. Maybe I'm looking for trends, and don't want to cancel out the very item where I think I see the "future" foreshadowed by "history," by averaging it with another where the "future" has not yet struck.[9]

Taylor's work was attentive to local context, animated by a desire to find solutions to pressing problems. His work had to evoke sympathy and invite solidarity; otherwise he risked being "too late" to affect the unfolding history of the moment. Most important, he was not going to passively observe, quantify, and average; rather he observed from close range, pushed forward into the issue, and took his findings directly into the political arena to advance solutions.

This approach was influenced by his military experience. As he combined his tactical skills and strategic experience to confront the concurrent crises of the Dust Bowl and Depression, Taylor grafted in other innovations such as using photography for visceral impact, publishing in nontraditional venues, and moving findings forward quickly at political decision points.

Like a Marine officer, Taylor entered difficult research settings as if planning a battle strategy—field observations, close reconnaissance, co-ordinated efforts, communication up a chain of command, and then attack as quickly as possible.

Crafting his own unconventional methods, Taylor followed no pre-scribed academic program and referenced no traditional academic approaches. His research was innovative and improvisational, partly because it had no precedent.

Agricultural Labor

In California, Taylor found an ideal context to study agricultural labor. With a grant from the Social Science Research Council, he received funding for six months of research, which expanded into three years of exhaustive field work. His inquiry into a rapidly politicized and polar-ized topic opened a Pandora's box—both on campus at Berkeley, where his unorthodox approaches drew rebuke from colleagues, and direct pressure later from California's powerful agricultural industry.

> Edith Abbott, chairman of the Committee on Scientific Aspects of Human Migration of the newly formed Social Science Research Council, was trying to find somebody who would study Mexican immigration. Since Mexican laborers were employed overwhelmingly in agriculture, her interests merged with mine. The outcome, with Social Science Research Council support, was that I spent three continuous years in the field, not teaching at all. I went all over the United States. That then led to an invitation from the Guggenheim Foundation. They wanted to begin a scholarly interchange with Latin Amer-ica. That was fine for me, so I said, "Sure, I'd be happy to go." So, I went down into Mexico and studied a community of origin of much emigration. I went there in 1931 and 1932 for a total of six months. I got deep into field research so I could meet and talk with people on their own ground.[10]

Taylor improvised his research methods, pushing across and through disciplinary boundaries.

My method of field work was just like going into a swimming pool by plung-
ing in!

I got myself a rough-riding, used Dodge roadster, so that I had a car and I
could go down the road and stop at a farmhouse anywhere I wanted. If I saw
a group of laborers, I could stop wherever I wanted, stay as long as I wanted,
and go on when I wanted. That was the way I did it. I would try to sample
officials, teachers, Americans who had contacts with the Mexicans—get all
the information I could from them. Then I would go among the Mexicans
and get everything I could from them—their wages, migrations, experiences,
problems, history.

My method developed by the doing of it. I don't know of any model
that I was following. I had no training at all in either anthropological or sociological methods. I combined the kind of work that a human geographer
would do, an anthropologist, and a sociologist, with my own background as
a labor economist having a strong interest in history. I kept asking questions
and seeking answers. What I did was choose (for the most part) a variety of
locations, areas, where Mexican labor was important. That's why the Imperial Valley interested me. While I was there, I studied a good deal about the
structure of agriculture into which they came, which was certainly a strong
contrast to the structure of Middle Western agriculture.

I combined an historical and a contemporary interest. I wanted a cross-
section of conditions Mexicans encountered in the United States, which ex-
plains why I went to places as diverse as Imperial Valley, Colorado, South
Texas, Chicago, and the Calumet steel, meatpacking, railroad industry center,
and finally the outpost colony of Bethlehem, Pennsylvania, steel and coke
works. Later I went back into Mexico to some of the origins of this migration.[11]

As he would throughout his career, Taylor encountered criticism,
pressures, and objections to his work—both within the academy and
beyond.

I can remember being told after I was out a couple years or maybe a little
more, by one of my fine professors, I mean a really good professor—this was
what was said to me: "Now it's time for you to come back and be a professor." You see, I'd been doing something else that wasn't being a professor!

My chairman said it to me this way: "Now it is time for you to come back
to the center of your field."

I replied, "What is the center of my field?"

"Oh," he said, "something like workman's compensation."

Going out to study Mexican labor wasn't working in the center of my labor economics field. I researched excessively; I was gone from campus teaching too long. I don't know that there are many who want to do what I did. I think anthropologists like to get out in the field. But I think people in economics don't generally feel the urge to do that now. I think I was a bit peculiar in that respect, partly inheriting the John R. Commons tradition from the University of Wisconsin.

I have not been popular down in the Valley, you can be sure of that. Pressure came from there too. Clark Kerr told me that when he was Chancellor under Sproul, and wanted to appoint me to the Industrial Relations Institute advisory committee, Sproul said, "Well, they don't like him very well down in the Valley."

Clark said, "I know it, but I want him anyway," and I was appointed.

I knew from my Wisconsin days that if I went into this labor field, I would encounter opposition. It was part of what I took on by choosing labor economics. Commons was under fire repeatedly. What I wanted to know here at California was, would I be supported with the freedom necessary to do the work.[12]

Taylor crossed the country, "searching out regions where Mexicans worked in agriculture or industry."[13] His work and experience were a revelation, teaching him how different agriculture in California was from what he had seen in the Midwest.

I learned my first lesson close to home in California. On the advice of a member of the agricultural extension service and overlooking the importance of seasonal migration, I got into my car early in February and drove to Napa Valley. There I found no Mexicans. I had come too soon. Mexican workers, landless and seasonal, would not find employment in Napa vineyards until summer. So, I turned back and headed southward.

When I reached Imperial Valley on the Mexican border, what I saw hit me in the face. I found myself in the midst of an agricultural society with a labor pattern the opposite of all that as a youth I had known in the Middle West. Production was highly organized by American managers employing Mexican workers off and on to meet seasonal needs. Mexicans

constituted more than one-third of the valley population. They were separated from the American population in domicile, in the schools, and in
employment status. For them there was no "agricultural ladder." In 1926,
a quarter of a century after Colorado River water flowed into the valley,
only six Mexicans had become owners of farm land, with a total assessed
value of $5,910, and improvements valued at $600. Mexicans and
Americans, I concluded, "live socially in two worlds."[14]

In these years of astonishing productivity (thirteen book-length
monographs for his Mexican labor series), he also first met, fell in love
with, and began a deeply intimate professional collaboration with Dorothea Lange.[15] During this time Taylor was regularly tasked with government assignments, and he brought her on board for these projects.

Toward the end of 1934 I was asked would I do research for the Division of
Rural Rehabilitation of the California State Emergency Relief Administration
(SERA). That was the state division of Harry Hopkins' Federal Emergency Relief Administration. The question was, would I do the research work to help
decide what rehabilitation program was fitted to the needs of rural California?

California conditions are peculiar and were largely unknown in Washington. Questions were: who was in distress, what was the nature of the distress,
and what would be a sensible thing to do to alleviate it?

When it was decided that I would do the research, [the project's director,
Harry Drobish] asked me what staff would I need? I told him what I would
need as field workers and as office workers, not many, but a few. Then I said
I would like a photographer. "Why did I want a photographer?" The answer
came slowly. Well, because we were going to go out into the field to see
what the conditions were. I knew in general what they were, because I had
done so much work among the Mexican laborers and was quite familiar with
rural California. Recently I'd been down to the cotton strike of 1933. So I had
a pretty good idea of the conditions I would be looking into. But knowing
the conditions and reporting them in a way to produce action were two
different things.

That was the main point I made. I said that I would like for the people in
the Relief Administration, who would read my reports, evaluate them and
make the decisions, to be able to see what the real conditions were like. My
words would not be enough, I thought, to show the conditions vividly and

Figure 2.2. Paul Taylor and Dorothea Lange. Copyright © Imogen Cunningham Trust.

accurately. Well, we talked back and forth a good deal. One of the questions was, "Would social scientists generally ask for a photographer on their research staff?" To which I answered, "No, they wouldn't, but I wanted a photographer."[16]

Taylor was given permission to hire Lange as a "typist," even though, of course, what she would do was photography. She accepted the position. Few relationships have been as potently productive and enduringly compelling in the cause of agrarian justice during the twentieth century. Amid the crisis of economic depression, and perhaps because of their collaboration, the nature of their work began to shift from documenting facts to *taking action.*

Working together, Lange and Taylor wrote and submitted a series of reports to the Roosevelt administration in Washington D.C. The emergence of Taylor as a politically engaged scholar becomes clearer at this time. One definitive result was the establishment of federally supported housing for migrant farm labor, which inspired Steinbeck's government housing camp in *The Grapes of Wrath*.

Lange and Taylor established the justification for the migrant housing camps in the valley during the Dust Bowl and Depression.

> In addition to the reports proposing program, we made some informational reports. One series we called "Reports from the Field." Its style was to carry a small notation in words (by myself), perhaps a paragraph, perhaps a page, and opposite the text to carry a relevant photograph. We wanted to bring conditions as we saw them into the offices and to the officials. You might call this kind of report an interim report to the division. One spiral bound report I encouraged Dorothea to make by herself, directly to the head of the Division, without me as intermediary. I wanted to elevate the status of her work in the Division, you see. Its message was, "Here's a photographer's report," a justifiable innovation from every point of view.
>
> [Y]ou see FDR—having new jobs to get done—set up new bureaucracies to do them that weren't crystallized in old ways. Through this newly created Relief Administration, under Harry Hopkins (who incidentally is also from Sioux City where he was a harness-maker's son), well, FDR wanted to do something in a situation that urgently called for some doing.
>
> When I undertook to prepare my researches, my idea was not just to study the conditions, but to use the studies to get something done. We had to find out first what it made sense to do, and after that how to get it done within the internal bureaucracy of the government.[17]

Lange and Taylor's most significant collaborative work, *An American Exodus*, was a direct outgrowth of their reciprocating innovations, shared devotion, and intense desire to assist the destitute in crisis.

Published in 1939, the same year as John Steinbeck's *Grapes of Wrath* and Carrey McWilliams's *Factories in the Field*, *An American Exodus* mirrored their previous integration of photographs and text to influence their audience in earlier government reports. Taylor also, again, "elevates the status" of Lange as first author of the book.

Photographs offered another mechanism to bring the story of home-less refuges and landless farmers directly into the imagination of the reader. Pictures told stories with nuance, texture, and immediacy—characteristics critical to bringing research subjects forward. Once that connection fostered empathy, it could leverage demands for public expenditure and responsive government policy.

During these years, Taylor's research and Lange's photography represented a plea not to turn aside from the crises. They wanted to bring forward the humanity of their subjects, for which Lange's artistry is now recognized worldwide. Their subjects' representations inscribed a political project into the book's narrative.

Not merely an exposé, the book offered structural assessment and critique to the larger and underlying economic system causing the suffering.

> In our concern over the visible and acute distress of dislocated people, we must not lose sight of the permanent farming organization which is being laid down. This grave question arises: After the sweep of mechanization, how shall our best lands be used—our southern plains, prairies, deltas, and our irrigated valleys of the West? Shall factory agriculture—our modern latifundia—prevail with its absentee owners, managers, day laborers, land-less migrants, and recurrent strife? Or shall other patterns be sought for the relation of man to the land?
>
> A very old American ideal, crystallized in the Homestead Act of 1862, holds that our land shall be farmed by working owners. But history has made serious inroads on this ideal. By 1935 tenancy had risen to 42 percent of all farms, and stood above 60 percent in many of the cotton states. Wage labor, standing at 26 percent of all persons gainfully employed in agriculture in 1930, reached 53 percent in Arizona and 57 percent in California. In order to preserve what we can of a national ideal, new patterns, we believe, must be developed.[18]

Assaulted by the expanding model of agribusiness, the plea to save the family farm—the most basic infrastructure of rural entrepreneurial small business—was becoming a search for a "new pattern" to be developed.

In time, Taylor confronted and challenged the power structure of California based in the state's system of industrialized agriculture, unequal

Figure 2.3. Paul Taylor testifying before US Senate Unemployment Committee. Washington, D.C., March 14, 1938. Alamy Stock Photo.

land ownership, and economic monopoly. He named the culprits while maintaining his modest Midwestern tone.

> The Associated Farmers was a natural, if excessive, response from the employers' side to labor's feeling that unionization was necessary to protect its interests. This phase had, and to a lesser degree still has, the violent aspects of some of the early efforts of labor to organize in coal mines, and the steel industry, where there were serious losses of life. This parallel came along in California's agricultural setting in a familiar chain of labor history.
>
> In California, farming is in a different position and is viewed differently than in the Middle Western states where land ownership is more widely diffused. Industry and agriculture are blended here in California as they have not been in the Middle West and Northeast, certainly not until very recently. Farming very early was regarded here as an industry,

rather than as a way of life for families on the land. That view has persisted to the present time; the term currently in use is agribusiness rather than industrialized agriculture.

The Associated Farmers sought to unite the larger agricultural interests with the Chamber of Commerce, which elsewhere represented urban interests. But here, they were blurred; they were blended. The pattern of employment and the attitudes that go with it are an industrial pattern. The laborer on the land is not the farmer owning his own land, but the man employed by somebody else to do the work.

The division between the landowner and laborer on the land came extremely early in California—in fact, virtually from the beginning of statehood it was divided that way. That is one reason why the remedies have taken on the aspect of industrial readjustments to conflict of interest; for example, unionization of workers met by employer resistance to unionization. Now that's just a brief, quick summary of a hundred and twenty years of California history.[19]

Building upon his agricultural labor studies, Taylor went on to enter, almost by happenstance, a subterranean war over a relatively unknown federal law guiding the development of water infrastructure. This procedural and administrative ground was the terrain on which Taylor would come to boldly contest California's agribusiness empire.

Confronting Californian Agribusiness: Reclamation Law

During the last 40 years of his life, Taylor confronted the most powerful political and economic interests in California, often in solitary battles on complex battlefields involving federal law and legislative process.

The salient point in this battlefield formed around an obscure federal law—the Reclamation Act of 1902. Quietly tucked into that law were provisions protecting against land speculation, countering economic monopoly, and instituting land reform in some of the country's most unequally owned regions.

The policies that were included and affirmed in the Reclamation Act of 1902 were based upon longstanding historical, cultural, and legal precedents. The earlier Preemption Act of 1841 and Homestead Act of 1862 had already established the democratic standard of 160 acres for land allocations dispersed or supported by the federal government. This policy effectively defines the democratic scale of a family farm as it favored "actual settlers against monopolists and speculators of that day."[20] Following this precedent, the Reclamation Act of 1902 mandated the same 160-acre limitation as a foundational centerpiece in aspiring to support family-scale agriculture and to ensure a more equitable rural society.

In 1902, the House Committee on Arid Lands that debated the bill that eventually became law stated, "It has been our time-honored policy to provide for the settlement of our public lands in small tracts to actual home builders."[21] As Congressman Mondell, chairman of that Committee during the 1902 debate, emphasized,

> in order that no such lands may be held in large quantities or by non-resident owners, it is provided that *no water right for more than 160 acres shall be sold to any landowner*, who must also be a resident or occupant of his land. This provision was drawn with a view to breaking up any large land holdings which might exist in the vicinity of government works and to insure occupancy by the owner of the land reclaimed.[22]

The first director of the United States Reclamation Service, which was established in July of 1902 after the Reclamation Law was signed, explained the law's purpose as being

> not so much to irrigate the land, as it is to make homes . . . It is not to irrigate the land which now belongs to large corporations, or even to small ones; it is not to make these men wealthy, but it is to bring about a condition whereby the man with a family can get enough good land to support that family, to become a good citizen, and to have all the comforts and necessities which rightfully belong to an American citizen.[23]

Congress specifically instructed the Reclamation Service not to subsidize water to large landholders, especially speculators of the sort characterized by Californian agriculture. Acreage limitations on government subsidized land and resource policies were conceived as a way of thwarting land speculation and aiding the broadest portion of the citizenry with the benefits of public resources. At its heart, it was an egalitarian policy tied to a foundational democratic principle in the United States.[24]

Support for principles of agrarian democracy and opposition to corporate influence were grounded into Taylor's character from his Midwestern upbringing. In time, he learned to play a meaningful role as an advocate and scholar in confronting entrenched and powerful interests.

> Corporations perform many valuable services, but they also affect our daily lives in much less useful, and I think in some ways very damaging. The questionable aspect is the power that goes with the corporation, and the inclusion of more and more people within a bureaucracy, whether government or corporate. Those organizations have enlarging power over not only economic matters, but over political matters as well. One result is that what we used to call "civic-minded persons" tend to shy away from what I regard as the more fundamental political issues, and to go instead into good "civic works" that avoid the deeper political questions.
>
> One day [Dick] Boke [who had been pushed off of the federal payroll after attempting to uphold the water law] asked, "How are you able to keep your position at the University?" Well, I was able to keep it because the University of California under President Sproul cushioned and rejected the pressures. Don't think I haven't been the object of pressures, most of which never reached me personally; the administration shielded me. Yet, my belief is that the administration has plenty of pressure upon it because of my views and what I had done in harmony with those views. Now that I am retired, I am, if anything, freer than ever. What are they going to do about it if they don't like what I do? They can't cut off my retirement pay. I assure you that there are very powerful interests in this state that don't like me. Since Governor Culbert Olson left office in 1942, I have received no state appointments, as I did before.
>
> People have asked me—Dorothea used to ask me, too—"Are you going to end up writing the history of your defeat on the water issue?" I never was able to answer that question with certainty. All I could say was, "They haven't defeated me, they've nicked me." I've had some "non-victories." But it wouldn't be an issue in the courts and Congress today if I, with the people who supported me, had not worked at it. It is an issue today because we had enough victories to make it an issue.[25]

Over his career, Taylor's research—and the focus of his engagement—shifted from agricultural labor to water. While never abandoning earlier lines of inquiry, he took up the issue of water as a politically engaged scholar, seeking to defend the enforcement of the 1902 Act's equitable, democratic policies.

Taking up the water issue, it was not long before I found myself very aware of, and active in, the political process. Did I get into this position by "accident" or by "chance"?

If I had to generalize, I would say that I do not know how, at the moment of its occurrence, to surely identify an important event, an important decision, and to distinguish it from what is unimportant. In perspective, the important event or decision may stand out clearly, but important things at the time often don't appear to be important. It's afterwards that they can turn out to be enormously important, and to be so recognized.

In 1943, construction of Central Valley Project had begun, and the Bureau of Reclamation was setting up a series of studies of 24 problems related to the project. They organized committees, or what today we call "task forces." Most of those would meet in California. One of the problems, No. 19, was acreage limitation. The question: what to do about the 160-acre law. By a series of "accidents," I found myself in the middle of the water issue, where I've been ever since. I had learned only a year or two before that there was such a thing as an acreage limitation law. That fact had been largely kept in the dark, smothered. I didn't know there was such a law until my friend and neighbor, Walter Packard, with whom I had served in the Farm Security Administration, told me.

Packard said, "They should *limit* the landowners to water for 160 acres."

I said, "You meant that is what they *ought* to do?"

"No," he said, "that's the law."

"Do you mean that that is the law now? That a landowner is not to get water for more than 160?"

He said, "Yes. That is the law now."

That is how I found out about it. When Arthur Goldschmidt took me on as a consultant [for committees in California], I began to talk with people who might properly serve on the study of Problem 19. I was in favor of that law. I watched as attention to the problem began to come to a focus. Soon it became clear that the large land-owning interests opposed to it had adopted a tactic of silence on the issue, in which they were generally joined by the Bureau of Reclamation engineers.

The Bureau of Reclamation administrators found that professionals from the Bureau of Agricultural Economics who were invited to participate in the studies—in fact they were even paid by the Bureau of Reclamation to do it—shared my view. "Why should the water be monopolized by a handful of big landowners?" We met and we talked about it together. Observing that word of the law's existence was spreading, its opponents got the Irrigation Districts Association to adopt a resolution asking Congress to exempt the Central Valley from this "unreasonable" law. With that, the issue began coming out into the political open.

Taylor's political engagement bridged the problems in the valley, his position as a scholar in Berkeley, and the federal politics of Washington DC. He had become adept at fluidly moving between and across these spaces.

I saw this. I didn't know how fast they would move, but they moved within a few months. Their tactic was to avoid any publicity on the issue that might mobilize supporters of the law. At House of Representatives hearings concerned with the project, they waited until hearings were over then slipped through with no advance warning what is called a "committee amendment" proposing exemption of Central Valley Project from acreage limitation law. So, no witnesses likely to oppose exemption were aware that such a proposal was going to be made.

The exemption amendment was learned by Bureau officials about eight o'clock on the morning of the day when it was going to come to the floor in the afternoon. That gave no chance to rally forces to block exemption. Congressman Jerry Voorhis, whom Richard Nixon defeated in the next election, tried to substitute a compromise with partial enforcement in place of outright exemption, but the effort failed. The exemption successfully obtained by Congressman Elliott from Kern and Tulare counties, slipped through the House on March 22, 1944, in about 20 minutes. By grapevine I heard that opponents of the law then expected to have their exemption through the Senate within three weeks. Well, they never got it. They didn't get it because the Senate had to hold public hearings on the bill including the exemption.

Do you want me to tell you what I did, from which I learned something of the importance of citizen participation? The Senate Commerce Subcommittee hearings on H.R. 3961 were held in May of 1944. I talked with friends who shared my views; some were in the Bureau of Agricultural Economics in Washington, notably Marion Clawson, and did their part in spreading word of the importance of the acreage limitation issue. I went to the AFL. I said, "Here is what is proposed; is this what you want?" "Oh, no, that isn't what we want." Before that, I had been to the AFL in San Francisco, and had told Secretary C. J. Haggerty the situation. He responded immediately. Labor didn't want the exemption. The labor people in San Francisco told the AFL in Washington that they didn't want the exemption. So, when I went to the Washington AFL and said, "The hearings are going to be held soon. Do you want that exemption to go through?", the response was immediate: "No, we don't want it to go through!" So, a representative of the AFL was at the hearings. All that was necessary was that they be informed. I went likewise to the separate CIO, to Robert Lamb, an economist whom I had met a few years earlier in Senator LaFollette's office. So, there was also a CIO spokesman at the hearings.

I had met James G. Patton, the president of the Farmers Union, when he was in Berkeley (in this room, incidentally). So, I went to the Farmers Union, and also to the National Grange. The Grange, the National Farmers Union, the AFL, were all there to testify against exempting Central Valley from the acreage limitation law. It was during the war and I went to veterans' organizations— Veterans of Foreign Wars and the American Legion. Their representatives testified against an exemption. You see, if irrigated land was to be opened to settlement, they wanted veterans to have opportunity to get land. That was the historic position of the government; veterans had a preference. So they wanted no exemption. Church organizations, too, were alerted. I didn't do all this informing in Washington. Some I did during the preceding weeks and months in California after I learned about the acreage limitation issue.

It was like punching a button. The technique of participation was simple. I went to speak to somebody, I knew what his attitude was, and I would say, "Is this what you want? Do you want them to exempt that project from the 160-acre law?" The response was, "No." "All right, be there at the hearings." They went. Of course, I was not the only person who alerted opponents of exemption. . . . [T]he issue had been building up, and we had been spreading information earlier in California. I don't remember all the things that I did, and I don't want to claim that I did everything—for others were active, too—but I did quite a lot....

The California Grange Master, George Sehlmeyer, moved because one local grange, the Farmersville Grange, down in the Valley, passed a resolution to support the acreage limitation. Robert W. Pontius, with Farm Security Administration experience, pushed the right button down there, and as a result of that Sehlmeyer took his strong stand for acreage limitation, and the National Grange testified. It was during the war, and the National Grange representative asked the Senate committee, "Who ever heard of a man shouldering his musket for his boarding house?" He'd shoulder his musket for his farm, but not for his boarding house. [laughter] That was his own idea. So you punch the right button and snap!—like that comes the response. Legislative representatives of national organizations didn't know about the acreage limitation issue in Congress until they were told about it. But as soon as they were told, they acted. So the Senate Commerce Subcommittee killed the exemption, and passed the Rivers and Harbors bill without it.

Democratic Senator Sheridan Downey undertook to do in the Senate what Congressman Elliott had done in the House, notwithstanding that the exemption had been struck from the Senate bill. Still thinking he could win an exemption, he obtained authority under S. Res. 295 to hold hearings in California in July. But these largely blew up in his face. Witnesses favoring exemption spoke, of course, but the surprise was the number of California witnesses who opposed exemption. Many people participated then. It was far beyond the early phase when two or three of us were the informed key people getting it started. It just fanned out and was picked up by many others, and they just snowed Downey under at those hearings!

What I'm telling you is that action came because of what somebody did. For my own part, I can feel the heat of the Washington pavement yet. There is a place that when I go back there I still remember that building and how hot it was that day. But that's the way you get things done! The net result was that the Senate Commerce Subcommittee rejected the exempting clause in the Rivers and Harbors bill, and the Senate did the same. But interests favoring the exempting clause were strong enough to have it restored in conference. So the fate of the exemption was tied to the fate of the entire bill filled with flood control and harbor appropriations for many places throughout the United States. The issue had reached its critical point—all

appropriations and exemption, or no appropriations. Well, I've told you earlier how it came out, with LaFollette forcing Downey to back down.[26]

The Central Valley Project, under reclamation statute, was poised to
place dams in the Sierra Nevada and canals on the valley floor, yet much
of the farmland that would receive the water was consolidated into large
landholdings. Since a limitation of 160 acres and on-farm residency were
required under reclamation law, the Bureau of Agricultural Economics
was brought on to determine if the law would be applied to the project.
The law promised to implement a gradual land reform to break up the
region's monopolized land ownership patterns, ensuring an equitable
economy of democratic scale.

The Bureau of Agricultural Economics then commissioned a study
(Walter Goldschmidt's Arvin-Dinuba comparison, discussed in Chapter
2) to determine if reclamation's provisions would be beneficial, if applied.
Taylor was involved in the case study's conceptualization. He influenced
its research design and mentored Goldschmidt (his previous student) as
the young anthropologist conducted the study in the early 1940s.

> I had nothing, directly, officially, to do with the Arvin-Dinuba study. Of
> course, I was deeply involved in the water fight over the acreage limita-
> tion. Marion Clawson of the Bureau of Agricultural Economics and Walter
> Goldschmidt of his staff were concerned with it, and they talked with me
> about it.
>
> They looked over the field, and I looked over the field. They chose Arvin
> and Dinuba. I recommended they choose Firebaugh or Mendota on the
> west side, rather than Arvin. Their objection I think mainly was that Men-
> dota or Firebaugh might be criticized as too extreme—an extreme example
> of a community dependent upon big farming, which, from my point of view,
> meant that it would show the contrast with a community dependent on
> smaller farms even more sharply than Arvin. I still believe that. But for what-
> ever reasons they didn't want to take such an extreme contrast as I thought
> would be good. But the contrast between Dinuba and Arvin, nevertheless,
> was sufficiently extreme to reveal the issue.
>
> So this study was embarked upon; Walter Goldschmidt carried it out.
> He is with the Department of Anthropology at UCLA and was chairman
> for some time. At the time of the study he was employed by the Bureau

of Agricultural Economics. His doctoral dissertation, which he wrote under me, grew out of this study. He took his degree in anthropology, but I was a member of his committee. Professor Robert H. Lowie, his chairman, asked me to take charge of the thesis because I had more familiarity with the general conditions of rural California than he did. His thesis was an outgrowth of the Arvin-Dinuba study, and is called "As You Sow." Most people know that what follows in the Bible is "so shall ye also reap."

The study was attacked bitterly while it was in process, and spread upon the pages of the Congressional Record by the hostile congressman from Kern County, Alfred J. Elliott. He attacked it on the ground (among other things) that they were asking crazy, irrelevant questions. The study was started in wartime and was also attacked as a waste of gas and rubber which shouldn't be tolerated. Sheridan Downey attacked it in his book *They Would Rule the Valley*. Senator Paul Douglas told me that one day he said to Senator Downey, "Sheridan, who would rule the Valley?", and Downey answered, "Yes, that's the question." A perfectly true answer if you knew what was behind it—the public through government, or the big landowners. Downey was objecting to the New Deal officials who had New Deal conceptions of a good society, and favoring the giant land-holding interests.

In 1946 Mary Montgomery and Marion Clawson came out with their *History of Legislation and Policy Formation of the Central Valley Project Studies*. It was produced in multilith form by the BAE, but never reached print. Not long after that the personnel of the regional office of the BAE began to shrink. I have no documentation for what I am about to say. I have not heard it from anybody inside the BAE. But I remember thinking at the time, and I continue to think now, that there were pressures upon Washington to keep these BAE people out of regional political issues. It was too hot and the pressures too great. I believe there were changes in personnel in the Department of Agriculture in the higher echelons unsympathetic to the position on acreage limitation taken by Clawson and the other members of his staff. They were under the influence, I believe, of the large landowners, and I believe that the regional offices were shrunk for the reason that I've described—it got into hot political questions. They were doing an excellent service in getting into those questions, in my opinion.[27]

Goldschmidt's findings, as we discussed in Chapter 2, were a warning about the effects of economic consolidation on community life and democratic governance. Tendencies of political pressure on scientific research, alluded to by Taylor, and apparent in Goldschmidt's experience, became characteristic treatment of subsequent Valley scholarship that challenged Californian agribusiness.

The historical precedents and legal points of the Reclamation Act of 1902 required that any acreage above 160 acres must be sold after ten years if the landowner was receiving federal water through a project constructed under this mandate. Many of the dams, aqueducts, and canals in the western United States, including those in California's Central Valley, were built under these regulations. Taylor fought to get the law "enforced" by the federal government.

The trend of non-enforcement had foreboding consequences. If a government cannot implement its own laws, or its civil society is unable to muster the political power to do so, then its authority is corrupted and is likely to continue to be abused. Just as cancer, left untreated, metastasizes, so the threat looms within the body politic of passively allowing the corruption of law, statute, and public process.

As Taylor began to examine problems connected to industrial scale agriculture, he identified and experienced political pressure and his questions turned toward understanding the "power structure" of California. He considered whether the law was within the people's control.

I don't know whether we'll ever make it or whether we won't. Or whether they are going to rivet on us this monopoly of land perpetuated with a monopoly of water. It is going to be very bad if that program goes clear through to the end.

If we were discussing the water situation—reclamation—I would read to you right now what Theodore Roosevelt said in 1911 before the Commonwealth Club. He warned the "very wealthy men" he was addressing of the "ruin that they would bring upon themselves" if they pursued on *exactly* the course they are pursuing today. I think a heavy price is paid both within the academic world and outside because instead of emphasizing foresight to avoid problems, we wait until the problems hit us in the face and then try to figure out what to do.

The land monopolists have controlled the enforcement of reclamation law and torn the law to ribbons. What bothers them is that controls over speculation and monopoly still are the law. They haven't been able to wipe them off the statute books yet; so they know they are in an uncertain, perhaps even precarious position, violating the law. They know it, but they keep the knowledge from spreading widely to the public.

I've exposed this in writing. The law journals are full of my articles on it. The *Bay Guardian* prints it—30,000 circulation, an underground sheet, they call it. I fill the congressional hearings, year after year, with my testimony exposing and documenting what they are doing. But nothing happened. What I say is buried in print. That is my frustration.

By administrative ruling, the excess landowner is obliged to sell the excess within ten years, and if he doesn't do that, then the Secretary of the Interior can sell them. That was the story of the DiGiorgio divestiture. They signed contracts in '52 and they did not sell by '62. So then the Secretary of the Interior undertook to pressure them into selling, and it was a grand mess. Although the law says the sale price is to be the pre-project price of the lands, the Bureau of Reclamation approved a sale price so high it was above current market value, and DiGiorgio couldn't get anybody to buy at that price. That gives you a little clue as to how pervasively the law goes unenforced.

The residency requirement has been unenforced for fifty-five years. A visiting federal district judge from Montana, sitting in San Diego, said, "You cannot invalidate a valid law by administrative inaction. Residency does apply." But where have the administrators been all this time? They allowed DiGiorgio to sell 160 excess acres to a shipping magnate and his wife living in San Francisco—legally ineligible by reason of residence to buy it. Now this law is torn to shreds by its administrators. The public doesn't know what's being done. They don't understand its full meaning and the repercussions from nonenforcement. It's easy to fool the public. You can manipulate people quite easily if you set your brain to it and if you have control of the media.

It's hard to make the average person understand what the issue has to do with him. It's so fundamental to the society in which he lives, yet it's hard to tell a Californian who runs California, and what giant landholdings have to do with it. As a Californian walks down the street and breathes the fresh air (when it's fresh), the question doesn't occur to him. He takes it all for granted without examining it. He doesn't understand the power structure that's been built up, nor on what it rests. Just try to tell even a university colleague that the drive to escape acreage limitation by creating the costly State

Water Project is a big factor behind the cutting of the education budget, and a factor in imposing student tuition. They shed it off like water off a duck's back. With most of them there's no use talking. Just try to tell the students why they're socked two hundred dollars a quarter in tuition.

Today California is increasingly urbanized, and the urban-raised generation thinks the family farm belongs to history, that it is passing out, and that efforts to save or revive it are "fuddy-duddy." Down in the valley, family farmers still don't think the family farm is dead, although they know it is under heavy pressure. But the city people fall for the argument that a farm has got to be bigger, because of bigger machinery, and to be more efficient. They swallow that propaganda. So today, you've got to punch different buttons than in the forties, although with some persons the "family farm" slogan still works. It doesn't work with the citified liberal: most citified liberals don't know what a farm is, anyway.

Now the buttons that you punch are called "conservation," "environment," "stop the urban sprawl," "preserve open space." Then you go to the educators and you say, "Under Abraham Lincoln you had land grants for education. How about water grants for education?" Educators rise to it, and they approve, but educators are not action people. Labor has been consistent in its support for acreage limitation all through. In fact, their battle against land monopoly in California dates from the 1870s.[28]

Taylor pursued this reasoning further. He built a coalition advocating for "water grants for education." He then drafted the legislation, and had it introduced in Congress. The story of this work reveals the innovative potential of politically engaged scholarship. It suggests how to affect national policies aimed to ensure fiscal stability and economic equity.

Long ago, Senator Paul Douglas told me that we wouldn't really get effective enforcement of the acreage limitation until the government bought the land. He also spoke of the land grants for education. After a long while I worked the idea over, got draftsmen to help on the bill, brought people together from the fields of education, conservation, and planning for open space, and labor to support it. The bill, HR 5236, was introduced in Congress through the combined personal efforts of representatives of the Sierra Club, the AFL-CIO, and the National Farmers Union.

The law says that the excess landowners are obliged to sell the excess at the pre-water price. Some people think that the government will have to provide millions of dollars to buy the land. I prefer to put it another way: If the government really followed the law, it could add millions upon millions of dollars to the United States treasury. We'd bail out the treasury from a lot of its indebtedness and we'd make possible public planning and we'd finance public education in the land-grant tradition. The windfall profits, or what Henry George called the "unearned increment," would go into the United States treasury instead of into the pockets of large private landowners. We're giving away the water now, not only for nothing, because it also costs to store and to move the water to private lands, besides. Of course, the excess landowners' spokesmen tell it just the opposite. They say we want to take their lands away from them. They avoid talk about the subsidy, or about the taking of the public water to private lands.

The government could either rent or sell, and receive the rent or selling price at the national treasury. I personally think it would be highly advantageous to lease the lands in the manner of present leasing of grazing land. Of course, there would be continuing pressure on the part of the renters to keep the rental prices way down, as they have done with the grazing lands, but there also would be balancing pressures of benefiting education to keep the rentals up to something approximately market value.[29]

Crafting legislation was tangential to Taylor's primary strategy to defend and implement reclamation law (and through this long battle, to engage a broader argument that an equitable economy is most suited to guaranteeing a democratic society). In this cause, his primary arsenal was built around numerous law review articles, which he wrote and published in some of the most prestigious journals in the country. As prophesied early in his career by E. A. Ross, Taylor did "argue" an important case before the Supreme Court, only he did it as a legal scholar rather than as a lawyer.

I wrote a series of articles in law journals from 1949 to 1965. They fine-tooth-combed the subject of land and water issues. They were done on my own time, researching my field in the university tradition. I was playing the game according to the rules.

I took the subject seriously, with never a question of motives on the other side. I knew all the time that the motivation was—and is—great private economic interest. They would just write the law the way they want to. If you have the interest and the power you just get the law written the way you want it to be written. It conforms to the long history of the disposal of the public lands in this country. The record is not a good one; it's a very bad one. It's a very bad one right here in California, and the tactic was first to grab the water, then the money to get the water to the land.

I wanted to zero in for those law journal articles. Instead of a scatter gun I wanted to hit a bull's eye. Then I stopped writing for the law journals and began to write for *American West* and *Bay Guardian*. Law journal articles are excellent vehicles for a certain type of work. The style is to document to a gnat's eyebrow what you want to document. From that solid base you can build in whatever direction you choose when action is what you want. Law journal articles themselves don't do the active job, but they provide the foundation, and they make a lot of trouble for officials who sometimes when they're called to account, have to meet what you say.

I was well rewarded for the Yale journal article—particularly well rewarded. The United States Supreme Court cited it. And on November 23 last, that good judge Murray decision on Imperial Valley in the San Diego federal court, that decision cited it, too. So I've had commendation at the very top in '58, and again in '71, at the very bottom of the federal judiciary hierarchy. That's a reward. Both of them good decisions.

I had lawyer's standards to conform to. You remember that at the University of Wisconsin I went half way through law school, so I had the grounding in legal training—not completed, but grounding. You document everything you say, right back to the source. After 1965, I felt that tactically I wasn't getting anywhere further writing law journal articles. Though I still write for law journals when I think there may be a practical result from it, and the recording of the situation may serve as a foundation supporting my side of the law in the courts.[30]

In 1979, Taylor compiled all thirteen of his law review articles into a single book: *Essays on Land, Water and the Law in California*. Taken together, they offer an overview to the water fight.

Taylor defined a democratic ethic linked to economic scale within reclamation law. He noted that its sponsors "presented their measure as one drawn with unusual care to prevent monopoly of water on reclaimed public lands and to break up existing monopoly on private land by denying water to it."[31] An essentially progressive act, the Reclamation Act of 1902 was designed to thwart speculation, prevent economic consolidation, and starve owners of plantation-like estates of public subsidy. Its value and purpose are that land and water are public resources and need to be equitably divided and shared. Most important, these resources needed to be protected from the narrow greed of a few individuals to ensure the basis of an economy that could support a democratic society.

Essays on Land, Water and the Law in California's articles emphasize the non-enforcement of reclamation law and examine concepts related to property. "Reclamation *creates* property values; that is one of its chief purposes," Taylor explained.[32] Capital valuation accrued both through asset appreciation and savings. By introducing water to arid land, the land's value markedly increased as delivery of publicly subsidized water resulted in the ability to produce more valuable crops and in substantial savings to farmers. In turn, the value of all farmland eligible for these water deliveries jumped immediately.

Water, also, became "property" (albeit briefly) through reclamation. "Appropriation, by customary California law, marks the *beginning* of a right to water, *use* is its basis, and *disuse* is its end."[33] A 1936 *Harvard Law Review* article that Taylor cited and quoted explained the temporary commodification of water from a natural, commonly accessed resource into private property via its use.

> The title or interest that one may acquire in the waters of a stream *is entirely different* to that which may be acquired in lands. Running water, so long as it continues to flow in its natural course, *is not and cannot be the subject of private ownership*. . . . This interest is *dependent upon* user and *it may be lost* when the owner ceases to make avail of the same. . . . It is the use of the water merely to which they may acquire an interest and not to the water itself.[34]

Since "ownership" was contingent upon use, it was also therefore provisional. The infrastructure provided by the federal government, such as dams and canals under reclamation projects, facilitated the use of water, in turn making a public resource into a transitory commodity.

Infrastructures created through the Central Valley Project therefore bookend the extraction of profit from a natural resource originally obtained from the public domain. Water, in this case, is then discharged as waste (in "disuse") into the underground aquifer, sediment ponds or waterways—back into the public domain, often as a liability and responsibility. (In the San Joaquin Valley, after agricultural use, water can be saturated with nitrates, fertilizers, pesticides, herbicides, salts, and other pollutants.) The costs of treating this toxic waste, after its use, is then passed back to the public and not charged to the polluter.

Property was a critically important facet of the reclamation battles. Taylor's democratic theory was based on his belief that "our entire society, like the law, rests on a principle of wide distribution of property."[35] He recognized, in his understated way, that concentrations of property in California were already perverting democratic governance:

> the excess land owners are sufficiently concerned over possible application of the excess land provision to resist it strongly. With this caution against published data as the *literal measure* of benefit from water development, it is appropriate to point out that an extraordinary concentration of ownership exists in the San Joaquin Valley, of a kind that has influenced Congress.[36]

He continued by noting that in 1947 the Bureau of Reclamation "told Congress that thirty-four corporations and individuals in the 'probable present and future San Joaquin Valley service areas of the Central Valley Project' owned close to three-quarters of a million acres."[37] These entities were not easily going to divest themselves of their land at the precise moment when its speculative value was poised to dramatically increase at public expense.

As the years passed, it was apparent that the law was being systematically violated. Taylor was put in the position of a citizen petitioning, with increasing vehemence, the government to follow its own law. Even worse, he witnessed an erosion of support for his position within multiple bureaucracies and constituencies. His tone began to express frustration and fatigue as the law was continuously "being violated through official nonenforcement."[38] Rather than pinpointing responsible parties (as he had done in earlier articles), he now broadly identified "concentrated and powerful opposition operating upon the law-making and law-enforcing mechanisms" as amorphous perpetrators.[39]

His later legal research then bore down into the most highly pertinent contexts and geographic anomalies, specifically the Federal San Luis Service Area with its 600,000 acre Westlands Water District. Areas like this exemplified precisely the characteristics of economic monopoly and consolidated landholdings that reclamation law was designed to reform. Taylor revealed that "seventy percent of the lands in the Federal San Luis Service Area are ineligible under the excess land law to receive project water because they are held in ownerships exceeding 160 acres and their owners have not executed recordable contracts to make them eligible. A single owner, the Southern Pacific, held nearly 120,000 acres."[40]

Circumvention of the law was conducted in the interest of large landowners and agribusiness in the San Joaquin Valley. Their political lobbying and legal maneuvers skewed traditional democratic governance and shredded the premise of an egalitarian economy. The issue, as Paul Gates mentioned in his foreword to Taylor's *Essays on Land, Water and the Law in California*, amounted to an economic strategy of agribusiness "to monopolize natural resources made valuable and available at public expense."[41] Boiled down into a simple axiom, the large landowners worked to privatize profits and socialize costs.

While some of the region's unequal ownership patterns pre-existed the construction of the Central Valley Project, they were exacerbated by the inability to implement reclamation law at the moment when public investments increased already owned assets of these wealthy individuals. Through Taylor's and subsequent scholars work, we are offered a window into the political corruption that follows gross inequalities in property ownership. At the same time, the values of progressive legislation, such as the need for land reform in places like the San Joaquin Valley, become clearer as future objectives.

The perversion of federal law was not the only public arena polluted by industrial agribusiness. The backstory that Taylor tells at the end of his life brings to light the efforts of corporate interests to pollute academic inquiry and scientific research. At the same time, his success in thwarting many of these violations offer lessons for future scholars.

Battle Tactics

Taylor's extensive experience as a politically engaged scholar taught him lessons that he passed on through his oral history interviews.

Do you want to hear about the ways of getting things done?

You see, on the one hand, you have the issue as an abstract political issue. On the other hand is the participant. I have been a participant; I've played a role. Some things wouldn't have happened if I hadn't happened to be at a certain place at a certain time. Like Dorothea, who happened by "chance," as the *San Francisco News* said, to be at Nipomo so she could photograph the "migrant mother." Was my participation by "chance?" I do not know how many "chances" I missed. But some I did not miss.

How do you take hold of a public issue and get something done about it? There are these two ways of looking at that 160-acre water problem, for example, or the agricultural labor problem. One is to discuss the problem— this aspect of it, that aspect of it. The other way is to play an active role as a person, as a citizen, as a professor.

I've played a role, seeking to get something done, namely, enforcement of the acreage limitation law. I haven't been content simply to record what happened, although I have done that, too.

I have learned, as an informed citizen, how to be effective. I have also learned some of the limitations facing a citizen trying to be effective. I've run up against the obstacles, but I think that subject might be an interesting phase which wouldn't come out if one said only, "Well, the 160-acre limitation, let's discuss its meaning, how it originated, and whether changing times have changed its usefulness."

You see? Analysis and action, altogether related, are two different things.

In commenting on the effective-citizen aspect of my work, I'd like to begin by dredging up memories of my studies of Mexican immigration. Both questions I have studied most intensively—agricultural labor and water— were public, political issues, and still are. I was not attracted to make my studies of Mexican labor because it was a public issue.

I learned quickly through experience the importance of public relations to the success of a program, but I did not learn this through direct political participation in the decision-making process.[42]

As an officer who led troops into battle, Taylor surveyed battlefields for tactical advantage. Later, as a scholar, he deployed these same skills to attack the foundations of California's power structure. Today, we hear his voice still, through his stories, as he offers advice for current and future battle.

> What I say to the young generation is this: Study your targets. Study what buttons to push and when to push them. Then push them, and you will get results.
>
> Young students are likely to pick the wrong targets. They have elevated Governor Reagan, I am afraid, to re-election, and to become a senatorial or even presidential possibility—well, that is exactly the wrong result. Why don't they take him on, for example, on *my* issue? They could tear Governor Reagan apart on the water issue; it would expose him. But they don't do it! They get rocks and throw them through the glass doors, they "reconstitute" the University, put posters all over the place, and all of that! And Governor Reagan loves it. The more the mess at the University, the surer he is of re-election. I say they don't know what buttons to push.
>
> If you want to break it down, there are really two answers. There are the people who don't want to deal from within—the outright revolutionaries. They want a mess! The saying is, things have got to get worse before they get better. Get everybody in a mess! I say they pick the wrong targets; they say, that doesn't make any difference. The students are here, so the University is the target. What they say in effect is, "Reagan? Yeah, sure we may be re-electing him now, but that will make things still worse, and that is what has got to happen before we have a revolution."[43]

Taylor used military tactics in his work on public issues. He approached them as life commitments, and he was willing to pay any price for the truth to be made transparent.

> I have a couple of causes about which I felt very strongly, very deeply, and I wasn't going to have them jeopardized by anything else, if I could help it. I wanted to deal with those issues on *my* ground, and not on their ground. That is one of the first things that you learn in minor military tactics. As platoon commander in World War I, what did I learn? To make the enemy fight you on *your* ground, not fight him on *his*. The issues are mine, and I want the fight to be on the *issue*.

The big landowners, like Kern County Land Company and others, wanted a state project as means of escape from the federal acreage limitation, in order to capture unlimited, unearned increment from public development of public water. Can you tell people that? Well, it takes quite a while to get around to tell anybody that. But if you can get on the same platform with them, then you can tell the audiences, and then you can expose them!

So, in my lifetime, I have had a couple of issues to which I have really devoted myself, that I put years into. I didn't want to scatter my shots, or expose myself unnecessarily, when it was so easy to throw brickbats and raise clouds of suspicion and so to make proof of anything unnecessary.[44]

Taylor was a scholar during the McCarthy era in the United States. Loyalty oaths and false innuendo were part of the national political and academic landscape. All of the early scholars in this book—Goldschmidt, Taylor, and Galarza—had to deal with this style of political attack.

Goldschmidt tells a story of going to Taylor and asking his advice on whether to sign the University's loyalty oath. What did Taylor do? He signed it and maintained his focus on the larger issue while personally supporting the academics holding their principled positions. He was not going to "scatter" his energy, but rather bring focused force to bear on his target.

I was not prepared to make the loyalty oath my battle, not to the bitter, bitter end. There were those who took it to the end and won the case. I was for them and contributed financially. I was always with that group, but it was just not my battle.

I never "scattered" my efforts and my energies for all the causes that I believed in, nor any large fraction of them. I've concentrated on one or two at a time. They have been, in general, lone battles. They have been my causes. The program of camps and other improvements for the migratory laborers, the water issue, those issues, I thought, were fundamental and closely interrelated. I still believe that to be true, and I still am interested in both.

While, of course, I am not the only person who has made these his causes, I have in a sense, made them mine from the 1920s to 1970s. I have been unwilling to take on other causes, in part for tactical reasons. The easiest way for your opponent to undercut you, to defeat you, is on his ground rather than on *your* ground. If he wants to defeat you on, say, a water issue, if he can find something utterly irrelevant with which to discredit you, building on people's prejudices, impugning your patriotism, that is the ground on which your opponent would *love* to fight you. I have been unwilling to offer them any openings of that sort that I could avoid.[45]

The McCarthy era politics were a terrain that Taylor had to negotiate. Repeatedly the FBI investigated him, making inquiries and interviewing acquaintances.

I remember saying to one of the FBI men referring to the battle over the 160-acre limitation, "I am not going to stop fighting for what I believe in on that issue. That is a gigantic scandal to capture hundreds of millions of dollars, contrary to law. I don't care what, I am not going to stop the fight on that issue!"[46]

In reflecting on this treatment in his oral history interviews, Taylor noted the intensity of the inquiry, and his suspicion that the FBI was unwittingly used by agribusiness interests seeking to undermine his academic research and policy advocacy.

It was not a happy experience to have your patriotism called into question, and to have those inquiries. I have a whole series of experiences—didn't you know that I had a full field investigation? I've been investigated from stem to stern. I have the final documents only. That investigation went on for maybe a couple of years. There were no charges made.

A political friend of mine—the Director of the California State Department of Agriculture when I was a member of the advisory board—told me that FBI agents came to him about me when he was on a trip in Minnesota. How many others they asked about me, I don't know. But you can see how they prowled around. There is one phase of the investigation where I suspect that the FBI was being used to try to "get" me.

They kept coming back. They would call me up by telephone of an evening and ask could they see me the next morning at ten-thirty or whatever. They would come always in pairs. They'd pick up something, I suppose, somewhere, that somebody would say about me, then they'd come and ask about it. I have the papers, their letter and my response, on campus. After the investigations, the next step in procedure was to give the results of the investigation to the agency of the government to which I was consultant, that is, to the Department of the Interior.

There were plenty of people around then—perhaps even now—who would like to have seen me out of the way. I am prepared to believe that. Who did this, of course, I don't know, but if my suspicion is true, it would be either big landowners, or big private power.

It was not my connection with the University, but my connection with the government that gave the ground initially for making the investigation under broad presidential order. The McCarthyites made trouble throughout the government, and all over the world. What I am telling you, when I speak of little incidents that cross my mind, is the impact of tactics like those of the McCarthy era on sensitive people who have causes that in the daylight are perfectly respectable causes. The McCarthy tactics are the tactics of throwing dust and dirt.[47]

The Basis of a Democratic Society

Opposed to subterfuge, suspicion, and innuendo, Taylor in his scholarship clarified democratic public policy, informed and agitated citizens through education, and promoted an equitable distribution of property. His work as a politically engaged scholar was firmly grounded in a view of what was required as a basis of an equitable and democratic society.

It was my belief in the desirability of holding people on the land in the status of owner-workers, avoiding two things: the split which we see in such extreme form in this state between landowners and their workers, and the sweeping of people off the land and into the cities.

People don't usually associate the two and say, "Well is that what we want from machines?" They kick about crowding the ghettoes, but seldom ask what created the ghettoes? The sweeping of people off the land with no severance pay created the ghettoes. How are we going to use the land is a really big question. Is the only criterion to be the advantage of big machinery to big land owners?

The political instability of our day is related to mechanization and displacement of people from the land. The distribution of property is no longer equal or equitable.

Look at the kind of society that you get when you go to a big-farming community. You no longer have a homogenous community. It's gone. You don't have the basis for a democratic society.

That's the conclusion from the Arvin-Dinuba study. That's why interest in that is being revived, even in Congress. It's a question of philosophy rather than agricultural economics. And political power. Look at Imperial Valley. It's a polarized society, a lot of landless people and a handful of landowners, largely corporate. It's the base of an egalitarian democratic society that is at stake.

It's interesting that the praise of large operation that you get from certain quarters on the economic side fits with the Communist argument. They're both for the big-scale operation. Well, you don't get a democratic society out of it there, and I don't think you do here, either.

Our Agricultural Extension Service and our Department of Agriculture assist those who are most alert in grabbing the assistance offered. As for the rest, let the devil take the hindmost. We are seeing the obliteration of our rural societies because of an overemphasis of that sort in the way we spread improvement in technology.

The inscription on Hilgard Hall, "To rescue for human society the native values of rural life" has had minimal emphasis, whether in California or over the United States, generally. So, we're seeing land and technology in the hands of a few, and a polarization of our society.[48]

Effective political actors, using scholarship in their struggles, generate empirical evidence to produce action. When the object of study is a defense of our own democratic institutions and values, the commitment of the scholar becomes tenacious.

In an article that was published in the *Journal of Social Issues* in 1947, Taylor wrote, "One may build from facts to principles, but the attempt to reason first from the principle to the facts is likely to prove ineffective in producing action."[49] Recalling this statement and article in his oral history interviews, he drove home a set of crucial principles.

I will stand behind what I wrote. It's facts that have weight rather than principles. You don't fail to relate them to principles, but it's the facts that carry the weight. I got the migrant labor camp program started by bringing the facts to the decision makers, visually as well as in text—making those reports of my text and Dorothea's photographs. They were showing field conditions, and they couldn't dodge them. What were they going to do about it? It's not enough to say, "There are an awful lot of people out there in the *greatest distress*. They *really* need some help. They ought to have a place where they can at least wash up, and where their kids can have some kind of stability and care." But if you amass the facts—words, numbers, maps, graphs, photographs—then they're uncomfortable if they don't do something about it.

That's the basis of your pressure. If you want to get something done, the best way is for somebody to say something to somebody else at the right time and place. Present them with the facts and make a personal contact. Most people just say, "Oh, my," and wring their hands: "Why isn't something done?" But things happen because *somebody does* something. And those somebodies, if they know what to do and when to do it—those somebodies can be the kind of people that often are considered nobodies. Most people haven't the faintest appreciation of the potential power they have if only they would use it.

In that article's last paragraph, on pages 55 and 56, I write: "The profession of social scientists can contribute much to make political decision intelligent, and its potential power is very great. If that power is ever to be exerted fully, the profession will have to come closer to grips with the processes of decision, in order to understand the rules of that game, and to know the obstacles to acceptance of its professional services. Its members will have to find the many ways, informal as well as formal, personal as well as official, by which our capacities to gather facts, analyze and interpret them, can be used to clarify issues and to raise intelligent alternative courses of action to the level of practical politics in those arenas where decisions are made."

Now most of our professional social scientists don't do that. They'll talk about the situation without going to the decision-making process. They will accept the decisions of those who make the decisions. They accept them without trying to influence them. But if you want to change the decisions, you've got to do something. I should be satisfied that I've helped to keep the 160-acre issue alive in the halls of government. Had we not been able to do battle on this issue from the New Deal of FDR and the Fair Deal of Harry Truman, the monopolists and speculators would have had the law wiped off the statute books.[50]

In 1982, the Reagan administration signed legislation passed by a Democrat-controlled Congress that increased the acreage limitation to 960 acres per individual. Growers also no longer had to be residents on their farms to receive the subsidy.

Coupled with loopholes for even larger parcel ownership, the issues of equitable land distribution and its effects on democratic governance were decided in favor of agribusiness. Taylor died two years later.

The struggle that he had helped to initiate, however, was just beginning.

3

Terror as Education

ERNESTO GALARZA

After driving through Palo Alto to Stanford University, Scott and I walk across campus feeling awe mixed with disdain.

The campus is laid out like a grandiose hacienda. Broad thoroughfares, large plazas, arches, and fountains. Spanish colonial architecture roofed with adobe style bricks. Like a national capital or medieval cathedral—a design that diminishes the individual before the institution.

A day after visiting the Bancroft, we make our way to the Cecil H. Green Library, its special collections and the university archives. Security desk just inside the doors. Identification confirmation, checkpoint protocols, rules to follow—all increase our impatience.

Allowed one box at a time, we take the first to a table in the back of the room. Sturdy, with manila files, its tab reads: Stanford University Library—Special Collections; Collection 224; Title: Galarza; Box: 65; Series: V; Folder: 1.

Diving in, we open the folder. The first document is a photograph of a man, shot, lying on the ground. Titled "Assassination attempt on James Price, DiGiorgio Strike, May 17, 1948," blood is pooling in the black and white still shot, staining the floor. An incongruous calm blankets the scene.

Smacked in the face, we pause, shocked. Survey more crime scene photos. Then, we move into the rest of the folders. Everything compiled here—weekly reports, research files, letters, photos—was organized by Galarza at the end of his life. His work, assembled and ordered, purposely handed forward, awaiting completion.

Now before us, artifacts easily excavated. A line of clues.

His lessons, an invitation.

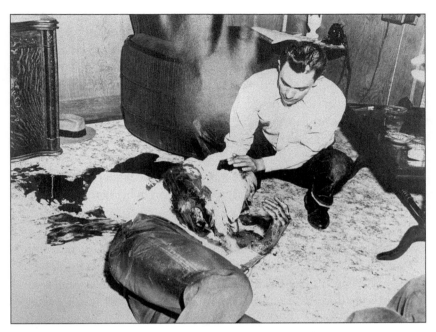

Figure 3.1. Assassination attempt on James Price, DiGiorgio Strike, May 17, 1948.
Courtesy of the Department of Special Collections, Stanford University Libraries.

From Farmworker to Scholar

Ernesto Galarza was in constant movement throughout his life and career. Born in Mexico in 1905, his family moved to the United States when revolution convulsed his homeland.[1]

As a child, he worked as a hop picker near Sacramento. At that time, he recalled, "I became a leader of the Mexican community at the age of eight for the simple reason that I knew perhaps two dozen words of English."[2] He took jobs as a newsboy, cannery and packing shed laborer, social work aide, interpreter, Boys Club organizer, elementary school teacher, co-director of a progressive elementary school and education specialist with the Pan American Union.

Galarza received a B.A. from Occidental College, an M.A. from Stanford University, and a Ph.D. from Columbia University. He taught at a number of prestigious universities, including the John Marshall School of Law, University of Denver, Claremont University, University of Notre Dame, San Jose State University, UC San Diego, UC Santa Cruz, and the Harvard Graduate School of Education. In 1979, he was nominated for the Nobel Peace Prize.

This journey was long considered, a diligent and earned preparation for public service to his Mexican community in the United States. Galarza's return to California as a farm labor organizer, after he finished his Ph.D. at Columbia, was the most intense application of that commitment.

In a 1949 pamphlet, titled *Common Ground*, Galarza concludes with a "Program for Action" and signals his intention to bring the fight out of the universities and into the fields:

> On this and other aspects of the changing context of the problem of the Mexican minority in the United States, an abundant literature has developed. This literature runs all the way from the serious, compact, and sustained scholarship of Dr. Paul Taylor's studies to the articles, newspaper accounts, and books of the "protest" type. In between are the shelves of catalogued masters' and doctoral theses, government reports, case studies, and monographs numbering thousands of items. Bibliographically, at least, the Mexican minority has come of age.
>
> By now the time has come for this minority to find the connection between the library card index and life. In the living and working conditions of this group certain problems have been isolated, defined, studied, and analyzed. Now they must be resolved.[3]

Rather than parley his Ivy League degree into an academic career, Galarza set out on this task of resolving the "living and working conditions" of farmworkers by taking a position with the National Farm Labor Union.

Between 1947 and 1959, Galarza worked as the Director of Research and Education for the National Farm Labor Union (NFLU), later reconstituted as the National Agricultural Workers Union (NAWU), both affiliated with the AFL-CIO. This effort to confront and organize farmworkers laboring within California's system of industrial agriculture arose as an outgrowth from the Southern Tenant Farmers Union (STFU).

The STFU were a tough, nonviolent, and bi-racial union that recognized all classes of landworkers, including day laborers, tenants, sharecroppers, and small farmers. Forged in the crucible of Southern planter reaction, where they faced extreme violence and waves of systematic terror, the STFU were steeled to face California's agribusinesses. The union, under the banner of the NFLU, entered the fields in 1947.

Galarza led the way, noting later that he participated in "probably twenty strikes," mostly in California but also in Florida, Texas, and Arizona.[4] From his position in the fields with the workers, he not only led strikes against particular farming operations but studied the broader, strategic issues and policy impediments facing farmworkers in California. His strategy involved attacking the "alliance" between agribusiness and government bureaucracies while introducing innovative approaches to labor organizing in the fields.[5]

With only a modicum of union support and financial backing, Galarza battled agribusiness for over a decade. As Joan London and Henry Anderson observed in their book, *So Shall Ye Reap*:

> His weapons were highly personal: the shield of research and analytical thought, the sword of the written and spoken word. Armed with these, he set forth to do battle with the fortified feudal cities of the bracero system, and the indifference of organized labor. His basic tactic was to document the flouting of laws—the abuses, the corruption, the debasement, the scandals inherent in the Braceros system—and to publicize his findings as broadly as possible.[6]

By standing on the ground and looking up through legal and political structures that hindered the farm labor movement, he identified specific objects for political engagement, most notably the DiGiorgio Fruit Corporation and Public Law 78, the authorizing legislation for the Braceros program. Both were audacious targets. DiGiorgio was the nation's foremost vertically integrated agribusiness, marshaling enormous political influence, while the Braceros program was a federally supported, international farm labor infrastructure funneling workers to the United States from Mexico. The exploitation of these bi-national laborers subsidized agribusiness profitability versus family farms and undermined farmworker union organizing in California and across the country.

Engage the Enemy!

In the years before his passing, Ernesto Galarza compiled his final teachings into *The Burning Light: Action and Organizing in the Mexican Community in California*. Published in 1982, two years before his death, the book includes a series of oral history transcripts, taped lectures, and interviews recorded between 1959 and 1981.

We begin with him looking back over his work in organizing farmworkers, with excerpts from a 1959 conference talk in Santa Barbara, California.

> I reacted with intense interest to a remark that was made this morning that one of the difficulties of the Mexican-American community is that it has not pinpointed the enemy . . . I ought to tell you that some fifteen or twenty years ago, more than that, perhaps, I asked myself the very same question. I had been working and living with farm laborers in this state, and I had moved with them up and down the state for many years, coming at last to the conclusion that one of our difficulties was that we had not defined the target: who was the enemy? So I spent some ten years of my life in an experiment. What happens to a Mexican-American community and those who presume to lead it when they do pinpoint the enemy? And we did. I helped to organize some twenty locals of farmworkers in this state from Yuba City to the Mexican border. It was our continuous effort not only to organize the farmworkers, but to try to help them to understand where the enemy was. I think we succeeded. In fact, the best evidence that we did succeed is that we were so thoroughly destroyed.
>
> In some ten years of what I like to call dynamic research (and someone will tell me if somebody else has thought of this before)—and by this I mean in areas of social experience where information is awfully hard to get because it's very closely guarded; the only way to get it is to go out and not ask for the information, but to challenge those who are keeping it to themselves—in California it became obvious to me that the way to get at the understanding of why farm labor was so exploited and lived so miserably in a hundred hamlets in this state, the way to do that was to engage the enemy!
>
> So we organized with the purpose of taking down a peg or two the power of the Associated Farmers of California, of the banks and insurance companies who have very high investments in agriculture, of other institutions that carry a role in the background as investors and as manipulators

Figure 3.2. National Farm Labor Union, late 1940s or early 1950s. Courtesy of Occidental College Special Collections and College Archives, People Files, Ernesto Galarza.

of wealth. Step by step, in a series of strikes, we challenged that power. We named institutions and we named persons. We named places. Through the years, the picture unfolded. But to the degree that we *did* define the opposition, the opposition grew in strength, in determination to destroy the union, and it did destroy the union.

I want to warn every Mexican American who thinks of himself as a leader. Before he puts together an organization of any kind that is going after specific targets of power, I want to warn him: he's asking for some pretty rough treatment. One of the things we found out, for instance, was that the agencies of government—and they are not Mexican-American agencies; they're not inventions of the Mexican peasant to come to this country—the agencies of state and federal power were conniving, collaborating and conspiring with the economic power structure to destroy the union. And they did!

Now the story of how that destruction was accomplished is a very important story. I've written a couple of chapters of it and I commend it to you with no sense of immodesty, because it not only describes a specific instance of the destruction of a growing community among the farmworkers in this country, but it describes how that destruction was accomplished. I think that any challenge to power in these democratic United States is going to, as of now, run into the same kinds of difficulties.[7]

Laying out a trail for others to follow, Ernest Galarza was systematic, explicit, and purposeful. Strategically, he taught and organized, always pushing forward.

At the United Farm Workers (UFW) boycott office in San Jose on May 7, 1974, Galarza sketched the history of his farm labor organizing, offered for perspective in the midst of the next movement for worker rights.

We had been in it, the union was out here since '46. The big strike was the DiGiorgio strike which started in October of '47 and the efforts to organize continued to the end of 1959. During those thirteen or fourteen years (to make a long story short), those ten years, '50 to '60, were years in which there was no hope we could organize farmworkers.

All we could do was to build our own knowledge of the *bracero* system and keep hitting at it till we could reach a stage where public opinion was so convinced that the arguments of growers was a fraud. And when that climate had been created, we could then move into the lobbying stage in Washington and gain enough support from friends of the union and those who were seeing the truth and that only then could we hope to repeal the *bracero* law. That we did, in '63, but our union was out of business in 1960; and we had to disband because we were not, from the point of view of the labor leadership in the U.S., an orthodox union. We were constantly stepping on the toes of growers and bankers and others who had their own understanding with certain other portions of the labor movement.

So we were a threat to the way in which power was put together in this state. And I never made any bones about it. I always said to our members and to whoever would listen to me that if our union lasted thirty years, we would change the power structure of California. That was our goal. And this was by no means a part of the philosophy of organized labor in California. So we lost ground until 1960, and then we were faced with this dilemma.

The State Federation of Labor had long cut off any financial support. I think at the top of our record the State Federation of Labor was giving us $2500 a year.

We started out with four organizers in California. We each had areas of the state. And by 1955 we were down to one and that was myself. Now obviously with one organizer servicing seventeen locals from Mexicali to the Oregon border, that's no labor movement. So part of the answer is that the growers wore us out. I was hospitalized for three months in 1959. I couldn't move. Just fatigue. The other reason was that by 1960 the leadership of the labor movement had made up its mind that we weren't a good bet. And so the word got around that we were inefficient. Here we'd been in the fields fifteen years and we had no contracts. We hadn't reduced any grower to terms. What kind of nonsense is this?

All during those ten years I doubt that we were getting more than $300 or $400 a month from organized labor, but even so we had proved to be incompetent; and by 1959 the suggestion came down from Walter Reuther to us that the best thing for us to do was to turn in our charter and give it to the Packinghouse Workers. And I told Walter to go to hell.

My advice to our president was, give the charter back to me; and he can do what he wants with it but we're not going to be ordered by anybody. So by 1959 we were in the worst possible shape: no money, no organizers, no support and all these suggestions coming to us to get lost quick. So from September of '59 to May of 1960 the liquidation process just went *fast*.[8]

Looking back now, we know that Galarza did actually change the power structure of California.

Recognizing that the UFW's organizing success had been reliant upon eliminating the Bracero program (created by executive order in 1942, and formalized through the passage of Public Law 78 in 1951), Galarza's persistent hammering opened fissures that later exploded into the 1960s farm labor movement.[9]

The UFW's first collective bargaining agreement was signed in 1966, only two years after the Bracero program was terminated. Since braceros were used as strikebreakers and oversupplied the labor market, depressing wages across the economy, the UFW fought on firmer ground than its predecessors.

Galarza's scholarship and organizing set the stage for the movement.

Politically Engaged Scholarship

Galarza's determination, resolve, and tenacity are exemplary for those seeking to follow the model he set as a politically engaged scholar.

Galarza understood research as a process as much as a product. His approach to social science was reliant upon long term engagement, even implying the need for a succession of scholars to engage intractable or inaccessible problems through innovative approaches to community-based research. A persistent refrain for him was to scaffold previous findings, then lay out still unresolved questions for others to pursue. This is why he often referenced his tables of contents to students, and then mentioned that his work was incomplete, inviting a next generation into the fight.

He was unrelenting in identifying the object of study, which for him, was the system of agribusiness weighing upon the Latino community as an oppressive force. In an August 12, 1960 statement to the President's Commission on Migratory Labor, prepared for the National Farm Labor Union, Galarza acknowledged that California's agricultural system was an "empire."

> The California Agricultural Code is careful to slight this connection. At Chapter 4, Section 1190, the Code says: "It is here recognized that agriculture is characterized by individual production in contrast to the group or factory system that characterizes other forms of individual production."
>
> The Code, in this respect, is as out of date as the crowns and scepters with which the pageantry of California's "agricultural empire" is adorned. In 1945, slightly more than 102,000 Class A farms, out of a total of some 5,850,000 farms in the nation, produced 20% of all farm products and hired over one-half of its hired labor. Over 17,000 of these farm factories were in California, and they produced over 65% of the value of all products sold.
>
> In a recent survey of land ownership in the West by the Department of Agriculture it was stated that corporation ownership and control have become a dominant characteristic of agriculture in this section of the country. . . .
>
> If the Commission were to call the roll of some of the outstanding "farmers" of this state, who would answer? The Standard Oil Company, with 54,000 acres in the San Joaquin Valley; Tidewater Associated Oil Company;

Southern Pacific Company; Shell Oil Company; Kern County Land Company; Van Glahn Lake Land Company; California Packing Corporation; DiGiorgio Fruit Corporation; Anderson-Clayton Company; J. G. Boswell Company; W. B. Camp Company; Boston Investment Company; General Petroleum Corporation.

Anderson-Clayton owns 40 percent of the cotton gins in the Central Valley. It owns three of the Valley's nine cottonseed oil mills and three of its eight compresses. Its tributary, the San Joaquin Cotton Oil Company, is the dominant force in the state's cotton industry.

A few more random facts will enable the Commission to focus properly on the economic and managerial structure of California's farm industry, the employer of the people whose conditions the Commission is here to study.

The DiGiorgio Fruit Corporation is a nationwide organization with plants or offices in seven states. Its ranch near Arvin measures 19 miles along its boundaries. The Kern County Land Company had a net income after taxes in 1948 of $11,292,854. It operated some 8700 acres in cotton, 3300 acres in potatoes and 1300 acres in sugar beets. Its current assets stood at $36,676,075. When its Board of Directors recently toured the company's holdings, they traveled by special bus for two days. One of the directors had to come from his home in England for the inspection.

This is the "corporation agriculture," the "finance farming" with which anyone who wants to appraise the human and social problems that have arisen in the rural areas of this State must be familiar.[10]

Galarza used his position and role as a scholar to battle the power elite of California. He took it upon himself to map, in fine detail, the industry he was organizing against. His research was enhanced by his close proximity to the problem. Social theories and scientific methods enabled him to see the structures he assaulted.

Books were at the center of Galarza's politically engaged scholarship and corresponding organizing strategies. Four of them stand out from his work with the farm labor union and interrogation into agribusiness: *Strangers in Our Fields* (1956), *Merchants of Labor* (1964), *Spiders in the House and Workers in the Field* (1970), and *Farm Workers and Agribusiness in California, 1947–1960* (1977). Only the first book was written while Galarza worked for the union.

Strangers in Our Fields

Strangers in Our Fields (1956), more pamphlet than book, had the educational and political purpose of undermining Public Law 78, which authorized the Bracero program.

The book documented this law's extensive problems by using accessible language, graphic photographs, simple statistics, and direct quotes from the braceros themselves. Its approach was reminiscent of Dorothea Lange and Paul Taylor's book *American Exodus*, as it had an explicit purpose to influence public policy. Galarza later admitted that the book was purposely provocative: "Presented with the experiences of the braceros in their own language, it was possible that the growers and government agencies would elect to challenge the material and thus bring the issue into the open."[11] As he was prone to do, Galarza baited his adversaries into overreacting.

As planned, the publication of *Strangers in Our Fields* instigated intense industry blowback. A resolution by the California State Board of Agriculture made numerous charges that it contained statements that were "derogatory," "unfounded," "inaccurate," "untrue, disparaging, or otherwise damaging," "erroneous and unjustifiably unfavorable," and that the report was published "without independent investigation and evaluation of the reliability of the research methods and statements of findings, or of possible motives for bias."[12] An October 1, 1956 letter from the San Diego County Farmers, Inc. found:

> The pamphlet entitled "Strangers in our Fields" by Ernesto Galarza, made possible through a grant-in-aid from The Fund for the Republic (Ford Foundation) contains a vicious group of false insinuations, and accusations. Its author, Ernesto Galarza, is well known in California for his active participation and leadership in creating labor disputes and social unrest. The convictions, and inferences recorded in this publication signify the author's contempt for the honest efforts of faithful representatives of the U.S. and Mexico governments. It appears to be a biased, prejudiced, one-sided opinion by one whose interest and leanings could be questioned.[13]

Agribusiness representatives tried to impugn Galarza's integrity and his research. Rarely in his life did he allow such a challenge to go unanswered.

Due to this backlash, the Department of Labor refused to publish the report. The U.S. section of the Joint United States-Mexico Trade Union Committee, which did publish it, agreed to investigate any discrepancies within the research. It later found no need for substantial revisions or corrections. Galarza responded in the second edition's preface:

> We remind those who previously denounced "Strangers in our Fields" and attempted to suppress it, that truth thrives on controversy and that mere denunciation never altered a fact. Censorship in a democracy is never called for except by those who fear the truth. On behalf of the trade union movement in both the United States and Mexico we pledge that organized labor will never cease its efforts in this area until abuses and exploitation of these Mexican workers as reported in this pamphlet are ended.[14]

The goal of eliciting a challenge, of baiting agribusiness and its allies, had been successful.

The straightforward booklet is a comprehensive, personalized account of the Bracero program's effects. It situates the voice and perspective of farmworkers out front, while its chapters offer a view into the daily life of the bracero's bureaucratized lives, smothering counterarguments in a barrage of detailed, first-person stories. Workers' grievances included dilapidated housing; insufficient wages, or outright theft of wages; over-supplying labor markets, causing depressed wages; overcharging for substandard food; inaccurate record keeping and inappropriate pay deductions; unsafe transportation; health insurance premium deductions for inadequate or non-existent coverage; use of the farm labor padrone system; lax enforcement of program regulations; and poor worker representation at all institutional levels.

The braceros were inherently vulnerable and exploitable within this labor system. One said, "These things have to be tolerated in silence because there is no one to defend our guarantees. In a strange country you feel timid—like a chicken in another rooster's yard."[15] Perhaps unknown to these workers, Galarza and his union were attempting to fill this role, starting by compiling documentary evidence and publishing the empirical findings.

A four-month survey enabled Galarza to collect first-hand accounts from braceros. He visited camps and worksites where he conducted interviews. Photographs emphasized his descriptions of housing and living conditions. *Strangers in Our Fields* begins with a Mexican farm-worker saying, "In this camp we have no names. We are called only by numbers."[16] From this statement, Galarza proceeds to ethnographically document the conditions of the braceros experience in the United States spanning the trans-border recruitment and migration from Mexican villages to work conditions in the fields.

The book remains close to its research subjects and readers, who are placed in the fields and work camps through his descriptions. From this first inflammatory account, Galarza followed with increasingly analytic scholarship.

Merchants of Labor

Congress terminated Public Law 78, ending the Bracero program, on May 29, 1963. *Merchants of Labor* was published the next year. It was therefore a requiem for a deceased institution. It also represents a validation and victory for Galarza, who had committed ten years of his life to the demise of the law.

The elimination of the braceros from the labor pool had been a goal dating back to the DiGiorgio strike in 1947. With subsidized braceros labor (used at times as strikebreakers, negatively affecting overall working conditions) purged from the labor market, the United Farm Workers union found traction and collective bargaining success immediately upon the defeat of Public Law 78, vindicating Galarza's strategy and objective.

Merchants of Labor, subtitled "An Account of the Managed Migration of Mexican Farm Workers in California 1942–1960," expanded the research of the preceding *Strangers in Our Fields*. It also fleshed out an evolving template for Galarza's later scholarship. One difference between *Strangers* in 1956 and Galarza's later scholarship on agribusiness was a shift in his position and professional purpose. The earlier work was propagandistic, more visceral and subjective than later, more scientifically distant and objective works. In *Strangers*, the reader felt the heat of the fields, squalor in the work camps, and grift of a society cheating its most vulnerable. Rather than being contextualized within social science literatures, its validity was substantiated within the struggle for existence among Mexican farmworkers. It was reminiscent of how Lange and Taylor's *An American Exodus* differed from Taylor's academic writing, for it evoked empathy and dared an ambivalent reader to avert their gaze at moral cost.

On the other hand, *Merchants of Labor* was a detailed overview of Public Law 78. It drew on academic literature; international, federal, and state documents such as laws, committee reports, policy briefs, hearings, surveys, and meeting minutes; newspaper and magazine articles; case law; popular literature; and publications from non-profits, unions, and advocacy groups. Onto this array of sources, Galarza wove a lyrical narrative reminiscent of a dramatic novel. His scholarship, linear and dense, weighted like a mace, was a heavy weapon for farmworker advocates. The book marked the beginning of a period of writing for Galarza: a turn from explicit advocacy through labor organizing to research and teaching through social science scholarship.

With this perspective, and limiting the study up to 1960, he began the book by framing his inquiry with rhetorical questions:

> Scholars will no doubt in good time weigh the truth of these matters. Then, also, questions not examined here will be raised: Are Mexican *braceros*, man for man, more productive than domestic laborers? Does the employment of *braceros* keep down prices of California products to consumers? Is the state's agribusiness so competitive that its very survival requires a permanent alien contract labor force? Is this indentured alien—an almost perfect model of the economic man, an "input factor" stripped of the political and social attributes that liberal democracy likes to ascribe to all human beings ideally—is this *bracero* the prototype of the production man of the future?[17]

These rhetorical research questions were left unanswered to frame Galarza's object of inquiry: how imported contract labor was being justified and used within California's economy. The functioning of the state's political economy was being called into question.

The breadth of *Merchants* utilized and expanded Galarza's previous experience with the Bracero program. Its scope now incorporated increased historical and analytical context and drew less from the personalized accounts of the workers. The chapters increased attention on agribusiness and the collusion of institutions—national labor unions, the federal government, and others—in the facilitation of or acquiescence to industrial consolidation and the marginalization of farmworkers.

The crux of his argument was that the Bracero program's initiation, cost sharing, implementation, and daily operations were borne at public expense. During the first three years, from 1942 to 1945, all program costs, estimated at $55 million, were covered by the federal government. After 1951, while employers covered transportation and subsistence costs, the government still paid $17.7 million from 1952 to 1959 for compliance and administration. In addition, the Farm Placement Service provided for certification and other program duties that were paid from federal unemployment taxes, which commercial farmers did not pay. This was an arrangement of public subsidy toward the industrialization of agriculture that found parallels in other areas like water supply and agricultural technology.

The managed migration of Mexican farm labor was linked to the maintenance and development of agribusiness.

> Of California's agriculture in the century that ended in 1960 it could well be said that the more it changed the more it became the same thing, for change in this case was but fulfillment, ever on a larger scale, of the original endowment.
>
> The holding and management of land was increasingly dominated by large units as the small, multiple-crop family farms withered. Corporations set the pace in technology and organization. Wealth production increased enormously. Productivity outran the national average. Competition was successfully met in markets 3,000 miles away. Specialized cropping took over. Field labor was assured through an improving system of administered migration which acted as the cost cushion of the industry. These factors, mainly, brought agribusiness to its maturity.
>
> As the sprawling land grants of the Spanish and Mexican periods were appropriated the amount of land under cultivation increased. Though in size the new ranches could not compare with those of the pre-American epoch bigness remained predominant. By 1959, California had 36,887,000 acres of farmland and of these 30,099,000 acres were in farms of 500 acres or more. Between 1950 and 1960 the acreage in farms of up to 49 acres decreased by 431,000 acres to a remainder of 925,000

acres only. The combined increase for farms with more than 500 acres during the same period was 2,097,000 acres. In the period from 1934 to 1954 farms with less than 1,000 acres decreased by 15 per cent while farms with more increased by 48 per cent.[18]

Requisite for these trends was the subsidy of braceros labor, which combined with other public financed benefits such as subsidizing irrigation infrastructure and its delivery of water at public expense. Clearly, non-implementation of federal reclamation law also fits snuggly into this managed program to consolidate economic production against public interest.

Large grower associations were formed to assist in the administration of braceros, with the Imperial Valley Farmers Association and the San Joaquin Farm Production Association hiring the most braceros. These two regions were most representative of industrial-scale agriculture in the state. Overall, the Department of Labor benefited from having to contract with fewer entities by using the associations. In turn, growers purchased labor in bulk, to their advantage. The Farm Placement Service, through research done at the University of California, was integral to this system. It certified the need for braceros and justified those certifications under the rules laid down by the Department of Labor. Galarza noted,

These rules grew out of the methods and techniques which had been worked out for establishing the validity of need by the Extension Service of the University of California during World War II. These methods did not change noticeably in the following twenty years. They proved ingenious, or perhaps ingenuous, enough to give statistical prestige to the imponderables, unpredictable and unknowns of labor shortage forecasting.[19]

A debate needed to occur. Could agribusiness have been initiated— and was it economically viable—without public subsidy? Were economies of scale eventually going to bankrupt smaller producers? And what socioeconomic effects would such change bring to local communities? Galarza also asked a different question: What were the ethics of offering public subsidies to a system that harms people and undermines the economic standing of a broad base of workers and residents?

The government and public institutions, including the University of California, were conducting transformative, real time experiment on rural California without fully understanding the repercussions of the changes that were being initiated and encouraged.

Ernesto Galarza v. DiGiorgio Fruit Corporation

Pushed out of the labor movement, Galarza moved into a new period of his life. Letters from that period illustrate his inclination to continue to work on farm labor issues and desire to stay in California.

A Christmas Eve letter dated December 24, 1960 to Congressman John F. Shelley was written just months after he left the union.

> Dear Jack,
> Without any doubt you have many more pressing matters to deal with than a letter from a non-constituent suggesting a job for himself.
> I am prompted to write you anyway, because my request lies in an area with which you have had a good deal to do, and so effectively.
> Since October 22 I have been out of work. That was the date on which the Amalgamated Meat Cutters terminated me from their payroll. They did have work for me in places distant from California, but I declined to leave.
> I would be interested in working on the staff of some House Committee with proper jurisdiction to investigate the Mexican labor program, if I would be assigned to California.
> Considering the fact that Public Law 78 will be an issue in the 1961 session of Congress, and the further fact that operation of this program has never been examined by Congress at its sources, I would suppose that some agency of the House would be interested in making careful preparations.
> Now a second point.
> It is not considered smear in a letter of application or exploration for a job to set forth your disabilities, if they be such. One which I am in all frankness bound to mention is that I am suing the DiGiorgio Fruit Corporation for libel in the sum of $2,000,000. I hope this would be no obstacle if there is a job somewhere of the type I have indicated.
> Best wishes,
> Ernesto Galarza[20]

Months later, on May 14, 1961, another letter finds Galarza excluded from the labor movement and unsuccessful at soliciting government employment. If he could not organize and educate workers, his default was scholarship.

Dear Fay,

After several months of trying, I am beginning to think the labor movement in California has no place for me. Government agencies who deal in farm labor do not respond to my inquiries either.

I have decided to try the Foundations for a grant to write narratively and analytically about the events of the last ten years.

Will you comb your contacts among such institutions and see if you can turn up one that will spend $3500.00 on me for such purpose. I estimate that I will need about 18 months to complete the research and write the first book—a little ahead of the next extension of Public Law 78.

With great expectations,

Ernesto Galarza[21]

Merchants of Labor was the book he referred to in this letter, but Galarza was already prepared to write books that chronicled his experience and lessons learned. In doing so, he secured these for history, and for us today.

Just as Galarza had written about his decade-long engagement on Public Law 78 for *Merchants*, he now revisited and wrote about a similarly prolonged political struggle in *Spiders in the House and Workers in the Field* (1970). This book detailed a series of strikes and lawsuits involving one of the largest corporations in the United States: the DiGiorgio Fruit Corporation. In the 1920s, DiGiorgio purchased more than twenty thousand acres in Kern County around Arvin and Delano, which were only part of its larger business interests and landholdings. By 1968, the corporation had $81,869,000 in assets and more than $100,000,000 in sales volume—ninth among the nation's top corporations.[22]

Spiders examined the strategic and tactical moves between DiGiorgio and its opponents, including Galarza himself playing a central role as participant and narrator.[23] The study covers the history of Galarza's union organizing with the National Farm Labor Union (NFLU) as it moved from Kern County picket lines to Californian courtrooms and

Congressional proceedings in Washington D.C. The analogy of a spider web was used to describe the intrigues and complex weave of traps set by DiGiorgio—the spider—while the corporation attempted to eliminate its opponents in organized labor and at newspapers. Intricate "webs" involved congressional procedure and protocol, the legal basis of libel and defamation, corporate structures and relationships, and illegitimate use of government reports.

The first web was constructed around a NFLU strike on DiGiorgio's farms. During that union action, a film titled *Poverty in the Valley of Plenty* was produced by the Hollywood Film Council (affiliated with the AFL). Portions of the film were deemed to have blurred the line between generalizations on agribusiness and DiGiorgio's specific business operations. Two initial lawsuits reinterpreted legal rulings around defamation, suggesting that a case for libel could be made against the union, filmmakers, and their representative leaders.

Decades of legal complaints ensued over this expanded interpretation of libel launching a protracted, subterranean war, with DiGiorgio bringing separate suits against Paramount Television Productions, the Hollywood Film Council, *Monterey Bay Labor News*, and the *Union Gazette*—just to name a few. These were acts in an economic drama playing out in post-war California between organized labor and the agricultural industry. At stake was the political sanction and legal leverage to gain superior position in that fight.

During the series of lawsuits over many years, the object of inquiry shifted. Originally it was the *Poverty* film and its characterizations of DiGiorgio's businesses. In later cases the object of litigation became a legislative document generated during the first lawsuits— Congressman Werdel's "Extension of Remarks to the House of Representatives." This document was vested with the authority of Congress and therefore had legal standing in court, which Galarza characterized as "borrowed dignity."[24] A portion of the report stated, "The processes of the Congress of the United States have been perverted and misused by the National Farm Labor Union in order to furnish a sounding board for its claims," when actually the exact opposite perversion of authority and process had occurred.[25] It would take years to untangle the web enough to understand what had transpired, and by then the damage was done.

The Werdel document had been signed by three Congressmen serving on the investigating subcommittee: Richard Nixon, Thurston Morton, and Tom Steed (Werdel was not serving on this subcommittee but was the representative from DiGiorgio's district near Arvin and Bakersfield). Upon initial release, however, it was "the perfect web" and highly damaging to the union's court case and existence. By the end of this period of lawsuits, the object of litigation ultimately had shifted to the U.S. Congress, its procedures, and how information was legitimized as public documents with legal authority. After years of investigation, it became clear that the Werdel document itself was a defamatory misrepresentation used by DiGiorgio against the union and other defendants.

The report's veneer of legitimacy was first substantiated by the findings of the initial court decision. Thereafter, its evidence and precedents were repeatedly deployed by the corporation in later lawsuits, newspaper reporting and other propagandistic purposes. It made four libelous charges against union officials: bearing false witness, making false statements for financial gain, collecting money for a nonexistent strike, and perverting the process of the U.S. Congress.

Recorded statements, such as Werdel's "Extension of Remarks," were a common and insignificant practice in the Congress. Galarza noted that the deliberate misrepresentation of them in this case became

> by all appearances, no less than a *congressional* arraignment issued in the printed pages of the *Congressional Record*. No common jury of ordinary citizens had spoken, or a judge sitting on a superior court bench in any one of three thousand counties. It was Federal power, in whose name congressional committees wielded what Edmund Burke called, "the thunder of the state." The Corporation could not desire more political advantage than this.[26]

In fact, Galarza was arguing that when the report was used in court it represented three "paper witnesses" who were the three congressmen who allegedly signed the document.[27] And because one of the charges in the Werdel document concluded that the union had "perverted and misused" Congressional processes, Galarza was aware that in the McCarthy era these claims could potentially be construed as "subversion" and "abuse" and lead to even worse outcomes for the defendants.[28]

Werdel's "Extension of Remarks" were catastrophic for the union. Within sixty days of the publication of the Congressional document the strike was defeated, picketing stopped, the union confessed to defamation and the film was discredited with all copies destroyed. The corporation did not allow striking workers to return, a dispossession that cast 1,000 of them out of work and home. In addition, the State Federation of Labor withdrew its support for the NFLU, permanently crippling it (it was reconstituted as the National Agricultural Workers Union). This first legal action and use of the Werdel report wove "the perfect web" as "a mesh of decisions, legal actions, deployments, understandings and moves that were calculated to prevent unionization."[29]

The bitter conflict between the union and DiGiorgio was not finished. A decade after its first showing, the corporation heard that the *Poverty* film was again being shown in the valley. The recently constituted Agricultural Workers Organizing Committee (AWOC), following Galarza's dismissal, were unaware of the previous lawsuit's settlement and its restrictions on showing the film. DiGiorgio rushed into legal proceedings on May 18, 1960 after only verifying that the film had been shown on May 13. It chose to ignore stipulations from the previous libel settlement under which it was supposed to give a thirty-day notice before suing other parties. DiGiorgio was also unaware that both Mitchell and Galarza were no longer working for AWOC, so the corporation unwittingly named them in the suit as well. Meanwhile, AWOC had walked into a web waiting to snare them.

Galarza, writing about himself, describes the game play and tactical moves that occurred between himself and DiGiorgio in the summer of 1960:

> In a hurry there was little time to weigh other considerations, among them how Galarza might react to the charges in the complaint and particularly those in the press release. This defendant was in some respects in a worse position than Smith and his [AWOC] associates. He, and not the others, was accused of failure to perform the terms of an agreement and of deliberately flouting (the press release said "flaunting") a court order. Against him and Mitchell [both of whom previously worked for NFLU] in particular were again arrayed the indictments published by Werdel, Nixon, Morton and Steed. Among these was the charge of perversion

of the constitutional processes of Congress, not precisely an accusation of treason but faintly suggesting it . . . As Galarza gave thought to these matters, Murray [Galarza's attorney] proceeded to instruct the Corporation and its attorneys on the unfortunate misstatements and contradictions in the press release. The short educational course was tendered at no cost to DiGiorgio on the supposition that upon discovering the truth, the Corporation would publicly disavow those portions of the release and dismiss Galarza from the suit.[30]

On September 13, the DiGiorgio Fruit Corporation did dismiss the suit against Galarza and Mitchell but did not retract its unfounded assertions or explain its reasons for bringing legal action against them. Two days later, on September 15, 1960, Galarza issued a complaint for libel against the DiGiorgio Fruit Corporation for malicious prosecution and publishing false news stories.

This lawsuit, and the intervening years since the first complaints of libel, had allowed Galarza and Murray to see that the Werdel's Congressional report was central to the case. They bore down into this document contesting the legitimacy erroneously afforded it in earlier trials. For their inquiry they utilized the legal mechanisms open to them through their lawsuit—subpoenas, interrogatories, depositions, and requests for admission. They called thirteen deponents, including a whole slew of DiGiorgio's top brass, Congressman Gubser, and then-Vice President Nixon, who had been a congressman when he supported the Werdel report.

Through the lawsuit, Galarza was able to make inquiries and elicit new details through sworn depositions in which false testimony was perjury. He focused on disentangling the web behind the previous four DiGiorgio lawsuits. The main questions were: Who were the authors of the Werdel report? Was the report considered a record of official proceedings of the House? What communications and connections were there between Congressman Werdel and the corporation before the drafting of the report? Was the corporation involved in drafting the Werdel report? And was there a connection between the corporation's legal actions, union busting, and the undermining of labor organizing efforts?

During the trial, Galarza and his lawyer established, through the use of expert testimony, that the same typewriter from DiGiorgio's law firm had been used to prepare legal documents in the 1949 court case and Werdel's Congressional report, which was supposed to have been written in Washington, D.C. A strong case had been made. The jury returned a split verdict finding some of DiGiorgio's actions were untrue yet astoundingly without malice. No monetary damages were awarded. The trial had taken four years. It had been a battle of attrition contesting representations of the truth.

DiGiorgio sued a few other newspapers for libel in 1964 and 1965, starting with George Ballis's *Valley Labor Citizen*, but the contest was spent. In his "conclusion without an end" after decades of grappling with DiGiorgio over libel and truth, Galarza wrote:

> So men make the choice how they will use the compelling exercise of mind they cannot avoid while they live. The true deceivers are faced with competition from truth searchers, who are even fewer in number . . . Given time and opportunity [the human mind] can find its way through the mists of possible truth and possible fiction that spread in all directions from a given fixed point of fact.[31]

After writing two books on Public Law 78 and another on the Di-Giorgio strike and court battles, Galarza's last book on farm labor and agribusiness provided a comprehensive historical overview of his work.

Farm Workers and Agribusiness in California

In 1977, University of Notre Dame Press published *Farm Workers and Agri-business in California, 1947–1960*. The book examines California's "agri-businessland," which Galarza had come to know from his direct personal experience and applied research as a union organizer, educator, and scholar.

The book is a three-part history of (1) the union's "intense, widespread organizational activity . . . into the structure of the agricultural industry," which primarily involved a series of strikes, between 1947 and 1952; (2) the period of "action research" between 1952 and 1959, when the union engaged "corporate agriculture" bureaucratically through legal appeals, and the union's propaganda focused on government programs colluding with agribusiness specifically codified in Public Law 78 and its Bracero program; and (3) reflections upon the dismantling of the union in 1960 and strategic decisions throughout its decades-long campaign.

As usual, the chapter titles and structure were purposefully laid out by Galarza for future inquiry and subsequent research, and also represented some of Galarza's last published scholarship on farm labor and agribusiness in California. His long crusade appears quixotic in the context of agribusiness, with the gargantuan scale of its economic interests, its willingness to use vigilante and political violence against unions, and the added weight of state and federal bureaucracies aligned against labor's position and interests.

In reflection, Galarza's presentation of these issues, because of his unique position in the research, required a different scholarly approach:

> In my encounters with those who administered the bracero system out of public view, the workers had no opportunity to act. In such situations I was often the only adversary, and I see no practical method of reporting these incidents otherwise. If this style suggests a certain nonobjectivity of the narrative, so much the better. The ultimate compass of what men say and write and do are values, which cannot be found anywhere save in their conscience, reflected in every choice of behavior self-servingly characterized as "objective."
>
> The academically minded may find the suggested readings too thin. A solid appendix of published references with a ballast of footnotes will no doubt be provided in time by those who might consider this text insufficient. For the convenience of such, I have given the Stanford University Library all the papers that I and my fellow-unionists collected during the years of action.[32]

His clarification invited another question: What qualifies knowledge as scholarly? As Galarza addressed potential criticism from campus-based scholars, we now consider the validity of his research juxtaposed against the backdrop of his lived experience.

For Galarza, knowledge is tested directly in trials that open the possibility to change history though action. Though institutional scholars may have reputations within certain journals or departments, most are not engaged *as scholars* in struggles in the field. As a scholar and an organizer, Galarza was at once a legitimate research subject (he suggests that there may not be anyone else who knows the information he does); an expert in the field of farm labor, agriculture, and immigration; and a scholar recording these events into a body of academic literature.

In this last book on Californian agriculture, Galarza described his research methodology, which he coined "action research" aimed at generating an "analysis of existing social power." It involved a process where

> the union's small but active cadres wrenched from corporation agriculture a picture of the bracero system, the mesh of American society—government, the universities, the rural press, diplomacy—was revealed. The accounts from the fields profiled the structure of power which the bracero system manifested.[33]

The organizing campaign was "a period of continuous forced entry and discovery in the face of great odds."[34]

In combining roles of teacher, organizer, and scholar, Galarza was a formidable adversary. Though initially under the radar, he prepared the groundwork for later labor upheavals by expanding leadership capacity, increasing worker education, and using participatory methods of gathering information to write newspaper and other articles for the union. He sought to translate analysis of "California's rural social structure," which appeared impenetrable and indomitable, into language that farmworkers could understand, adapt, and adopt. Galarza described his approach to crafting his own worker education program:

> At this core of organization, with Galarza in charge as director of education and research, the Union maintained a program of information, discussion, analysis, and techniques of group action suitable to the requirements of the strike. There was a strong mental appetite among many of the members to understand the social forces that for all their concealment by the mists of "high edgication" were bearing down on Local 218. Into these dim, outer margins, the Union laid a course of guidance and instruction. The curriculum was not the facts of work and life, which the workers knew better than the Union officials. It was the meanings of these facts when related to one another in patterns that had not been noticed before. . . .

Taught to appreciate the meaning of routine details in the daily work experience, the members of the Union became the eyes and ears of a research operation such as agribusiness had never been exposed to. However remote the places where agribusiness planned its strategies to manipulate the labor market, in the end these strategies took concrete shape in Wetback pools, bracero crews and the hundred ways in which the domestic workers were harassed and displaced. Union intelligence was simple. It consisted of listening to the members, checking their reports, assembling these in outlines for discussion by study groups, and equipping the members to look more closely and carefully and to report again and again. These were the sources of the press releases and reports that the Union issued in its nationwide propaganda which provided a protective shield for Local 218.[35]

The three-year DiGiorgio organizing campaign's successes were found in its racial inclusiveness and diversity. Galarza noted the ethnic diversity of the workers—Filipinos, Mexicans, and southern whites— where "the mingling of the races did not reduce the distance between them that contractors and employers encouraged. In the Union meetings this distance was shortened by a deliberate effort to overcome the barriers of prejudice and language." In addition, Galarza continued, men and women took roles of leadership with "a shambling reluctance and a shy speech to the effect that 'I hadn't oughta do it fer I ain't got no high edgication.'"[36] Though unsuccessful, the campaign had illustrated that a sustained organizing effort could be undertaken against the most powerful economic interests by the most vulnerable workers drawing upon the strengths of their diversity and intimate knowledge of their own oppression.

By 1952, it had become apparent to Galarza that their action research had not been successful. It did, however, eventually overturn Public Law 78, cutting off the braceros labor supply, which had been one of his primary goals.

The attack on Public Law 78 rested entirely on the vigilance of the local volunteers, their training in what the law, the contracts, and the international agreements provided as to the rights of both domestics and braceros . . . The increasing capability of the volunteers to confront the

agents of the Farm Placement Service at any level drove them to conceal-
ment and hole-in-corner intrigues. When the records of the Department
of Employment were finally opened for local inspection, the volunteers
quickly became familiar with them and used them effectively. Grievances
brought by braceros were attended by the volunteers, who became adept
at using the work contracts to press the complaints and add to the union's
knowledge on that score.[37]

This statement of the union's work illustrated the educational outreach and development necessary to build volunteer capacity. Once
trained, workers became advocates increasingly proficient to argue the
fine points of bureaucratic legislation and labor agreements to the government authorities charged with their oversight and implementation.
The volunteers were acting as an applied research team.[38]

Galarza needed to teach these volunteers, and the broader public.
He also needed not only to inspire them to act, but to see that change
was possible. For that he needed to demystify the imposing edifice of
corporate agriculture. In the introduction to a section he called "Agri-
businessland," Galarza discussed research related to social systems. He
focused on the object of twelve years of labor organizing and much of
his scholarship to this point, seeking to disrupt this "immovable social
institution" so that it can be seen as a process, in play, at present:

There is a deceptiveness about social systems that beguiles those who
view them, because of fondness, interest, or perversity, as a product exclusively, ignoring them as a process. The present is only the front end
of a culture. On its surface it is possible to trace boundaries, categories,
types, classes, and settlements that can be isolated for semantic treatment to the delight of scholars and the advantage of politicians. It is like
viewing a kaleidoscope clamped firmly in a vice so it will not turn even
slightly and scatter the charmingly frozen image. There is a certain peace
of mind in peering at such images, as there is in gazing at seemingly immovable social institutions.

From a distant perspective, Agri-businessland had that look when the
Southern Tenant Farmers Union under its new name, the National Farm
Workers Union, went west. It came upon one of those cultural artifacts
fashioned over time by the winners of the West, the agri-businessmen.[39]

While history framed strategy, empowerment necessitated resolve. In this case, agribusiness presented itself as an all-powerful institution, creating an aura of invulnerability. Galarza referred to this "social power" at various points. His task was not only to educate volunteers on the technical aspects of law; he also needed to motivate them through their own values and commitments. The past was being written in the present— and everyone contributed to its story.

The past can be a compost pile of recollections of the disasters of the many and the triumphs of the few. In it anyone may dig out of curiosity to uncover some missing piece of lore, to fertilize a silting nostalgia, or to settle with faded chronicles a scholarly controversy. History practiced in this way can satisfy those who view the past as residue, as a postmortem of successive epochs in which most men appear as subjects of history, not as its agents.

The past can also be prologue to those who are willing to learn from it. But to what purpose? To offer such minds a place and a role at the forward edge of the search for meaning where time, space, nature, culture, men and their conflicting interests and even disasters mingle to resolve their never-ending tensions.

Even more important is the sense and the will that, once a historical process is understood, a choice can be made as to one's place in its next moment, and the realization that the best history is that in which one has had an effective part. A mind placed at the forward edge of events and guided by knowledge uses the past, affects the present, and possibly helps form the future.

The action is where people are, and a place among them is the crux of everyman's search. Human society is an organized complex of settlements, among which men sort themselves into universes of commitment and communication and cooperation reduced to the human scale in which a man's grasp can equal his reach, physically and intellectually and emotionally. But in time these settlements become the foundations of social power. Gradually they reach out, absorb, integrate, merge, and acculturate other less vigorous settlements and distort if not destroy their human scale.[40]

By organizing community, Galarza worked to undermine and sever the cultural tolerance and institutional supports of agribusiness. We can see this as an educational mission, a pedagogy of empowerment from the fields.

Intellectual Migrant

On April 20, 1977, Galarza spoke to UC Berkeley Chicano Studies students—reflecting on his work, encouraging them, offering advice. That day he was asked to speak on "the role of the Chicano graduate student on campus and in society" before an audience with whom he had perhaps the most affinity and affection.[41]

> We have to take a closer look at the academic world itself. I guess I have taught in a half a dozen universities in California. I'm now teaching a course in the politics of bilingual education at UC Santa Cruz.
>
> So I've had an opportunity—really I'm something of an intellectual migrant—to look at the establishment in all of these places. At first I wasn't aware that I was a professional intellectual migrant, and really the circumstances of my personal life were such that I just couldn't sink roots on any campus. But those circumstances gradually led me to look at the establishment in which I was working temporarily with a much more critical eye, and gradually I developed an attitude.
>
> And the attitude, which I expressed to a couple of my colleagues at Santa Cruz, was this: I am there temporarily filling a slot, holding it for another person who will be coming in the fall as a permanent faculty member. And the talk was whether or not I would consider applying myself for that slot. It pays well, tenure to start with, nice campus, a maximum of maybe two courses a week, two lectures a week. I said no. They asked, "What is your reason?" My answer was maybe a little disrespectful, but I meant it.
>
> I said, "If I stay here much longer than three quarters, I'll feel that I am sinking roots into a cemetery." I really mean that. The intellectual fervor at campus, the ferment of ideas and that kind of recklessness that comes early in your life when you discover the possibilities of following an idea through and down and over until you are on top of it and can speak about it with authority and with honesty—that is going on in the Santa Cruz campus, not among the faculty, but among the students.
>
> So if I could invent some way by which I could maintain my relationship with the students and take them off campus with me a couple of times a week and do things in the community, I'd accept that job. But those weren't the terms which I was offered. So I'm again about to move my tent to some other campus.[42]

Figure 3.3. Ernesto Galarza. Courtesy of *Syndic Literary Journal.*

Scholarship, for Galarza, did not require having a position in a university, nor having academic credentials. In fact, he questioned and spurned these positions. He moved, staying abreast of the issues, in step with his community. Relevant research necessitated direct engagement. Learning occurred, and solutions were found, where the problems reside.

Aware of the difficulties and limitations, Galarza incited graduate students into action. He offered sympathy, counseling them around difficulties, as he propelled them forward into position as politically engaged scholars.

> Most of the students that have been coming to me for the last ten years have given up, have abandoned the idea of doing any research that interests them and has some relationship to the community, to California, or the southwest.
>
> A few hang on. But if they hang on, they run into a different set of problems. Those problems have to do with the Chicano experience of the sixties. That experience brought to a peak all sorts of awareness, one of them being the role of the university, the role of the campus Chicano, in the affairs of the community.
>
> I have had this experience at San Jose State University. I taught one seminar in the School of Social Work for two semesters. We began by a discussion of theoretical foundations of community organization, and we ended by my seminar being discontinued because during the middle of the year we split up into teams to examine what was going on in the various barrios of San Jose. We assigned ourselves tasks of very serious, hard research to find out what was going on. So that seminar was not cancelled, it was not suppressed, it was not discontinued, it just *fumore*—it disappeared as so much smoke and fog.
>
> You Chicano scholars who are here now today must recognize this drastic change on the American campus, and begin to ask yourselves, must we abandon what's here for us? This campus contains immeasurable treasures for all of us. Here is an accumulation of experience that should be open to us for each one of us to analyze and evaluate and put to our own uses. And you can't get it off campus—these magnificent libraries and research facilities. These are public facilities. This is public wealth organized and set up here for your use.
>
> Please think very carefully before you abandon this place because of certain difficulties that you're having. The thing to remember is that the training, the capability in the law, in sociology, in whatever these disciplines may be called, is available only here. Unfortunately, it is under the control, under the vigilance of people who don't share your motivation. But that is no reason why you should abandon your claim to these resources. You do have a claim to them.
>
> The point of view that I'm asking you to consider, of course, is not an easy one to carry out. One of the difficulties that we as Chicanos and Mexicans

have always faced is that our universe in the university is so unfamiliar and so distant from the community from which we come.

It's awfully hard to explain to your families and to your neighbors—neighborhoods that are constantly in turmoil and in the process of change—what it is you're up to, what you're doing, what your difficulties are. There's a gradual alienation between us on campuses and those in the community. I contend that the solution or the effort to overcome that alienation is ours and not the community's.

We understand what causes it. We know why we are victimized by it. We know why the community itself is victimized. But you cannot ask a person who has not had your opportunities to become mentally critical and professionally competent to dig at, to go at the fact that you need to establish a thesis.[43]

Similar to how the Marine Corps recruit kids in working class neighborhoods—"it will be the toughest job you'll ever love"—Galarza entices the graduate students by telling them how difficult the work will be in fighting for their communities, in the farmworker towns and barrios of California.

Never one to sugarcoat or coddle, Galarza always offered brutal invitations. Why bring in someone not tough enough to see the work through?

I'm often asked about these books that I have written, how long it took me to do them. I'll tell you how long it took. *Spiders in the House*, the research on that began in 1952 and ended in 1974. This book that is to be published by the Notre Dame University Press, *Farm Workers and Agribusiness in California, 1947–1960*, [1977], the research began in 1947 and it ended two years ago.

If you want to compare the discipline, the persistence, the diligence that's required to do a piece of research in the field of social science, you will find that if your subject is important—more than that, if it's vital—and if it does not fit in the mood of these times and these days, it's going to take you a long time to do it. You have to determine that it is an important subject. To me, this was an important subject, and after twenty-two years of researching it, I wrote it.

And it was important to me because the structure of California politics and its very society have been molded by agribusiness. You can't touch any part of California society that you don't put your finger on some aspect of this structure of power. I thought it was important. My own satisfaction, my own curiosity was being driven to get that answer, and I think I have a part of it here. But only a part of it.

I want you people in this room to remember as graduate students that when you read the table of contents of this book, it's really an outline for your research. There are some forty-five important topics in this table of contents. I have dealt with each one of those, first because it was important to my story; but secondly because I wanted to put enough facts into that particular section so that others might come along and say, "Look, this is not the complete story. There's a lot that he's left out of here. Where *is* the rest of it?"

That's what I'm hoping this book will be—a directory, a guide, a list, a topical list of the research that needs to be done to tell us what's happened to us in the last fifty years in California. The time that it takes you to do a research job in whatever discipline is only one of the difficulties. Where are the materials? Where do you get the data in these areas of our social experience that nobody has bothered to look at before?

I happen to think that this is precisely the aspect that brings out the best possible qualities of scholarship. I've been told so many times that there is no information on this, but my response is, if it happened in human experience somewhere there must be some evidence of it. And if I've got to go out myself and look at it, eyeball to eyeball, that's what I'll do. As time goes on, you'll find that the pieces begin to fall together. You find evidence in the most extraordinary places. One of the best documents in this book is a memorandum that I found in the wastebasket of a farm labor placement officer in Modesto. He was receiving every week a pile of stuff from the central office in San Francisco, and he'd look at it and throw it in the wastebasket. One day I was visiting him to help with a bit of trouble he was having and the conversation brought us to the wastebasket.

He said, "I've just thrown away a document that maybe helps me understand what's happening." He had been canned by the regional director of the Bureau of Employment Security because he had been enforcing the *bracero* law. Probably the only enforcement officer in California who was doing it. And for that, he was canned. In his wastebasket were some routine papers about his job.

So I said, "Well, let me look at them." We turned the wastebasket upside down on a table and I ploughed through that, and there was one document—some twelve pages—entitled "Minutes of the Regional Farm Labor Operations Committee." Never heard of it before. I said, "Bill, what is this?" He said, "Oh, that's some outfit that meets now and then. They have dinner and talk about a lot of things. These are their minutes." I said, "Well, let me have it." *Damé. Aca.*

I read the document that night, and I discovered that there was in California at that time a kitchen cabinet of about twenty agri-businessmen and politicians who met every two or three months with the top officer of the Department of Labor here in San Francisco or in Sacramento or elsewhere, and that is where *bracero* policy was made. In those minutes there was a statement from the director of the regional office and the [U.S.] Department of Labor promising—whether he did that on his knees or not, I don't know—but he promised at that meeting that he would never issue a regulation before clearing it with the presidents and the officers of the Associated Farmers and the local associations. Now, that was Minutes #7. They'd had six meetings before, and maybe they'd had another three of four afterwards. So I wrote Mr. Brockway in San Francisco asking for a set of all the minutes. "Minutes of what? Minutes of what? Don't know what you're talking about."

So I started a pilgrimage around the state of California, emptying wastebaskets. By the time I got through, I had all the minutes, the complete set. And if any of you ever want to go into this special feature, go to the Stanford Library and ask for the minutes of the RFLOAC. And you will be able to expand this chapter and point out things which I have no knowledge of because I didn't follow up on them.[44]

By this time in his life, Galarza understood that the fight was going to extend beyond his own life. He had carried the torch for a while, but others were to finish it. So, we witness him here recruiting future scholars to enter the fray and pick up the work.

Work on Something Real

We encounter Galarza after he has passed away, which tends to elevate his stories. They appear as objects on which we project our hopes. His accomplishments seem extra human. Yet his experiences are not extraordinary. They are a product of holding a steadfast commitment to core values.

Let's return to Galarza's 1977 discussion with Chicano Studies graduate students at Berkeley. After his lecture, he took questions that were also recorded and transcribed. His advice and lessons are still applicable to any student looking to make relevant change in the world.

Student: What do you see happening to graduate students or any Chicano that goes into higher education? You mentioned some people that are now in the hierarchy, the power base; it had a bad effect on the community . . . Is it that we have to stay in the institution, try to change the institution to our perspective of what we have to do?

Galarza: I don't think so. What I've been driving at all this morning, is that if you stay in an institution—I dislike the thing that happens to your mind—you become institutionalized. But if you stay within it and try to come to terms, or rather accept its terms, for your survival, you will have to become one of the Chicanos who will become a fixture on the totem pole. And from that time on, his assignment is to make it easy for the institution to turn its face away from reality.

Student: What does a student do that's caught up in that thing now? Would it be a solution to try to set up parallel institutions, a people's college of the law or apprenticeship programs?

Galarza: No, I don't think so. Because these parallel institutions, if you look at them closely, have a lot of similarity with their prototypes. I think the only way to go is for students who have the luck to survive four or five or six years in an institution, is to milk it. Get all you can, all the techniques, all the skill—you have to become as articulate as the best of them. But don't lose sight of the fact that politically you are a sitting pigeon, if that's where you're going to stay.

Student: What percentage of people do you think will go into an institution of higher education and be able to maintain the ability not to get brainwashed?

Galarza: How do you maintain an attitude and a value? You maintain it by keeping in touch with those people who represent that value. That is to say, you know something about bilingual education, you know it's going sour, you know it's not doing what it should be doing—then you make, and maintain and keep, contact with people in the community who are affected by that problem. You get to know them. You win their trust and their confidence, and over time, you become their advisor, their fellow worker, and their participant in action.

Student: I believe I agree with you, that probably one of the greatest concerns that affects us now at the university is the production of intellectuals, who in clothing and in speech speak radically, but who have in essence become this bulwark or beachhead for traditional and even reactionary ideas. We see it here at Berkeley, among a lot of the students, a lot of the professors. What are some of the reasons for that? I'd appreciate an elaboration.

Galarza: Yes, I think the main reason for that situation is that there is a vested interest in the past, and the way it views intellectual endeavor. And the degree to which it accepts it, I call the pigeonhole mentality. Pigeonhole mentality is the division of intellectual interests into disciplines. You become an attorney, an anthropologist, and sociologist, an economist—and so on. Now, in my judgment, that is an inevitable sort of necessary evil, because the field of knowledge is vast. And you want to organize it provisionally, so that you can make some sense out of the field that you have selected as your interest.

I say provisionally, because, in my opinion, the usefulness of a discipline is the degree and the way in which it becomes useful to society. And so we have, for instance, the problem of Alviso. First thing I did was to set up a team of seven of us—you would have described it as an interdisciplinary team . . . We joined our forces because we had skills—in the law, in economics, in research—but the purpose of it was to get to the bottom of what was happening in Alviso. Because our aim was to save that town! That was the focus of our endeavor. We were all, I think, fairly qualified technicians in our respective fields, but the object of our getting together was to save this little town. And we did save it.

In the American university, I think if you look at it closely, you'll find that the departments have their vested interests. They want to turn you all into illustrious anthropologists, and after that you can talk about nothing but anthropology, but you won't know that in East San Jose we have some very crucial problems that require anthropological brains to help us! That's the choice you have to make. Find those people in the community who can use anthropological counsel (call it whatever you will; but it's the discipline from which you're coming), apply it to a situation that is urgent—and it's important because these people are losing their homes and their jobs. And you're there to help them.

So, my suggestion is to think in terms of a structure that brings you from the academic campus, a community group and some legal support together and go to work on something that is real and pressing and urgent to all of us.[45]

More than a year and a half later, at his San Jose home on December 7, 1978, Galarza sat for another interview where he offered a "personal manifesto."

Galarza: There is a limit to what you can ask one individual to do, and I think that limit has been reached with me. Fortunately, we have taken the precaution of leaving a record in various places—in Alviso, in San Francisco, Berkeley, Santa Cruz. So I don't feel that these are blank pages that still have to be written by *me*.

In fact, the whole theory on which I operated for years is that if I wrote *books* in detail, with documentation listed, and bibliographies, that that would be *my* contribution to the history of my time. But I keep getting calls from people who keep saying to me, "Come and teach. Come and give us a lecture. Teach us this. Fill in these gaps."

With all the young Chicanos who are in this now, who are taking courses, who are going into graduate school, who are looking for things to do, I'm saying to them, "The system is still there. If you're young and energetic and if you agree that something's got to be done, go do it! You have enough of a background in the records I've left behind to give you a start."

But this is a tough assignment! The idea of reading the past in order to do something about the present and the future, is *not* something that you learn in institutions.

Interviewer: The kind of energy and dedication you've put in it is probably a little terrifying to some people who haven't . . .

Galarza: That's right, and I want to keep them terrified.

Interviewer: They may wonder if they can put in it what you have.

Galarza: That's right. Experiencing that terror is part of their education.

Because it is a terrible thing to have spent most of your life working with people . . . and to be forced by circumstances to realistically analyze a social system that's there in front of you—it's terrible! It takes a kind of grit that the schools of education—graduate schools—don't tell you anything about.

You have to *experience* the *awfulness* of a stratified social system that will not become human.

Interviewer: Even though it's made up of individual human beings.

Galarza: That's right.

Interviewer: Is it terrifying to look at a social system and see that it's rigidi-fied and needs change, from the aspect of how do you make a start?

Galarza: I made a start. In my case, my life is well enough known to a number of people through my books, my writing, my letters, in the docu-mentation I've left behind. You see, I've always had this concern for thirty-four years that this might be significant to people who follow me.

I'm not in the position that most people are who talk into your micro-phone. What I say into your mic is really a fringe benefit because the people who have left a record in oral history are not people who have written their course. They're not. I know many of them. And they're glad of the opportu-nity to live in oral history because they haven't taken the time nor had the interest nor the skill nor the opportunity to leave a record of documents and papers behind them. I have. And they are in archives.

In time, if these issues remain alive, it will not be difficult for them—for my successors—to find out from me, from what I've written, what happened and my views of what happened—my appraisal, my analysis—it's all there. Some of it is still too scattered, I'm afraid—but it's there.[46]

Reaching across time—enticing, warning, teaching—Galarza's un-relenting resolve offered little refuge for the less committed. Like Fred Ross finding organizers, Galarza demanded life commitments to disrupt mechanisms of injustice and engage structures of oppression.[47]

In turn, he showed the way for those select scholars who followed. Leav-ing a line of bread crumbs, a detective's trail of clues within the unfinished explorations from his own set of inquiries. He invites us to take up the cause, in effect joining him, engaging together in carrying on the work.

And that brings me to the concluding two points. I've said before that in my judgment the War on Poverty at this stage is a mere skirmish.

I don't think it's going to become a war until the amount of money ap-propriated by Congress enables us to mount a massive attack on the problem of unemployment. I mean by that not just the problem of creating jobs, I mean the basic decisions that our society is continuously making; such as, for instance, the allocation of resources: where money in vast quantities shall be invested, and how it shall be spent. This is what creates jobs.

To those decisions the poor are not parties. I suggest we have got to keep battling for what I call anthropomorphic education. It's a terrible phrase. What I mean to emphasize there is that we can't stop pressing the schools to teach us as if they were teaching children and not systems. Do you know that in certain parts of Los Angeles many people have made a wonderful discovery? They've discovered that one teacher with fifteen children and an expert assistant can do a better job than one teacher with no assistance and forty kids. The question is no longer discovery and demonstration, the question is now: can we hold the line so that ratio of one teacher to fifteen children can become universal? I hope that we don't give one inch.

And I trust that the restructuring of educational methods, the downgrading of status and authority where it now is in the upper strata of administration will be accelerated. I hope the time comes when the greatest prestige, the largest salary, the most attractive emoluments in a public school system will be those of the kindergarten teacher. In reverse process, when we get to the superintendent of schools, he will be a guy who's around to be called on when he's needed.

I want to conclude by saying that, again, I haven't been talking of fundamentals really. Not until this economy provides all men with sufficient income—I'm not talking of the income of a day or a week; I'm talking about the income of a year—so that their wives and the mothers of their children can stay home and take care of the families; obliterate the slums and make it possible for other slums not to take their places; until we reconsider such things as urban development so that they become other than weapons for displacing these doughnut communities from one part of the landscape to another, I don't think the job will have begun.

I close with the question: Are the Mexican Americans ready? That I don't know. But I think some of us in this room intend to find out.[48]

Like Antonio Gramsci's "organic intellectuals" who explicitly identified with their economic class, Galarza's values were deeply integrated with his community. There was no separation here; he was in service to them. Solidarity gave weight and substance to his work.

No other scholar's life had a greater practical impact on me than Galarza's brutal invitations, visceral commitments, and life-long dedication to the cause.

In essence, lead from the front and stay in the fight as long as you can.

4

In Front of the Bayonet

DEAN MACCANNELL

In June of 2006, I reached out to Dean MacCannell, just as I had emailed Goldschmidt.

Though I had gone to UC Davis, and studied in an academic department that once housed him, we had not previously met.

Professor MacCannell,

I am currently a doctoral student at Cornell in their Adult Education and Extension Program. I attended UC Davis from 2000 to 2002 getting a M.S. degree in International Agricultural Development. During that time, I got to know Isao Fujimoto and his work in the Central Valley.

Simultaneously, I worked with Cooperative Extension in Knights Landing for two years under a RAship and conducted a critical ethnography of social segregation in public institutions, in particular schools but also housing, churches, and local political bodies like the area's water district.

While researching broadly around the question of the reproduction of inequality, I became familiar with Walter Goldschmidt's work. Though I did not emphasize it at the time, I have since continued to be troubled by the extent of the poverty and environmental problems within a context of such wealth.

This July, I will be going to the southern San Joaquin Valley to explore research collaborations with various community groups in the region. Before I head down there, I will be visiting Davis between July 7 and 11th and would value any advice you have on approaching the research topic.

I have read some of your work on the topic, specifically around the Westlands, and the general context of the social and economic repercussions of industrial agriculture. Cornell Professors Lyson and Geisler refer to you regarding this topic.

I hope you have time to meet.

Thank you,

Dan O'Connell

On June 30, 2006, MacCannell responded:

Dear Daniel,

Thank you for the note. I'm always interested in supporting further research on the valley.

I am in Europe lecturing right now, and will not return until July 9. I have no plans to go to Davis (I live in the Bay Area) during the dates of your stay.

Depending on your schedule, we could meet in Berkeley on the 10th or 11th.

Best wishes and good luck with this important research.

Dean Mac

We met a few weeks later for breakfast at Saul's Delicatessen in Berkeley. An apt setting—immersed in the aromas of Jewish soul food—to digest a cascade of harrowing stories.

Dean was already sitting in a booth with Juliet, his wife and partner, when I arrived. A renowned scholar in her field of comparative literature, Juliet was, as I came to realize, essential to MacCannell's journey—emotionally, politically, and intellectually. There was no way to lead a personal life away from the pressure they experienced together due to his work.

They brought me back through their lives, with humor and at peace. The upheaval in the sixties, confronting the Westlands growers, and dramas negotiating the politics of higher education. Most remarkable—still with me to this day—was the recounting of the UC Davis Chancellor Jim Meyer warning MacCannell that John Harris, a powerful westside grower, was capable of killing him and others to silence his research. As we talked, I regretted not taping what I was hearing, craving to safeguard and secure the stories. I could barely control my desire to jot down notes, which I fudged by taking a few on a napkin.

In the café that morning, a backstory presented itself. Clear and simple, pleading to be brought into the light, it was laid out for me like a line to follow. Beyond the *Chinatown*-like political backdrop was the scientific "retest" of Goldschmidt's hypothesis. First censored and suppressed by the federal government in the 1940s, MacCannell had led a team of researchers for over a decade, to eventually validate and confirm the original Arvin-Dinuba findings.

Leaving the restaurant, I felt like a beat reporter with the scoop of a lifetime. Over the years to come, with kernels planted, I returned numerous times to harvest and clarify the saga.

The testimony from that day grew into a full indictment of industrial-scale agriculture and birthed a theory that agrarian democracy is premised upon economic equity.

Becoming a Scholar

In the 1960s, a new generation of social scientists began to work in the Central Valley. For the first time, rural sociologists were permitted, authorized, and funded to research the social cost and effects of agribusiness consolidation and economic monopoly.

In the history of the University of California, there had never been a rural sociology program or department. In fact, as far as known, there had not been a rural sociologist hired by the U.C. system as a professor authorized to use that title. Isao Fujimoto and Dean MacCannell, both coming from Cornell's Rural Sociology Department, were the first known hires allowed to practice their discipline with institutional deference and support from within California's land-grant complex, including its flagship institution at Davis.

A multidimensional scholar, MacCannell was an adept statistician with mastery over quantitative methods who was equally versed in social theory, philosophy, and semiotics. No apparent aspect of his preparation was overlooked as he headed to Davis to conduct the Goldschmidt retests in its new department of Applied Behavioral Studies.

To arrive there, however, he was trained, educated, and mentored from his earliest years by some of the most renowned scholars of his day.

My father was a professor of sociology at San Diego State where Frank Young had his first academic appointment and I began school before transferring to Berkeley. He started in my freshman year, so Frank Young was my first anthropology professor. He taught me Anthro 1.

Frank arrived with a lot of drum rolling. He acted like that, too. He was working on a book, a cross-cultural study of male initiation. He came into the first classes and said, "I just discovered that there are no graduate students here, and I have to have a research team. So I am going to give an examination. The top tier of students on the exam, even though you are undergraduates and you are not supposed to be doing this, will be a part of my research team. You will get out of all work for the class. You don't have to write term papers or take any of the other exams. You are only going to be graded on the quality of your ability to take orders and do the research." I was up for that! I became a part of Frank's research team as an undergraduate at San Diego State. I did coding and made tables for that study of male initiation ceremonies.

All of this was happening as I shifted from San Diego State to Berkeley. I was a five-year undergraduate because not all of my credits transferred. My Berkeley faculty in anthropology were horrible as far as teaching was concerned. There was nothing that resembled a Frank Young. They were old. Opinionated. It was supposed to be the best anthropology department in the world, but it was a freaking disaster from an undergraduate student's standpoint. Goffman was in sociology though. I audited Introduction to Sociology from Erving Goffman as a junior. I couldn't take sociology at San Diego State because it would have been taught by my father or a close family friend.

I was determined to get back to Frank Young, or something like Frank Young, for graduate study. They wanted me to stay at Berkeley in sociology, but I went to rural sociology at Cornell exactly when Frank was in his complete ascendancy after returning there. All graduate students wanted Frank on their committee. If you were really lucky, and part of the elite, he was the chair of your committee. He was putting together his Frank Young paradigm. Assembling it, in seminars, piece by piece, so we watched his thinking process as he created his three systemic structural variables of differentiation, solidarity, and centrality. He shopped out the variables to the dissertation students. I was actually known in graduate school as "differentiation man," because that was the variable that I was going to be working on. This was the way he had everyone going.

Frank was a structuralist. He was in the process of building a mega-theory, like Talcott Parsons. Though structuralism was coming in Europe, he was doing it over here independently—totally American. It came out at the same moment as what was happening in Europe. He was the only guy in the United States that was doing a rigorous, theoretically deductive, structural model for analyzing the ways that communities or regions undergo change and development. It is still potentially interesting, if it still existed today. It is still teachable. It could still be useful; but it died somewhere along the line. It just lacks any kind of human life. It's like Frank—too arid.

I was writing about tourism as a graduate student. I was interested in doing a dissertation on border towns and tourism. I had sent my proposal to Goffman. He really liked it and sent me back good comments on it. After I had sent it to Goffman, I gave the same proposal to Frank Young. The committee huddled, then concluded out of my presence that they would not accept the proposal. They were nice. They said, "It's a great proposal. It will be a great book. But you are on completely unchartered territory here. It will take you probably ten years to do it, if you do it the way you want to do it. We don't want you around here for that long, so just propose something a little more conventional and get the hell out of here."

Though I always have had a troubled relationship with Frank, we got along fine. He was the chair for my dissertation. Signed it off. He nominated me for Rural Sociology Society's "Dissertation of the Year" award, and I got it. He had to write that letter. We've never had a break. The dissertation was theoretically high wire, the most methodologically sophisticated thing you could do at the time in a positivist mode. I did it, just the way they told me.

Macrosocial Accounting

My dissertation method was macrosocial accounting.

The development of macrosocial accounting, the term and the idea, was Frank Young. I was the first person hired at Cornell to head its Macrosocial Accounting Project.

I finished in '68 and had this nifty job as a Senior Research Associate to start up and coordinate Cornell's Macrosocial Accounting Program. I had all of the perks and salary of an Assistant Professor. I was teaching a seminar. I even taught Frank's methods course when he was on sabbatical at Stanford. It was clear that my status would have been converted as soon as a faculty position opened up. But we knew that there were not going to be two positions in Ithaca for us. We agreed that if Juliet could get a faculty position in either Boston or Philadelphia, I would go to Boston and study with Chomsky, or Philadelphia and study with Goffman. Even if I didn't have a prospect, I would go. My main goal was to take a year and write *The Tourist*. When Juliet got a position at Haverford College, I quit.

Later, everything we did in macrosocial accounting in the valley, and probably everything that Young ever did using it in Mexico, would be done in GIS [Geographic Information System, a sophisticated tool related to spatial and geographical knowledge]. Let's say macrosocial accounting never existed and Frank Young was an Associate Professor at Cornell and I was a beginning graduate student, GIS would be the method. But we would not be doing it in a kind of a brutish, empiricist, inductive way. Sometimes geographers using GIS don't have an idea in their head, or they will chase something really low level and find things by accident. We would never do that. We would have theory. We don't find things by accident. We would be harnessing GIS to the theory in order to try to have this powerful method to illustrate conceptual relations.

We would be taking exactly the same sets of variables, like Young's variables—differentiation, solidarity, rigidity—or others and attempt to see how they can predict such things as poverty and what have you. Since everything that we did was laid out in space, connected to geographic entities like towns, it would be the perfect matrix for us to just grab a hold of and use its robust capacities for handling data.

Macrosocial accounting was originally conceived as these giant repositories or archives of data at the community level that we could then examine for relationships that existed within the data sets. That's the GIS system. As long as your unit of analysis is a geographic entity, which ours were—always towns or counties or whatever—it would be perfect.

The regression method, once considered by Goldschmidt for his second multi-community study, was now in place and ready to be applied. Macrosocial accounting was ideally suited to retest the Arvin-Dinuba values with a much higher degree of scientific confidence.

Macrosocial accounting was a quantitative research method that investigated community and regional structures, described local economics, assessed civic participation, and measured community well-being.

MacCannell was among the first to adapt and apply this tool to agricultural regions most indicative of monopolized industrialization.

Macrosocial accounting utilized research methods similar to agricultural economics.[1] The primary difference was that a sociological framework broadened the level of analysis. MacCannell commented:

> The difference between MSA (macrosocial accounting) and economic approaches is the level of analysis and the types of models which are made. Economic analysis of agricultural systems focuses on the integration of business enterprises in markets, and it models costs and benefits of different policies and practices at the level of the firm. As its name implies, the goal of MSA is to describe regional social structure.[2]

Statistics bolstered the method's credentials. Its findings were rigorously scientific.

In an early article, Young fleshed out this method's evolving themes and framed them as "sociometric" as they described the connectivity between multiple layers of society—the state, regional affiliations, intervillage networks, villages, and individual informants.[3] These "inter-system relationships" were linked to "variables of community structure" that could be quantified.[4]

A year later, Young and Fujimoto suggested "the possibility that communities can be ordered on a single dimension of complexity and differentiation" using "community as a unit of analysis."[5] By 1967, Young and MacCannell had standardized a model stable enough to measure across geographic, social, and cultural contexts.

A key description of macrosocial accounting, written by MacCannell in 1978 for a layperson's understanding, was titled "The Elementary Structures of Community: Macrosocial Accounting as a Methodology for Theory Building and Policy Formation." Three themes were designed to be inclusive of almost all aspects of community life. MacCannell defined them:

> ... the notions of community "spirit" or a "sense of community" are aspects of *solidarity*. A community's "isolation" or, alternatively, its "importance" are functions of its *centrality*. And *differentiation* incorporates what we ordinarily think of as level of economic or social development.[6]

Differentiation, in particular, was useful in codifying institutions and groupings of community in order to construct a baseline to make comparisons over time or with other locations:

> Once analysis of component groups was begun, it became quite clear that communities are only expressions of underlying structural codes similar in some respects to the genetic code or to a grammar of a language.[7]

These variables of community included such institutions as churches, schools, hospitals, libraries, unions or newspapers; the presence of services like public transportation, taxis, recreation, water supply, or electrification; and facilities like types of housing, number of roads, or other types of infrastructure. Once counted, they could be compared.

Social structural differentiation, expressed in community variables, was seen as interconnected rather than random. The institutions and services of community formed a network reliant upon each other in a reciprocating structural system. This hypothesis opened the door to changes in community development theory, potential policy adjustments, and real-world applications. If associations within this structure could be determined—like increasing the number of schools to promote long-term economic development, for example—then investments and programs could be directed to maximize beneficial outcomes. The application and utility of determining structural differentiation seemed accessible and unlimited.

Not the method for romantics, macrosocial accounting did, however, prove to be a potent weapon when used to analyze the social effects of corporate farming on California's rural communities. Before that, though, the MacCannells were tossed about by the upheaval of the 1960s.

Scholars in the Counterculture

> We returned to Philadelphia [from a year in Paris]. It was great because Goffman, Juliet, and I were there together and visited. The Center for Urban Ethnography had just been started. Students were doing ethnographies in the ghettos. Around 1971, I taught the first graduate course in the United States called "Semiotics, Ethnomethodology, and Social Change" at Temple.

Figure 4.1. Juliet MacCannell, Dean MacCannell, and Isao Fujimoto at a demonstration in support of the establishment of African American Studies at Cornell University, April 1969. Courtesy of Dean MacCannell.

I survived all the University's cuts from one-year to three-year. Then, midway through the third year, Isao called and engineered the move to UC Davis.

Isao Fujimoto was my graduate student office mate at Cornell. Frank Young was his major professor, too. We were close. He was ahead of me by a couple of years, and I was assigned to him as his little brother. He was my graduate student pal to get me through the first year. They did that back then. Every incoming graduate student was given somebody who had been there a year or two to advise them. They housed us together with two graduate students per office in the basement of Warren Hall. They put me in with Isao. He was my guy. He was as activist then as he is now. Everything was starting up—the war, African American Studies, everything. We were all off protesting together as often as doing all the graduate student stuff.

The grounding that Young gave us in social analysis using empirical indicators was equally influential for Isao and myself, but neither of us were slavish Youngians. We both used macrosocial accounting. Isao was an innovative user of it; in his hands it got embroidered upon. Still, we were probably the least likely of Young's students to follow him right down the road and do exactly what he told us to do, which doesn't diminish the importance of Young's teaching for both of us. It was crucial.

Young was innovative with social indicators. He wasn't interested in just grabbing the standard set of demographic indicators. He was constantly teaching us that *everything* was a social indicator. You just have to figure out how to quantify it. The paint on the side of a house was a social indicator. Was it peeling? Was it new? The depth of tire treads was a social indicator. He was poetical in his application of empiricism, if he let that side of himself go more.

One of his first published articles was done up in Canada on a small community. It was called "Tombstones and Social Structure." He went into graveyards and weighed the tombstones. He took the years off of them to chart the community's economic cycles for the last century by measuring the average aggregate weight of the tombstones by year. He had all sorts of ways of analyzing the cemetery. How were family sizes fluctuating during different eras by looking at children's tombstones? What was the average age of death for the people? He was able to paint this detailed picture of the life of that community for the last 100 years in quite imaginative ways. He had his antennas out for that kind of stuff. It was *that* Young, who was most appealing to Isao when Isao came to Davis.

Isao was one of the first rural sociologists to come out to Davis. They hired him after he had been in the field to do his dissertation, but he hadn't really started writing it yet. We were coming out of the Ivy League. If you were hired as an Assistant Professor at Cornell back then, you would have no teaching responsibilities for a year, but he was teaching a full load. Isao took every responsibility Davis handed him very seriously. He didn't say no to anything. I could see that he was being used up. Every time they needed anybody who was a little bit different for anything—to be a public face, to start a program, to work with a student who was different, whatever—it was always his job. They overused him. Overload. There was no way he could have finished his dissertation.

They brought him to Davis at a moment when everything was in ferment and turmoil. The Chancellor, Jim Meyer, had to deal with students laying down on the railroad tracks in Davis to stop the munitions train from going to the weapons station. The students weren't going to classes. They were holding rallies all the time. Education stopped. Meyer personally told me a story where he called in the students. They demanded "relevancy" and gave him a cafeteria menu of recommendations. So, he said, "I went to Sociology and Anthropology and Economics. I asked them if they would be willing to accommodate within their curriculum some courses that the students would regard as 'relevant.' They all slammed the door in my face saying that under no circumstances would the curriculum of their august sciences be shaped by some hair-brained, spur-of-the-moment student demand." It was a shutout.

Meyer had been the Dean of the College of Agriculture. Up until about ten years ago that was the only stepping-stone to being the Chancellor at Davis. It was automatic—you were the Dean of the College of Ag, then you were the Chancellor. He still had good contacts back in Ag since he had anointed the next Dean. So he went back to his old college and laid out the problem. They said, "No problem. We will just start a whole new division here. It will be the 'relevant' division." That is how Applied Behavioral Science was born, with Orville Thompson as the head. It had Native American Studies, Asian American Studies, International Ag Development, Human Development, Child Development, Community Development, and Landscape Architecture and Design.

Orville had been a Cornell Education guy. He was an astute institutional creator who managed to nurture that impossible entity into a fairly powerhouse department that was hated by almost everybody on campus. One of the first hires that Orville made was Isao. As I mentioned, Isao got overextended right away because he got put in charge of everything relevant. We were waiting, hoping and praying, back at Cornell that Isao would be submitting his dissertation any time. But events just conspired against him. There were too many things for him to be doing in California and at Davis.

Around this time, when I was at Temple, Isao called and said that Applied Behavioral Sciences was taking a lot of heat from the conventional social sciences and humanities, even the science sciences, on campus. It was a hot bed of activism. They were doing things like laying out the bicycle paths, starting the farmer's market, getting the free clinic going, protesting the war. Isao said "Look, we have to have someone on our side who can lend an aura of legitimacy to this thing." By this time, *The Tourist* had been accepted for publication and a couple of other things, so the administration could see me as one of their kind of players. They brought me out for an interview, and I got the job.[8]

When I arrived at Davis, Isao had been there for five or seven years. We drove straight to his house. We were that close. We didn't go to the university. We didn't go to find a realtor. We went straight to Isao's house on Linden Lane.

I was perfect because all of the enemies of Applied Behavior Sciences said, "This guy would never do anything with Ag—*The Tourist*, structuralism, semiotics. Absolutely. Ideal!" I got a complete pass! Not only a pass but an enthusiastic welcome. Charlie Hess, the Dean, called me into his office and said, "I am sorry I have to tell you this, but as far as I'm concerned, you are a flower growing out of a dung heap!" The dung heap was Applied Behavioral Sciences.

After arriving, I immediately got funding from a device the legislature had started up. The legislature was interested in trying to shape UC research programs so that they would in fact address some of the real problems of that moment. It was a nutsy time. David Saxon was President of the University, after being fired for not signing the loyalty oath years before. Jerry Brown was Governor. Carter was President.

The legislature was on our side. They were offering $50,000 grants to UC faculty that would propose to do something that would be relevant and geared to the current crises. They were called "policy seminars" or "Legislative Grants for UC Policy Seminars." I immediately got the first one—straight into old Behavioral Sciences, the dung heap. It was for the "California Agricultural Policy Seminar."

I pulled together a consortium of people on several campuses. I went out and found people in the state doing alternative research to ag business—Frank Cancian at Irvine, Bill Friedland at Santa Cruz, and a couple of guys at Berkeley. I was able to put a little money into their research programs and got a publications series going off of that support. Charlie Hess and the people at Davis were quick to match the money that I brought in. They said, "Yeah, for your own research, if you are doing all this, we will make sure you will be able to do your part."

My part was to do the Goldschmidt retest.

The Goldschmidt Retests

The retests of Goldschmidt's Arvin-Dinuba findings now moved forward.

After years of recalcitrance and resistance, California's land-grant establishment, specifically at UC Davis, stood aside and allowed the science to tell its truth. Even California's state government directed funding for an extended research program to understand the state's agricultural economy from a sociological lens.

Scientifically, the testing of Goldschmidt's hypothesis amounted to a technical problem for which MacCannell had all of the tools to answer and solve: testable theory, sound research design, previously implemented methods, access to data, improved computers. It was a straightforward research project. Yet, past controversies and ongoing political volatility were in the air, pressuring the work from the start. The historic absence of rural sociology as an academic discipline within the University of California illustrated the difficulties of the work ahead.

I have this wording in my head that after Goldschmidt and Taylor, the state legislature, with pressure from the Ag guys, passed a law saying, "It is forbidden to use state money or facilities to conduct social surveys in rural areas."

It would be interesting if it is apocryphal because even if it doesn't exist, the University of California is the only land-grant institution in the entire U.S. that did not have a department of rural sociology. What happened to produce a situation in which the UC felt that it was inadvisable to establish a department of rural sociology? I feel fairly certain that there is a law. There has to be. I don't think that the University of California would have uniquely turned its back on rural sociology unless there was more than "we don't like your kind around here."

Coming out to an Ag School, I arrived asking, "Where is the rural sociology?" For the first few years, I was the only Ph.D. rural sociologist in the state. Isao was really the first, but they tripped him. He had given me a report on how crazy things were, so I was somewhat prepared for the turmoil. I arrived with this strong sense that some of my research program, not all of it, ought to be on rural and ag issues. I felt that it was my responsibility to stir that particular pot since I was the first guy the university hired to do that stuff.

I was naturally drawn to the controversy, aware that that was a good way of becoming visible inside the university and beyond. But I also wanted to go to the Ag School because I knew what was going to happen to the social sciences on the general campuses after the Vietnam War. They were going to croak. Sociology had been a big, robust, important, socially-discussed, Op.

Ed.-present field in the fifties and sixties. I knew that given the things that I wanted to do I had to have a stronger institutional base.

I was interested in an Ag School because otherwise I would never survive an academic career.

The problems in the San Joaquin Valley had persisted, and in many respects, had worsened. In fact, they were spreading to other agricultural regions of the United States, first in the Sunbelt states and then across the Midwest. The model of industrialized agriculture and corporate farming was now affecting places where family farms were once the foundation of cultural life, local economies, and civic vitality in thousands of small towns across rural America.

California's San Joaquin Valley was an ideal context to apply macrosocial accounting. While Young's method had been designed for international contexts, the valley represented many characteristics of a "developing" country. MacCannell conducted statistical regressions measuring variables of social conditions (for example poverty, substandard housing, education levels) against variables of industrialized agriculture (such as farm size, residency, chemical use). For the next decade, innovations of this research design were repeated in various forms and with increasingly nuanced interpretation. Again and again, Goldschmidt's original findings were supported and affirmed after repeated, numerous, and academically rigorous studies.

I never once tried to formulate an alternative theory of ag and social conditions. I did everything as a retest. I used Goldschmidt—a very simple and clear frame—to put my efforts around from the first day. I conducted research that would demonstrate conclusively whether or not Goldschmidt was correct in the way that he analyzed those relationships.

My position was clear: "I don't care how this comes out. I *really* don't care how this comes out. I am going to set the research up in such a fashion that we will have a definitive answer to the question: What is the relationship between farm size and capitalization, and community conditions? I'm going to win either way. I am a young, brash assistant professor. I am going to prove Goldschmidt was wrong, and that will be fine; or I will prove that he was right, and that would be fine."

The leftist kids inside the program were really sitting on the edge of their seats. Some of Isao's students were really angry. They said, "What if it comes out the wrong way?"

I said, "If it comes out the wrong way, I confess it will sadden me personally, but I am okay either way as a scientist. Either I find that Goldschmidt was mainly correct, maybe even more correct than he thought he was, or I find that Goldschmidt was never correct. I will come forward with it no matter how it comes out." I set this thing up in such a way that the chips will fall. I do confess that I am happier that it came out the way it did.

In some cases, 80% of the variation of the type of things that Goldschmidt was concerned about—quality of life issues using his causal variables of farm size, absentee ownership, etc.—were in his direction. Bear in mind that the big farmers would argue the exact opposite: "Our huge, robust, marvelous farms are actually beneficial to these communities because of trickle-down economics. Without us they would be much, much worse off." They would argue in the opposite direction.

After testimony before a House Committee in D.C. in the immediate aftermath of the Westlands study, their in-house technical advisors remarked that the design was such that had this not been the case it would certainly come out in the research. If large farms were beneficial socially, these technical advisors in the House Committee said that that would have come up.

Major retest research was conducted over the next decade. The first straightforwardly expanded the originally planned Goldschmidt follow-up study of agricultural communities in the valley. The second burrowed into the westside of the San Joaquin Valley, an area most representative of industrial agriculture. And the final analysis looked at the regions within the Sunbelt states of California, Arizona, Texas, and Florida most expressive of large-scale agribusiness domination.

The earliest findings were first presented at academic conferences. Of these, the most significant was the 1978 Rural Sociological Society (RSS) conference held in San Francisco. It was here that the first Goldschmidt retest findings were publicly presented. On Friday, September 1st at 5:00 pm, MacCannell discussed the paper he had submitted to the conference, titled "Retest of Goldschmidt's Arvin and Dinuba Findings Using Macrosocial Accounting Methods." (Remembering that day, Juliet commented, *"Everyone was on tenterhooks waiting, waiting for Dean to present the findings at the Rural Sociology meeting. You could hear a pin drop. Dean came out and said the results. The whole place erupted—Goldschmidt was right!"*) The following day, on Saturday morning at 8:00 am, Goldschmidt himself, together with Fujimoto and others, participated in a conference panel reviewing and updating his 1940s research. After the RSS conference, MacCannell continued to broadcast his findings. In December 1980, at the Interreligious Task Force on Food Policy in Washington D.C., MacCannell gave the keynote address titled, "The Effects of Agricultural Structure on Social Conditions in Small Communities." And in October of 1981, he traveled back to Cornell, where he presented the "Preliminary Results of the Goldschmidt Restudy" to graduate faculty in agricultural economics and rural sociology.

A 1981 report, titled "On the Relationship of Agriculture to Rural Community Conditions in California," co-authored by Dean MacCannell and Jerry White, was retained by Goldschmidt and gifted to me in his files. The report represents the data and findings that MacCannell was likely presenting at these conferences, presentations, and lectures. This paper applied macrosocial accounting to 83 rural California communities in an explicit retest of Goldschmidt's findings, even referencing his disallowed second study. The first sentence acknowledged that it "was conceived as a retest of Walter Goldschmidt's study."[9] The authors emphasized (perhaps for political reasons) the Goldschmidt retest as solely a scientific study. No more, no less. But they likely knew better, and the particular care they took in situating their study away from past controversy and back into the realm of scientific inquiry hints at this study's potential volatility.

This retest improved on Goldschmidt's earlier BAE research design. It took his original premise, expanded the number of variables, applied statistical regression, and made sociologically grounded interpretations of the data. The research design was broader in scope geographically, and added many more quantifiable variables of both industrial agriculture and community well-being. Rather than simple averages gathered through surveys and observation, macrosocial accounting primarily accessed, compiled, and analyzed measurable public data.

Variables of industrial agriculture beyond the Goldschmidt variables or farm size (SIZE ACRES) and residency (ABSENTEE) were added to the study. Four additional variables were included: (1) the size of the adjacent or surrounding water district as measured by its annual operating revenue (H2O DISTRICT $); (2) whether the governing structure of the water district was democratic or undemocratic (NONDEMO/H2O); (3) whether the farmland in "committed crops" was like citrus or grapevines (CITRUS and VINES); and (4) how diverse were the crops grown in the region immediately surrounding the town (CROP DIVERSITY).

Dependent variables were run against these independent variables in tests to measure "agricultural rigidity," economic well-being, education, housing, social insecurity, service professionals, medical professions, and retail trade. Data gathered for these variables was thorough and extensive, and the study's findings, validating Goldschmidt, were presented in antiseptic findings stripped of emotion:

> The regressions reveal a consistent pattern of correlation between the structure of agriculture and social conditions in California's central valley communities. Between 20 and 50 percent of the variation in social conditions between the 83 communities can be accounted for by differences in the surrounding agriculture. We think it is unlikely that any single other system of practices (e.g., industry, retail trade, communications, etc.) could be shown to account for the unexplained variation, although there is certainly an implied challenge to social and economic science here. Until proven otherwise, on the basis of our research, we suggest that agricultural structure is the single most important determinant of social conditions in California's central valley communities.[10]

The report concluded, "The results of our research provide overall support for the form and direction of the relationship of agricultural structure to community conditions as this relationship was described and analyzed by Walter Goldschmidt almost 40 years ago."[11] Its final "policy implications" also supported and reinforced the original findings.

> Our research clearly shows that the original Reclamation law was intelligently conceived given its expressed aims. We cannot address the continuing validity of those aims, but we have shown that the acreage and residency requirements of the law, if enforced, would produce the effects desired by the law makers in their original statement of intent and subsequent

reinterpretations of the law and its intent. Both local residency of land owners and limited scale of land holdings are determinants of strong rural communities as measured by a broad spectrum of standard social indicators.[12]

The next MacCannell retest of Goldschmidt's hypothesis examined questions related to the construction of the San Luis Unit, the last phase of the Central Valley Project. In this sense and others, its purpose mimicked that of the original study in clarifying the effects of government investment in California. Once again, the federal government, through its Office of Technology Assessment (OTA), was asking for a determination of the social impacts and economic costs of publicly funding and building water infrastructure, now on the western areas of the San Joaquin Valley.

The research findings were published in two related reports. The first was in the OTA's 1983 *Proceedings of the Workshop on Policy, Technology and the Structure of Agriculture*. It was titled, "Agribusiness and the Small Community." A year later, in 1984, MacCannell and White published this research in a book chapter titled "The Social Costs of Large-Scale Agriculture and the Prospects for Land Reform in California."[13] The chapter was concise. Once again, the numbers told the story.

The findings were especially revealing because the research design highlighted and analyzed the Westlands Water District. The Westlands was a 600,000 acre special district. It was a focal point of controversy, reclamation policy contradictions, and academic engagement in the 1970s and 80s. Except possibly for the Imperial Valley, no other geography in California was more expressive of the contradictions and problems associated with agribusiness concentration and inequitable landownership.[14] MacCannell and White's research distilled outcomes that illustrated the problems of industrial-scale agriculture.

In making "The Westlands Case," MacCannell and White contextualized the region by comparing it to the rest of Fresno County and the United States as a whole. Not only did they choose a region highly characteristic of factory farming, they also looked at its most vulnerable residents to understand the social costs of its agricultural economy. Some of their statistical variables specifically documented Mexican-American well-being and hardship, as they comprised most of the region's agricultural labor force.

Figure 4.2. Dean MacCannell, in the 1980s preparing congressional testimony. Courtesy of Dean MacCannell.

The book chapter MacCannell and White wrote focused on the five census tracks that overlapped the Westlands Water District, with particular attention to the largest town in each of these tracks: Coalinga, Firebaugh, Huron, Mendota, and San Joaquin/Tranquility. The U.S. Bureau of the Census research data established key findings:

1. The growers in the Westlands were not (and had not been) compliant with reclamation law. There was not a single 160-acre farm in the entire service area and only twenty percent of the farmland owners—individuals or corporations—had addresses in or near the district. The average size of a farm in the water district was 2,200 acres. MacCannell and White noted "the current operating scale, residency patterns, and social conditions are precisely those the [Reclamation] act was passed to prevent."[15]

2. Substantial public subsidy and investment had been allocated and spent in the region. The authors found that of the $600 million total project cost, $265 million was from the federal government amounting to a $1,540 per acre subsidy, or over $3 million for a 2,000-acre farm. These expenditures artificially inflated indicators

for employment and infrastructure changes for this sparsely populated area over the time period of the research.

3. In the twenty years since the water infrastructure was constructed,
   it was apparent that opposite policy outcomes had resulted from
   public investments through reclamation in the region. MacCannell
   and White stated that the "peculiar way that the Reclamation Act
   has been interpreted in the Westlands has contributed to the great
   local disparity between the rich and the poor."[16]

The economic outcomes for residents of the Westlands was detailed
through six categories: housing conditions; poverty and inequality; income, employment and affluence; education; and infrastructure changes
from 1958 to 1978.

The results were dramatic:

I. Housing Conditions. There was an overall reduction in the amount
   of housing (an explicit goal of reclamation was to construct rural
   farmsteads and towns), and many of the existing housing facilities were substandard. MacCannell and White found that "[t]en
   percent of the homes in the Westlands lacked plumbing in 1970, as
   compared with 3.4 percent for other rural and small-town areas of
   Fresno County. Almost 20 percent of the homes in the rural area
   around Firebaugh lacked plumbing." Overcrowding also characterized accommodations: "Over 18 percent of the Mexican-American
   population lived in homes with more than 1.5 persons per room,
   and the figures were as high as 43 percent in the Coalinga tract."[17]

II. Poverty and Inequality. In the Westlands, MacCannell and White
    established that "[i]n some census tracts the proportion of the
    Mexican-American population living below the federal poverty
    standard in 1970 ran as high as 35 to 53.7 percent. Almost 84 per-
    cent of the Mexican-American population in the rural Firebaugh
    tract lived at or below 1.5 times the federal poverty standard . . .
    [Mexican-American] families were subsisting on about $3,000 a
    year. Less than half of them were receiving any form of public as-
    sistance."[18] The region exhibited an odd characteristic juxtaposing
    high levels of employment (which usually improved the lives of
    working families) with economic destitution.

III. <u>Income, Employment, and Affluence</u>. MacCannell and White used 1970 census statistics to find that "Median family income for the rural areas of Fresno County was about $4,000 lower than for the rest of the state, and income in the Westlands was about $2,500 lower than for the rest of rural Fresno County. The family income of the Mexican-American population of the Westlands was another $1,000 lower."[19]

IV. <u>Education</u>. Seemingly contrary to other findings and difficult to interpret, residents of the Westlands (for most census tracts) had more median years of education than people in other rural areas of Fresno County.

V. <u>Infrastructure Changes, 1958–1978</u>. Under this heading, MacCannell and White measured macrosocial differentiation by collecting data from telephone directories for 1958, 1968, and 1978. During those two decades notable declines including the loss of five doctors, four local newspapers, and four taxi services. The findings in this category were uneven as some sectors experienced growth— for example, in banking or government services such as welfare.

The MacCannell and White chapter appeared in the book *Land Reform, American Style*, an appropriate title because a function of reclamation law was to implement gradual land reform in regions like the Westlands. Emphasizing this point, the authors reference the unanimous 1958 U.S. Supreme Court *Ivanhoe Irrigation District v. McCracken* decision, directly quoting the court's decision that the project's benefits "be distributed in accordance with the greatest good for the greatest number of individuals," and that "the use of federal reclamation service for speculative purposes" should be prevented.[20]

Further establishing reclamation law and its values, the chapter also quotes U.S. representatives speaking in 1959, only one year after the *Ivanhoe v. McCracken* decision, and referring to the application of reclamation law to the Westlands' San Luis Unit. Senator Douglas articulated and rightly expected that reclamation principles would be implemented and applied:

> The people of Illinois are paying taxes, and have paid taxes, to build these CVP (Central Valley Project) dams, reservoirs, conduits, and irrigation

systems. They have paid taxes against their own economic interests, because they believed it was in the national interest; and are ready to continue to do so, but on condition that the money which we contribute shall be used to maintain agrarian democracy, and not huge agrarian estates. We are willing to have money spent for a democratic . . . farm system, but we do not want to have it spent to build up the power and strength of huge landowners . . . We do not want a system with a big manor house on the hill, and farm laborers living in hovels. We want a system in which the owner is the cultivator. That is the basis of American agrarian democracy.[21]

The added indignity, by 1984 when the MacCannell and White chapter was published, was that the federal reclamation law had already been overturned. The Westlands, anathema to the concept of agrarian democracy, was now positioned to receive a huge infusion of taxpayer support and public largesse contrary to the original law's intent, purpose, and explicit direction.

If the reclamation law's progressive land reform statutes were enforced, society could be different, MacCannell and White remind readers by quoting California Congressman Sisk in 1959.

If the San Luis Unit is built . . . the present population of the area will almost quadruple . . . . Why will this land support four times as many people if this project is built? Because it is inevitable and historic that under the impact of reclamation laws, as well as the economics of farm management and operation, these lands will break down into family-sized units, each cultivated by individual owners and their families . . . We are seeking to make our greatest land resources available to provide more and better living for more people. This, I believe, is the real and ultimate goal of the reclamation policy laid down by Congress more than a half-century ago—not merely to irrigate land and produce crops.[22]

Writing a quarter of a century later, MacCannell and White's research was a survey of lost opportunities as much as a chronicle of outcomes. Their research documented federal law being ignored and openly violated, even after unanimous direction by the U.S. Supreme Court in 1958. "Every petition of the large Western growers for relief from the Reclamation Act has been denied," MacCannell and White wrote, "and yet there has never been a scale-down of agricultural operations to the level required by law."[23] The inability and "failure to enforce the law" as MacCannell and White concluded, was perhaps the most damning indictment that industrial agriculture was essentially undemocratic.[24]

MacCannell's last published "retest" in 1988 incorporated a much larger region and sample size than just California's Central Valley. It also presented the information in prophetic terms applicable to policymakers and the general public who were witnessing the mid-1980s agricultural crisis bankrupting Midwestern farmers.

Originally written as government reports, this research was subsequently published in an edited book, *Agriculture and Community Change in the U.S.: The Congressional Research Reports*.[25] As he had done previously, MacCannell aimed at the locations that were highly representative of the trends and problems he sought to understand and study. His sample was from 98 counties in the four Sunbelt states of California, Arizona, Florida, and Texas. Forty-three counties were among the top 100 counties in agricultural sales for the United States. An additional 83 counties were included because they had high sales relative to their populations (eventually 26 Texas cattle counties were excluded due to their very small populations). Nine indicators of agricultural industrialization were used to predict regional social outcomes:

- The percent of the farms in the county organized as corporations
- Farm size in acres
- The percent of the farms in the county with more than $40,000 in sales
- The percent of farms with full-time hired labor
- The cost of hired labor per farm
- The cost of contract labor per farm
- The value of machinery per farm
- The cost of fertilizers per farm
- The costs of other chemicals (including herbicides and pesticides) per farm

Industrialization was no longer a regional phenomenon. Agricultural production and rural economies were consolidating across the country. And, again, the social conditions in communities where factory farming was practiced were much worse off at statistically significant levels than other comparable places in each state.

In these Sunbelt states, rural tracts dominated by large-scale agribusiness had poverty rates beyond all normal thresholds. Rural communities surrounded by large farms had "bimodal income distribution" between the wealthy landowners and poor farmworkers.[26] In Arizona, the agribusiness tracts had poverty rates around 20 percent. In Texas's agribusiness tracts the rates were five to 40 percent above the national average. Looking exclusively at Spanish surname families, the poverty rates were additionally higher by five to 20 percentage points in all tracts. All told for the 98 counties, over 40 percent of the increase in poverty was "directly attributable to farm size" with "the greatest increases associated with the largest farm sizes."[27]

These findings showed a social system transformed beyond Goldschmidt's observations and warnings. In the 1940s, many of the farmworkers Goldschmidt encountered were Dust Bowl refugees who were United States citizens. In contrast, MacCannell found communities dominated by immigrant laborers who were hired at low wages with little job security and limited work benefits.[28] These changes resulted in a "simulacrum of a Third World economy" being established within the United States.[29] In many places, immigrant workers were numerous enough to alter the social and cultural identity of communities. At the other end of the spectrum, the landowners were even more divorced from the geographies where their fields were located. Following and going beyond Goldschmidt, MacCannell wrote:

> Even under conditions where the industrial farmer is a person rather than a board of directors, and even when he actually lives on or near one of his holdings, his unprecedented wealth and primarily urban orientation, combined with modern transportation and communication technologies, permit him to operate outside of the local community in all of his social, economic, political and cultural affairs, with the single exception of his need to obtain a steady supply of inexpensive labor. And even in this latter regard, international law and relationships are the ultimate determining factors in shaping local community and labor relations.[30]

Strikingly, the middle class were mostly absent from these communities, and this both affected the civic capacity of the rural towns and limited economic demand by reducing local purchasing.

After a decade of retest studies, MacCannell had a body of empirical evidence supporting a sharper "industrialization-degradation hypothesis" that extended Goldschmidt's conclusions. Scientifically, the retests had unambiguously upheld the original findings for the San Joaquin Valley. The Sunbelt study in 1988 established corporatized farming as a national trend not limited to California's agricultural valleys.

As the evidence became more conclusive, the spread of the industrialization problem accelerated and became more pronounced:

> A convergence of social, geographical, technical and political factors have permitted the development of a new form of industrial-scale agribusiness which is now powerful enough to operate mainly outside the constraints of nature, national policy, moral and ethical norms, and local markets.[31]

While reaffirming previous findings that "rural community stagnates or declines in the context of increasing agricultural productivity," the theory had evolved with the increasing complexity of an industrializing and consolidating food system throughout the country.[32]

MacCannell's particular talent at research design became evident through his retest studies. He constructed studies that presupposed critiques, answering them by bounding specific geographic areas that would best explicate theory. Take, for example, his Sunbelt study conclusion:

> With some qualification, the relationship of agricultural structure to rural community conditions throughout the study area supports the industrial-degradation hypothesis: as the degree of agricultural industrialization increases, social conditions in the rural communities become worse. This test of the hypothesis can be considered rigorous because (1) it measures social impacts of agricultural structure at the county level where any such impacts are weakened by other economic and sociodemographic factors, (2) it tests for the relationship across four states, 98 counties and over five million people, and (3) it is restricted to rather small variations between counties preselected to represent only the highest levels of industrialization and intensiveness of agriculture found in the U.S. today. All of these factors would tend to obscure the strength of the relationship between agricultural industrialization and community conditions. Nevertheless,

many such relationships have been found at statistically acceptable levels of significance. Repeated tests have consistently shown that increasing farm size, mechanization, and gross sales significantly predict declining community conditions not merely at the local agricultural community level, but in the entire county.[33]

MacCannell's later research admitted a more explicit political position beyond the strict scientific neutrality of his earlier valley scholarship. He expanded his rhetorical range to include advocacy, policy suggestions, and predictive warnings:

> It is probably not an exaggeration to suggest that what happened near the southern borders of the United States in the last three decades will prove to be as important during the next 200 years as the pioneer experience was during the last 200.[34]

MacCannell's forewarning was similar to that of previous valley scholars. Perhaps the best example of this turn was found in the paper's first prefatory words:

> This is a report on social conditions in rural communities of four Sunbelt states: California, Arizona, Texas and Florida. There are *two* main findings: (1) an advanced industrial type of agriculture is now fully established on a regional base in the U.S. Sunbelt, and (2) there is evidence for substantial deterioration of human communities and living conditions associated with the new form of agriculture. These findings will require careful consideration as they challenge widely held assumptions about the generalized beneficial effects of economic development. The people of the U.S. must prepare themselves to consider either structural or community development solutions to the problems described here. Specifically, it may be necessary to enact legislation that will have the effect of reducing the size of the nations' largest farms. Alternatively we will have to create costly new social and environmental programs to repair the damage to human life and the environment which is endemic to the unrestrained industrialization of agriculture.[35]

In referencing and bringing his case to "the people of the U.S.," MacCannell shifted his original narrow position from only answering research questions on industrial agriculture and its socioeconomic problems to also advocating broad, public interventions to counter the damage of "industrialization-degradation" on rural communities.

The study was conducted against the backdrop of the Midwestern farm crisis of the 1980s. Its forewarning has arrived—industrial agriculture and economic consolidation were now devastating the country's heartland.

* * *

Given all the extended academic relationship between the two scholars, it is somewhat surprising that MacCannell and Goldschmidt failed to work together directly. Though they tried on one occasion, in crafting a rebuttal to an article in *Science* critiquing some of Goldschmidt's ideas, and the viability of small farms.[36]

A correspondence of two letters between them at this time illustrates their differing approaches, and hints at reasons they were not able to collaborate:

Walter Goldschmidt
978 Norman Place
Los Angeles, CA 90049

August 3, 1987

Dear Wally:
Thank you for taking the initiative with our paper. I am circulating your letter to everyone with instructions to do their part. Trudy has been on vacation for about 10 days but she will return on Friday, and her responsibilities now seem to be minor in any case.

In some ways it is hard for me to respond to your concerns about the 83 town study and the OTA report. Of course the raw data exist. In the case of the OTA [Office of Technology Assessment] study, most of it was reported in the original, in tables A2 A through H. I think you have these tables, but I am sending a second set in case you do not. These data provide some of the detail that you want, but never as vivid as the ethnographer's datus. Still you are correct in noting that it is this kind of information that gets the message across to the non-specialist public. It was these tables which

were excerpted and given greatest play in the *California Farmer* and the
Phoenix newspaper accounts of our work . . . .

Our work in the Macrosocial Accounting Project has been to test the
strength of the relationship of industrial agricultural development to community underdevelopment in such a way as to maximize the possibility
of disconfirmation of your original findings. By dealing with 83 towns or
100 counties, selected at random, we lose ethnographic detail, but we gain
the power to test the assertion that small farming communities are just as
likely to be poor as large farming communities. What is important in our
work is not the tables of descriptive statistics but the regression equations
in which farm structure characteristics appear as independent variables
used to predict differences in community conditions. As you know, all the
tests we have conducted along these lines, in which a significant relationship appears, either supports, or at least does not disconfirm, the relationship you originally described: i.e., the industrial agricultural development-
community underdevelopment hypothesis.

Some of these tests have provided very dramatic support for the hypothesis. For example, we were able to predict 31 percent of the variation
in the growth in family income *for all families in 100 agricultural counties*
during the 1970s using farm structure variables alone, with slow growth or
negative growth associated with the largest farms. This is highly significant
when considered in the light of all the other factors known to affect family
income. [This was the finding singled out for a special note (p. 226) in the
OTA final report to Congress on their technology study.] Now the question for the critics is, Can they still believe that small farms communities
are just as likely to have slow income growth as large farm communities?
The answer is Yes, of course. But they cannot dismiss our finding on the
ground of case selection. If they want to hold to their position, they *must*
do research, using essentially the same design, in which they introduce new
variables and demonstrate that the farm structure-community conditions
relationship we have discovered is spurious. Any lesser response will reveal
the *criticism* to be politically motivated. We have not yet moved to this
stage in the debate.

Olmstead and others are just waking up to the fact that the Macrosocial Accounting Project studies cannot be classified and criticized as being
"small-farm-community-large-farm-community" comparison.[37] And, of
course, to the extent that they have relied on common sense assertions,

"small farm communities aren't really that different, things are tough all over," etc., the critics have enjoyed 40 years of the luxury of not having to come up with a well-formed alternative hypothesis. Now the ball is in their court.

Anyway, the simple point I am trying to make is that the descriptive MSA findings are not as important as the analytical findings, and it is the latter which should be emphasized in any summary. I suggest that in addition to any descriptive data you want to highlight from tables A2 A-H, we reproduce two or perhaps three of the regression equations from the OTA study and report the existence of a series of similar equations with proper referencing. If this [is] agreeable to you, Ed and I will make the selection, have the tables prepared in publishable form and write a brief summary of what they show.

We hope your Catholic Conference went well and are looking forward to hearing from you.

All our best,

Dean

MacCannell, positioned here as a quantitative social scientist, was lecturing Goldschmidt the anthropologist on the scientific process; in particular, how the regressions insulate the findings from the charges of political bias that were leveled against previous work in the genre. He was also offering strategic advice on how to win a scientific argument, and his recommendation mirrored Taylor's position that "it's facts that have weight."

Goldschmidt's response came ten days later:

August 13, 1987

Professor Dean MacCannell
Department of Biobehavioral Sciences
University of California
Davis, CA 95616

Dear Dean,
I was pleased to get your letter of August 3, indicating that you are inspiring everybody to get going on the materials that I asked for.

I am responding because I want to hasten to add that my comments about the number crunching did not mean that I was opposed to them or did not recognize that they are absolutely essential for the purposes of validating hypotheses. Certainly all of your statistical analyses and the regression curves you speak of should be included in the paper we are preparing. After all, as you know, I had intended doing that very kind of thing for the Upper San Joaquin Valley in 1944 but was stopped from doing it; a lot of other people realized that a statistical analysis of 25 cases would be much more effective than a comparative examination of two.

The conference in Minnesota went very well. I found it extremely interesting to be among a group of unfrocked (not defrocked) priests and unhabituated nuns; seeing them in slacks and jeans respectively came as a shock to me, but it enabled me to find that there are real human beings with real problems among the clergy as well as among the laity. What was particularly interesting was the pressures upon these liberal clergymen and women by the powers that be endeavoring to keep them from speaking out on issues of small farms. There is a very active concern among church people over the farming issues of the day.

I look forward to hearing from you and your co-workers in due course and hope that we can get this thing off our hands.
Warmest personal regards,
Walter Goldschmidt
Professor Emeritus

In the end, the *Science* rebuttal was left incomplete. Outlines and early drafts from its collaborating scholars (Dean MacCannell, Jerry White, Isao Fujimoto, Trudy Wischemann, Joan Randall, and Walter Goldschmidt) were retained by Goldschmidt in his files. Differences in style and approach were too great for the two scholars to overcome and successfully collaborate.

More important, the decades of research and final correspondence between Goldschmidt and MacCannell establish and present the case—an ongoing challenge and demand—for the academic community to definitively acknowledge their findings, continue further studies using modern technologies like GIS, and begin to actually impact and remediate problems. At the least, the onus to refute their work is now on those who propose counterarguments to actually demonstrate their positions through scientific research.

The narrative history of political pressure on both scholar's experience in California adds weight to the argument that industrial agriculture is detrimental to society and democracy. In MacCannell's case, nowhere was this more evident than on the westside of the valley, an area so exemplary of inequality, injustice, racism and oppression.

Westlands Water District

The lesson that economic monopoly and consolidated ownership of natural resources had drastic negative effects on the quality of life and governance of rural communities was nowhere more apparent than within the Westlands Water District.

MacCannell's personal experiences with attempted bribery, misinformation campaigns targeting his research, moles planted within his research team, and outright intimidation, threats and coercion are testament to the caustic behavior of large landowners and major industrial interests controlling the San Joaquin Valley.

In the early 80s, Congress decided to amend the acreage limitation law toward the receipt of federally subsidized irrigation water. They were under pressure from all sides—small farm and big ag interests. The law at the time was 160 acres maximum for a farm receiving federally subsidized irrigation water.

Small farm advocates had been lobbying to enforce the law, and the big guys wanted it to be changed so they would not be in violation of it. Their position was then, and continues to be, that they were never in violation of the law because the federal government delivered water to them therefore making them innocent of any wrongdoing since the very government whose law it was, was giving them water. Apparently, there is a legal basis for that claim. Still, they were uncomfortable with laws that were on the books that restricted it to 160 acres.[38]

There was no farm in the Westlands Water District that was compliant, and the Westlands Water District was the greatest recipient of federal largesse in terms of water subsidy with the building of the Central Valley Project canals. The legislation eventually went through. The big, westside farmers who early in the process thought there was a good chance of prevailing with their plan of removing all acreage constraints on farms getting subsidized water, ended up with legislation that basically lifted the 320, or the 160/320 rule, to 960. 960 acres—leaving them still non-compliant.

The Office of Technology Assessment (OTA), a research organ of the US Congress, was charged with the responsibility of preparing an Environmental Impact Statement (EIS) on the effects of changing the limitation law. Its task was to estimate probable impacts of varying scenarios of changing the law. One scenario would be enforcing the existing law. The other scenario would be the removal of all restrictions. And the third scenario would be to set a higher limit, somewhere above 320 acres. OTA outsourced its research to Harbridge House Incorporated, a global consulting firm that started out in Boston by faculty from Harvard. The Harbridge people were told by OTA, even though they outsourced the work, to include certain OTA-named scientists on the research team. I was one of the OTA-named people.

Harbridge House did in fact hire me to work with them on preparing this EIS. I was in charge of the social component of the EIS. We decided that we would focus our energies on the Westlands Water District as a test case. It would not be the only area affected by the law; however, it would be the area most likely to be affected by changes in the law. The Westlands Water District was thought to be similar enough to other areas where large-scale agriculture was occurring that it would give us the conditions in other areas in the American West covered by the limitation law. There were people who were looking at every aspect of it: things like environmental impacts, soil compaction, water drawdowns, all of the technical aspects.

My group was responsible for the social issues component of the report. What would be the social impacts of the three scenarios? It was in that context where the indications appeared again that very large farms, as Goldschmidt had shown earlier, do have a range of negative impacts on local communities and populations. We used the best available methodologies to look closely on the Westlands, and eventually at the whole Sunbelt, especially on California, Arizona, Florida, and Texas. This work went on for a couple of years. Eventually, two published studies came out. The EIS was eventually published by Geisler and Popper. The Lou Swanson volume is various work that was done for OTA but not connected to the acreage limitation series of studies.

When I submitted it to Harbridge House and the Office of Technology assessment, I was worried that some of the things that I was saying would be anathema to Coors. He was on the board of Harbridge House, or at least had some cozy relationship with them. I was concerned that by the time my raw reports got through the vetting process, the impact of the findings would be blunted in the editing. I will confess to it—I don't think it was illegal, but it was probably unethical—I did send the draft to the National Farmers Union. They were concerned about these same issues. Wendell Berry was on their board, and I admired some of the activists they had working for them.

The National Farmers Union immediately reproduced the report and sent it to all of the members of Congress. I did not know they were going to do that but I did not ask them to retain confidentiality, so technically I did not care. By that time, I guess I knew enough about the politics of this stuff that I wasn't under any illusions; if it was useful to somebody that had it in their hands, they would make maximum use of it. I didn't know that they would go that far and give it to everybody in Congress. It was apparently read with interest.

The people at Harbridge House got royally pissed. I was called down to Washington D.C., but somebody in the Office of Technology Assessment got back to Harbridge House and told them that under no circumstances could they fire me. In the end, versions were published in the Congressional record. Harbridge House and OTA did not suppress anything that I did, but they cut it up in these bite size chunks and distributed it through the massive report in such a way that you were never able to get the focus of it back. It had no singular impact.

It was politically effective to send the EIS draft to Congress. By the time the finished product finally arrived, the ball was already rolling. Soon after, I got into trouble with John Harris and the Westside Farmers Association. The valley farmers found out when Mrs. Harris visited her Congressmen at the time. She was a lobbyist for the Westside Farmers Association. He gave her a copy of my report and asked her what she thought. She read it and wept, literally wept. Not from the pathos of my report, but from the new difficulty it had introduced into her role as lobbyist. She told me, "I used to enjoy going to Washington D.C. I'd go up to Washington once a month and used to enjoy my trips. I really liked dropping in on my Congressmen and on my Senators. We always enjoyed our conversations together. But now when I go to the door of their office, they hand me *this*." She burst into tears in front of me. "It's not fun anymore." Basically "this" was more or less what got published in the Geisler and Popper volume. It was a well-documented analysis of levels of poverty and income inequalities of the four or five towns that are inside the Westlands Water District—places like Huron, Mendota, Five Points, Tranquility.

When the EIS came out, the Westside Farmers Association made a phone tree. They were calling the Chancellor's office, the Dean's office, my department, and our house, every hour, all day and into the evening to complain about what I had done. At my house, it was just vituperative and ended in the evening; to the Chancellor it was "you have to get rid of him." The Chancellor's office had to set up a sub-department with two or three secretaries who answered the "MacCannell complaints" trying to do it in a way that would not violate me, but also in a way that would calm down their biggest research donors. It was headed by a professor of Ag Econ who directed their activities. John Harris is on record saying that he would withdraw a million dollars in funding to the University—or that he would actually *give* a million dollars of funding—if they could successfully get rid of me.

I was chair of my department at the time. When they called and asked to speak to the chair, they would get me. So my conversations were somewhat stymied, because they were calling prepared to complain to my chair about what a rotten person I was and how I really shouldn't be allowed to teach impressionable young kids.

I would say, "I will take that under advisement, but you are speaking to Dean MacCannell."

"Oh!" a deep voice on other side of phone would reply.

One that sticks in my mind was a guy who was yelling at me: "This study is completely biased, you can't have possibly interviewed everybody down here."

I said, "Well, no, we didn't. Actually, it is a sample."

"Well, you didn't sample anybody like me—I'm rich!"

Right in the middle of this, John Harris, speaking for the Westside Farmers Association, called the Chancellor and asked him to send me down there to answer their questions about what I had done in the EIS. The Chancellor, who was still Jim Meyer, had asked me to keep him informed of every aspect of this thing. Shortly afterward, I went to the Chancellor.

"Harris has offered to send a plane, pick me up, and fly me down," I said. "I really don't want to do this. If anything happens in this meeting, where I do decide that I have to soften what I've written—perhaps they show me something I needed to know that I didn't know before—it may look like my taking an airplane ride with them had influenced me. I want to keep my options open."

The Chancellor said, "Under no circumstances get into that plane. They would think nothing of wasting a plane and a pilot on you." We drove down.

The stance of Charles Hess, the Ag Dean, was completely supportive of me at this time. They had reviewed the work. What could they say? Hess sent Bill Weir, an Associate Dean, with me, literally as a bodyguard. Nearing retirement, Bill was older, respected, and staunch.

But the Chancellor was clear. He told me, "Look, I *don't* like what you are doing! I really wish you would stop what you are doing! You are costing us plenty of money. My great preference would be for you to cease and desist. But I can't order you to do that. There is no way. I am aware of that." He was sort of like, "Please?"

So there was a lot of drama surrounding my visit to the valley. Everyone was worried: "Should I even go at all? Won't they assassinate me?" When we got down there it was a big public affair, a roast with speakers like Mrs. Harris taking turns. The only purpose of the meeting was to insult me. That was the only purpose of it! First of all, for him to try to buy me off. Second of all to intimidate me. And finally to just yell at me. They were venting.

Before the lunch and the big public meeting, I met with Harris privately. I was led into his study; it was separate from the main house. In fact, it was in a building that was probably 200 or 300 yards from the house, and it was a *house*. The study was a house! He had my report sitting in front of him. He opened it up and the first thing he said was, "This is lovely . . . . We are still pretty far apart on these numbers."

He's referring to the data on poverty and other statistics in the report. This opening gambit is like we're doing a real estate deal, and I have made him an offer or something—"we are still pretty far apart on the numbers." I explained to him that there was nothing I could do about that because they are mostly from public record like the census.

His next gambit was, "Well, what will it take to get you to *change* these numbers?"

"It can't be done because it is public record. Even if I wanted to, and I have no desire to, any undergraduate in Ag Econ would be able to take a quick pass through the data and say, 'Something is fishy here.'"

So then he said, "What would it take from us for you to *recant* your report?"

I said, "I don't do stuff like that. It isn't my style. You're talking to the wrong guy." They would clearly do anything. Later, they sent letters to the *Fresno Bee* signed by me that made me sound like a total crazy man. The paper called me up to verify and reads me these letters and saying, "Did you write this letter?"

"Well, no!"

We were then taken to a foreman's house for lunch (I was judged to be too low class to be a guest in one of their homes). They sat at least 75 people down to lunch in the dining room, and no one was bumping asses with anybody in the foreman's house! This is where they tried to poison me. Everyone was being seated when a woman came up with a tray and a cocktail on it.

She said, "This one is *just* for you." There was something about the way she said it that made me wonder. I stuck my tongue in it, just the tip of my tongue, and my entire tongue went to sleep. I set that one aside, so I was able to jump over that particular little hedge.

Afterward, he put me in a car with a couple of thugs. They really had to struggle to engineer a separation because Bill Weir was very protective. (I was told I was never to be separated from Bill.) They drove me out into the country. I really thought this is it, but all they did was act tough. Talk tough. They weren't physical. They were just saying things like, "How long do you think you can get by with pulling crap like this with us!" Verbally intimidating stuff like that, which has never bothered me just as long as that is as far as it goes.

Then they drove me back to the lunch where everyone stood up to testify against me, including Mrs. Harris. They were all saying what a horrible person I was. Bill then told them they just had to accept it. He said, "Look guys, you are going to have to get used to this. We have been doing research for the last century that you have benefited from enormously in terms of new varieties, new practices, new machines. Now, for the first time, we are starting to do 'human research' into the human factors involved, which as far as we are concerned is just part of our mission. You were willing to receive the results of our previous research—now we do this as well. Live with it!"

I have zero complaints. They were tough guys. Even though they are in the back pockets of these big farmers and all of the R&D is for them, I discovered that there was secret liberal in some of those production ag people. Many of them had grown up on small family farms. They were doing research that was building these mega-farms and a lot of them did have a guilty conscience about it. They were perfectly happy that someone else was in front of the bayonet, but they weren't yelling at me all the time, as one may have expected.

On a different occasion, but similar context, I was asked to attend a meeting with Fazio, farmers, researchers from the University, entrepreneurs, and others. They were asking what we could do to stimulate the agricultural sector's economy. Everyone was talking about how times were tough. This was in the early eighties. Everything was bad at the same time—regulations, acreage limitation law, things like that. Fazio is taking it all in, listening to everybody.[39]

Then, the conversation drifted. They were talking about how difficult, even impossible, it was these days to make a new millionaire.

"It used to be easy. We just pick out one of the brightest young guys from high school or junior college, we give him a $10,000 loan and let him start sharecropping out here on some acreage. In three of four years, he would be a millionaire. We just can't do that anymore. It's just out of the question!"

Then this old Extension agent said [gruff voice], "I'm sorry. I disagree. I think it is still possible to make 'em millionaires. It's not by any means impossible. I just won't be a party to this saying it can't be done. It just takes a whole hell of a lot more poor people to make one millionaire today than it used to." That was said in the positive. They just assumed I would be in complete agreement.

Around this time, I also had a mole in my shop who was being paid by the westside farmers to produce findings that countered mine, which he was doing. He had been a professor at Oregon and his wife had been hired by Extension here. He was a Cornellian. Out of pity, I said, "Well, he has a Ph.D. in Rural Sociology from Cornell. He's got skills." Shortly after I hired him, he got bought off by these guys.

Then things started to happen. One time, we were sitting at dinner and somebody knocks on the door. He was well dressed, probably a lawyer. "I'm the man from across the park and I am a part of the Save the Bay Coalition. We have this report from your research organization at Davis. I just can't believe that you wrote this?" On the SARE [Sustainable Agriculture Research and Education] letterhead there is: "Dean MacCannell, SARE." And it's a total concoction. A complete fabrication. It had been circulated to this attorney for Save the Bay probably because it was water related. It recanted all of my findings.

I went to Orville and I said, "Hey, this guy has been taking money, writing reports on our letterhead with my name on them, and sending them to the westside farmers. I've got to get rid of him." It was perfectly in my purview to simply fire the guy since I was the head of the Macrosocial Accounting Project. He was my employee and wasn't protected in any way.

But Orville said, "Isao and I both have to be there when you tell him what you are going to tell him." Orville was so cool about it. At the time, I thought, "What are they going to say—that I can't fire him?" I invited all three of them. I never quite understood that. Perhaps it was to shame him. His name was Doug Gwynn.

Last I heard he was working for the westside farmers trying to do consulting work. They let Gwynn's stuff into the record, and it was garbage. The science was bad. Later, I was brought in to refute it, and since he had been using my letterhead, to let them know that it wasn't done under my auspices.

Later, after he was fired from UC Davis, Gwynn transitioned fully into positions where he worked for agribusiness interests by producing research and testifying in court proceedings. Goldschmidt's files included transcriptions of official testimony before the California State Water Board where a contest of dueling scholars cast MacCannell against Doug Gwynn and Refugio Rochin.

Over the years, I visited with the MacCannell's often to clarify and fill in the narrative of their valley work. Juliet was with Dean at every one of our meetings, and clearly she had also been directly involved in the dramas around his research. During one of these visits, I recorded our conversations and later transcribed them into research notes.

Remembering, Juliet said, ". . . and then we got involved with all of the Congress meetings studies. They did allow him to testify once. It took years and years, because the lawyers for the Westlands farmers would never let him come up to just say anything at one of these Congressional or State . . . What do they call those? They aren't inquests. They were like hearings."

She posed the question more to Dean than to me, but he did not hear her from the other room. She continued, "Well, they wouldn't do it. This story was amazing. Every time, people were working against him. Very pernicious interests. They would say, 'Okay, we want you to be appearing in Fresno,' and he would go down. Then the lawyer on the other side would say, 'We are barring your testimony.' Finally, they let him testify in Sacramento. I don't remember what year. It was a huge auditorium in the State offices in Sacramento where, for the first time, I saw reporters use laptops. They were kind of tall and had these reddish screens. It was a long time ago and late in the game."

As Dean returned to the room, Juliet asked him, "When did you finally get to testify in the hearings in Sacramento?" Dean was slow to respond, so Juliet continued her train of thought. "Anyway, the moment he began to speak you could have heard a pin drop in the entire auditorium. Everyone was poised . . . ."

Later, I asked Dean about this testimony. He said, "They fought for an hour over having me speak. They raised objections. It was one challenge after another. Everyone was waiting. All it did was make it all the more dramatic."

"I didn't recognize it at the time, but it was structured as dueling reports—mine and one from Gwynn, long after he was severed from me. He had done a restudy of his own in which he found no relationship between farm size and capitalization and social conditions. Their lawyers somehow did not have enough social science background, and our lawyers were actually letting him get by with it up to this moment—arguing from non-correlation! In other words, he had no correlation, so he was claiming no relationship. He had a whole raft of non-correlations.

"So, as part of my testimony, I had to do Research Methods 101: 'Do not argue from non-correlation. There is a host of reasons why a correlation doesn't come out, such as your measurement is wrong. We are instructed in graduate school that this is not publishable, and you cannot base any argument pro or con on it. You can only base argument on statistically significant relationships. And there is one statistically significant relationship in the Gwynn report—and it is in the Goldschmidt direction!' The lawyers for his side spun to him, and I heard a chorus of, "Is that true?!" Gwynn could only sit there.

* * *

Transcripts from the California State Water Control Board's "Bay/Delta Hearing," on December 14, 1987 includes the examination of

Figure 4.3. Dean and Juliet MacCannell. Courtesy of Dean MacCannell.

MacCannell by Timothy Ernst of the law firm of Pettit & Martin representing the Bay Institute, opposing attorneys representing Central Valley agribusiness interests, and the board members themselves.

At this late date for MacCannell's valley research, under "direct examination" and with the retest studies complete, he brings forward what can be considered his most distilled and potent finding. One that encapsulated more than a decade of research, his many data points, analysis of a still expanding problem, and a summation of their meaning.

Responding to a question by Ernst about his findings, he answers,

> in the research we did before and after the building of the Central Valley Project [San Luis Unit], that is, before 1968 and after 1978 study, taking into account the decade of water delivery in the Westlands Water District, we found a 300 percent increase in sales from agricultural production and a 10 percent decrease in real wages of agricultural workers measured in constant dollars.

In cross examination, this finding was questioned, and MacCannell responds,

> The problem is that the development of a particular type of agriculture may pit the interests of agribusiness against the interests of the people in the communities.
>
> There is no denying that there was a 300 percent increase in agricultural production and sales in the crops grown in the Westlands Water District in the decade of '68 to '78. The issue for me, as a rural sociologist, is does any of that tremendous profit and benefit ever get translated into benefits at the local community level?
>
> We take a great deal of trouble to try to measure that, and the best measure that we can come up with suggested, that, no it did not. And in the case of the wages to farmworkers' families, there was an actual decline, inexplicable, but nevertheless there, and a decline in the real wages of farmworkers during the same period.

University-based, publicly funded inquiry into the Central Valley Project and reclamation law were drawing to a close. Agribusiness interests had successfully maneuvered to get the water without following the law. Even though government funded research studies (including Goldschmidt's BAE research and MacCannell's OTA studies) together with unanimous Supreme Court decisions substantiated and supported declarations of the negative effects of sending water to industrial scale growers, the law remained unenforced and was never implemented.

A lesson bridges the history of non-enforcement of the legislation from Taylor and Goldschmidt to MacCannell and later scholars: if you don't control the sheriff, or are unwilling to call in the National Guard, the law will be made moot if the interests opposed to it are powerful enough to disregard it. Even worse, California water districts, like the Westlands Water District, were undemocratically structured, with voting based on property ownership rather than the traditional standard of one person, one vote.[40] Foundational democratic principles were actively being undermined in the state by private interests. Over time, the distinct outline of a neo-feudal undemocratic infrastructure, institutionally constructed, emerged in the San Joaquin Valley.

In response, the work of scholar's shifted toward direct engagement and community organizing linked with academic inquiry and experiential education. To make change, the focus shifted into the valley as research capacity and student activists became involved in specific campaigns with local communities.

5

Take a Bath among the People

DON VILLAREJO

Don Villarejo occupied spaces outside of the university.

The offices of the California Institute for Rural Studies (CIRS) were literally located a few blocks from the UC Davis campus: a prominent perch from which to access resources as well as agitate, given the university's past omissions of farmworker interests and sociological research.

In effect, CIRS was formed as an applied rural sociology department. Yet, even more potent, the nonprofit research organization felt no reservations about feigning neutrality in its values nor apprehension in expressing its principles. If anything, it was less encumbered by political constraint as the organization allied with social justice and worker movements at a moment when they were mobilizing for historic change.

While in graduate school at UC Davis in 2001, I visited the CIRS offices on G Street. Waiting in the common room, I looked over their displayed publications, many written or co-authored by Villarejo. My affinity with the organization was obvious from the start.

A few years later, I emailed Don to schedule a time to talk. Still fleshing out the dissertation's narrative thread, I intuitively followed lines of inquiry by accessing how much risk particular scholars had taken and how much controversy they opened up.

We met in Davis, downtown at Peet's Coffee on E Street in 2006. The café was busy, filled with students and the ferment of ideas. Don was systematic and practically helpful, laying out his history for me in a matter-of-fact line.

As I learned over the coming years, Don easily structured complexities.

Chicago, Physics, and the New Left

While I always had a range of interests, including politics, economics, sociology, and science, at a relatively young age I learned that I had talent in mathematics. Throughout my education, mathematics was always the strongest subject in school.

In 1955, I graduated from Hyde Park High School in the Southside of Chicago. At the time, there was a great interest in the nation's scientific workforce. I decided I could make a living using my skills in mathematics. The question was, how should I do that? I thought about physics.

Physics was much more difficult than I had ever expected, but I liked the challenge. The first day of physics class at the University of Chicago they said, "Look to the left of you, look to your right. The purpose of this class is that only one of the three of you will be here in the end." How's that for encouragement!

Eventually I got a Ph.D. at Chicago in experimental physics. While a graduate student, I was sole author or co-author of nine papers published in peer-reviewed scientific journals, six in experimental physics, and three in theoretical physics. My career path seemed clear.

As it happened during that period, there were other things happening in the world that were of interest to me. I became active politically at the University of Chicago as an undergraduate student in '56. There were qualities I had, as a personality and as a scholar, that were attractive to this rag-tag bunch of social science and humanities majors. Hot issues were things like Strontium 90 and nuclear radiation fallout from testing of nuclear weapons. People who didn't have a clue about that found it wonderful that I could write coherently and explain it in lay terms.

Along the way, some colleagues and I created a magazine called *New University Thought*. It was one of the first of what became known as the New Left. The London *Times* reviewed our first issue in 1960 and cast it as a "breath of fresh air from the States" in terms of the political thinking of the country. Young scholars, mostly at the University of Chicago but also from other places, brought it together as a combination of scholarship, political awareness, and action. Out of this political work, we hooked up with young folks at the historically black colleges and universities of the south. Some of the first leaders of the lunch counter sit-in movement came through Chicago, into Madison, and eventually as far as Berkeley to spread the word on a tour that we helped to organize. Before the major media had made much of it, we were raising money, awareness, and recruiting students to go south. The sit-ins were started by people we had previously worked with politically at the National Student Association annual convention in Ann Arbor, Michigan, during 1958.

The first thing I wrote in New University Thought was about Cuba. As it happened, we started the magazine just when the Castro revolution succeeded. I've always had an interest in structures of power and relationships in society. I felt that Americans knew little about Cuban life and the role of American imperialism in the sugar and nickel mining industries. So I wrote about that in an article called, "American Investment in Cuba." It's in the inaugural issue of New University Thought. The next big piece that I wrote was "Stock ownership and the control of corporations," published in the Autumn 1961 issue of our magazine. The paper suggested that a sizeable share of the 250 largest U.S. industrial corporations were demonstrably controlled by wealthy families whose inherited wealth was their base of power. Of lasting importance, that paper developed my understanding that primary documents were essential to understanding economic and social structures. I used that knowledge over and over again in my future political work.

That period was so fruitful in terms of political education and action. We rented a house as New University Thought on the southside of Chicago near the University of Chicago campus. The acronym of course for New University Thought was "NUT," so it became known as the "Nuthouse." In the Nuthouse, there were weekly meetings. Meetings ranged from people organizing the annual Easter Peace march in Chicago to people from northern parts of the world—Minnesota, Wisconsin, the Dakotas—coming through, having a place to stay on their way south. It was all a natural part of what I saw as life.

I was also productive in physics at that time. I published about six articles in a two-year period in physics journals. I found physics to be engaging as a problem-solving exercise, but it was compartmentalized. It was separate from this other life. There were people who were even unaware of the other life. My thesis advisor, after becoming aware of it, was shocked and distressed.

During this period from 1958 to 1968, I got an opportunity to become more engaged in political work. There were times that I just focused on physics, when I said, "I can't come to meetings; this is what I've got to do."

Then there were times when somebody was in town for a day, such as leaders of SNCC [Student Non-Violent Coordinating Committee]. You don't pass that up. I also met people who were later connected with the Weather Underground, but never worked with them. They had a fantasy world that had nothing to do with the world of real working people. As far as I was concerned, you start in the understanding that real working people have a lot more at stake if they stand up politically than people who come from affluent, comfortable backgrounds.

Later, while doing anti-war organizing at UCLA, there was another crazy faction saying, "It's time to pick up the gun." I said, "I am supporting an end to the war because I want the National Liberation Front to win. I want them to persist and throw out western imperialism. They fought the French; they are fighting the Americans. That's what it's about. They have fifteen divisions. They've got tanks. They've got howitzers. What have you guys got?"

We're not holding ourselves out to carry guns. What we're really trying to do is to educate folks who have a lot more at stake and help them to understand how they can take effective action. That's the only way to get change in the long run.

Activist Scholar

I finished my Ph.D. in '68 and went to UCLA. I had a faculty position as Assistant Professor of Physics. My wife told me that she had envisioned me wearing a tweed jacket with leather patches, holding a pipe, and saying nice things. She had a Ph.D. in Biochemistry from Chicago, but did not have a regular faculty position. She was able to initially obtain a half-time research associate appointment while having primary responsibility for our young family and household.

My wife, Merna, is precocious and, in many ways, smarter in science than I am. She is a very good scientist, but it was difficult for women in science at that time, particularly since we had young kids. Eventually she was hired through a connection at the UCLA med school. It was an opening for her to keep her biochemistry research and publication record active. It paid off later when the physics department at UCLA found me growing my hair long, doing all kinds of weird things that they didn't think were appropriate for a physicist.

The physics department faculty were unhappy with me. They had wanted this high-level scientist. They got something they didn't expect: a person who had a wide range of interests, who was unconventional but initially appeared to be conventional. When I went out to interview at UCLA, I gave a seminar. I had spoken at several physics meetings. They had seen my publication record, and I had good recommendations. Later, while there as a professor, I was recognized as an outstanding physics teacher. On the other hand, I did not aggressively pursue grants, as I was expected to. I did not publish, as I was expected to. I devoted my energy to teaching.

At that time, there was an unusual faculty committee called the Committee for Educational Development (CED) that I agreed to serve on. It was the only one on the whole nine campuses of the University of California that had the power to grant credit and hire faculty for experimental classes without any additional faculty review. We had 11 FTE to play with. This was won as a result of student demonstrations and combat on the campus, demanding other kinds of alternatives to mammoth classrooms filled with automatons. The students called for more socially relevant classes.

When I agreed to serve on the CED committee it was an opportunity to do all kinds of interesting things. Together with colleagues, I created a whole program for community work. Students volunteered to work at a free clinic, an afterschool program, a trade union, or for the ACLU. It was a twelve-unit, three quarter long sequence. As the faculty sponsor, in my view, I had responsibility for being an equal participant in the activities, except for the field placement. I didn't have time to do that since this work was in addition to my regular teaching load. Sixty students were doing this. We had weekly meetings with the students placed at the different locations. I was responsible for health and science with students working in places like free clinics. They would do twenty hours a week of volunteer work. Readings were collectively agreed on. Everyone had to keep a journal. We had men's and women's groups for consciousness raising. The physics department faculty had thought that I had lost my mind. It was great fun and important for me to explore ways of learning and teaching that were not possible within the physics department.

After the Cambodian invasion in 1970, the student's response shut down the whole campus. I had become a well-known speaker against the war. I had short hair and was a traditional physics teacher in some respects, but students also turned to me for advice on what to do. I said, "There are a lot of things you need to do. You need to organize yourselves. I can help with that, but you have to do it." They decided they needed a communications center to communicate with campuses all over the United States. The question was where they could get access to a phone. I said, "My office is a great place—go for it, guys." So, my office became the communications center. Those characters even got the inside line to the White House somehow. They were unbelievable.

A real, ground-level political action and political education program was happening. The physics department was very concerned about all of it. They questioned, "What are you doing?"

I said, "The students are not throwing rocks. We have been doing something they believe in. It's totally nonviolent. They're learning something. The community is learning something. I have a bunch of people sitting on a phone all day. What the hell do you want?"

In the midst of that, the television people wanted interviews. I got selected to speak at a convocation called by the UCLA Chancellor at Pauley Pavilion where the UCLA basketball team plays. The entire university, 20,000 people, were given official time off by the university from their regular employment to attend the event. The media selected me to be a spokesperson along with student leaders and the faculty spokesperson. I gave a one-minute rap that made national television and brought down the house. Everybody was jumping up and down applauding. The theme of my message was that the whole nation should to go on strike to stop this war.

My wife was so upset that she fell on the stairs at Pauley Pavilion. She cut her leg bad enough to require some medical attention. She goes back to her office to fill out a worker's compensation form and listed "the invasion of Cambodia" as the cause of the accident. She was also upset because her department chair had spent twenty minutes at the doorway of her small office, not even coming in her room, yelling at her about her husband's behavior. I was seen as a lightning rod by faculty who were supportive of the war, who were pro-military, who were conservative Republicans. They saw what I was doing as damaging to not only the nation, but also UCLA. It was one of the most trying times of our marriage. I didn't back off, but we also reached certain understandings about what I would do and would not do.

After six years, the physics department met with me. They said, "This is not working. This is not a good fit. You are a talented person, but it's time you considered working somewhere else." They gave me a terminal contract, which was the right decision, given their value system and what they were trying to accomplish. I did not fit, given my interests and what I had become. It was a relief for me. I felt an exhilaration, saying, "Physics is over. What am I going to do next?" It occurred to me that I ought to find a way to (A), support myself and my family, and (B), find out how I could do that in a different way in a different context.

Then a miracle happened when my wife was offered a position in Biochemistry and Biophysics here at Davis. It saved our family financially. At the end of that one-year terminal contract, what did I have? I had nothing—no job. I wasn't stressed because I had been self-supporting since nineteen. I had worked in factories to help put myself through school. I knew I could get work, but I didn't know what. So she and I reached an understanding that she would become the primary breadwinner.

We both wanted to work in the same community. I took primary responsibility for the household and the kids. She developed her career full bore, to have an opportunity to grow not only as a scientist but as a professional in the world. We did that, and moved to Davis in August of '75.

Shortly after we moved to Davis, I met Isao Fujimoto, in early '76. He is one of our local heroes in terms of his commitment, his dedication, his teaching. There was a birthday celebration for him. I had not previously met him, nor had I known of his work. But some of the activists that I was involved with at that time said, "There is going to be a birthday party for Isao. You really have to be there." I couldn't get there at the start of the party because I was responsible for the kids. When I walked into his house on Linden Lane, there were several dozen young people sitting, completely covering the floor. I was at least twice as old as they were.

Isao was sitting in a chair. Each person spoke. When they were done, somebody else stood up and spoke. Each of them talked about what they were now doing in the world with their lives. Somebody had started a food coop someplace. Somebody else had started a community cannery. This was their birthday presents to Isao. These were his students. It was the most moving experience to understanding Isao's importance and influence here— that as a teacher he had inspired and taught all of these young people, and they had come back. It was beautiful. That is Isao.

Organizing Farmworkers, Creating Institutions

Thanks to Merna's appointment, I was able to get half-time lectureship at the physics department at Davis. Then I went to work on some political campaigns up here. Most notably, I was recruited by Tom Hayden to volunteer to work on his 1976 primary campaign to replace then Senator John Tunney as the Democratic Party nominee for U.S. Senator from California that led to becoming a volunteer with the United Farm Workers union for their Prop. 14 campaign in the November 1976 general election.

In my view, [the UFW] had an even greater need for a research department, with people who could understand agricultural trends, who were knowledgeable about agricultural economics. People who could help to develop the skills needed when you sat at the table and bargain with a business. The UFW was bargaining with businesses that had thousands of employees and hundreds of millions of dollars at stake. They have economic decisions they make. If you aren't at that same level, how the hell are you going to argue in favor of something? There was a disagreement around this in the Fall of '76. César didn't see the need to have a research department. When this possibility ended, I continued to maintain that it was something that was clearly needed, though I was not sure how to go about filling that need.

During the Prop. 14 campaign, which was initiated when the funds ran out to implement the brand new 1975 California Agricultural Labor Relations Act, the first law ever designed to protect the right of agricultural workers to engage in collective concerted action, I became a public spokesperson for the campaign in the Sacramento Valley region. After I participated in a live radio interview, a woman named Katherine Bertolucci called our home, and said she wanted to volunteer in the campaign. She joined our happy crew that very day.

The need for a labor-oriented research organization—even if the UFW rebuffed the invitation—and the history of the University of California's enabling of agribusiness set the stage for the creation of the California Institute for Rural Studies.

The California Institute for Rural Studies was started in 1977 by Paul Barnett, Katherine Bertolucci, and myself. Paul had been active in the UFW previously, working in their legal department. And Katherine had a Master's in Library

Figure 5.1. California Institute for Rural Studies (CIRS) and California Agrarian Action Project (CAAP) staff and volunteers, 1984. Courtesy of Don Villarejo.

Science from the University of Chicago. She knew how to organize information. Since the union did not want a research department, but was interested in that work, we agreed to explore starting a progressive research organization that focused on agriculture, farm labor, water policy, reclamation law, and rural issues in California. As part of that exploration, we traveled around the state and met with key people regarding the following questions:

- Was there a need for such an organization?
- Would it compete with any existing organization?
- What would be the key topics that the organization would focus on?

We spent six months answering those questions. We didn't want to go out and start a serious organization and compete for funds if there were other groups who were doing the same work. Then there's no point. We met with knowledgeable people around California to see if there was a real need and purpose for a research organization.

The first place we go: Paul Taylor. We spent two days meeting with Paul Taylor in 1977. It was fabulous. Can you imagine what it was like to ask Paul Taylor everything you ever wanted to know? It was very special. The time with him was limited to maybe three or four hours a day. He was ill. He was walking with kind of a shuffle, but he was prompt. Right on time. Just full of life despite the physical limitations.

He told us, "You ought to work on the reclamation issue. Did you know what they did in the Sacramento Valley? They used as the basis for the annual yield the highest value ever measured in the flow of the Sacramento River. Then they used that as the base for the amount of water that should be allocated. I have an article on it!" His office was a total catastrophe. There were piles everywhere. He said, "Now I'm going to find that article." And by God, he got up, went to some pile and pulled it out. "Here's this article. I want you to read this." He was a great mind.

Taylor was generous in sharing documents with us. He referred us to published papers and other materials with a focus on the acreage limitation law and what he considered to be the systematic violation of the intent of the 1902 Reclamation Act. We took that to heart and made it a principal focus of our initial year's work. He gave clear instructions on where to find papers and field notes in the Bancroft library. We went to the Bancroft and spent several more days in his uncatalogued cartons. It was a fabulous treasure hunt, like kids in a candy store going through and finding all of these materials.

We discovered from our conversations with Paul Taylor and others that there was a great and real need for a research organization focused on agriculture and farm labor. The University of California was not adequately addressing these issues. And there was no other institution that was adequately addressing them. Labor unions have their own purpose and were not likely to be interested in doing the work that we thought would be interesting, as I learned with the UFW.

George Ballis was another person we visited. Since we were trying to create an organization to do research on farm labor, rural poverty, agriculture, land use, reclamation policy, he was knowledgeable and experienced in these broader topics. Reclamation policy, however, was the only thing he was working on at that time. It was his thing.

George had an office in downtown Fresno and was living on the western edge of the city. He was kind enough to put us up. We had no money. We slept wherever we could find a place to sleep. I remember him saying, "OK, you guys can sleep out there." There was this old bus that he used for his tours of the valley. We had our sleeping bags. I slept on the roof of the bus in George's backyard.

As an unexpected coincidence, the National Land for People (NLP) lawsuit against the Department of the Interior was won that same year, in 1977. It led to the promulgation, for the first time, of regulations to implement the acreage limit provisions of reclamation law. The lawsuit was *NLP v. Andrus*, who was then Secretary of the Interior in 1977. The federal court ruled in favor of National Land for People. It said that Interior had failed to promulgate regulations to enforce the acreage limitation provision of federal reclamation law and that the absent regulations led to demonstrable harm. The demonstrable harm were the folks who were individuals named as plaintiffs in the lawsuit. These were farmers unable to get access to land in the Westlands Water District, or who otherwise demonstrated harm caused by the production and competition from the illegally subsidized corporate farms of this district.

NLP had standing in court because George had recruited people who had some evidence of demonstrable harm caused by Westlands. The charge was a simple one: the government and landowners never complied with the law. The reason they hadn't complied with the law was that Interior had never made regulations and therefore had never enforced the requirements of the law. It was a brilliant lawsuit. It won in 1977. The federal court ruled in favor. We were all celebrating, but were eventually outwitted by an alliance of the growers and environmentalists around the 1982 Reclamation Reform Act. We made reclamation policy and the 1977 court decision our initial focus. Since NLP's federal court case was to promulgate regulations for the implementation of the 1902 Act and the 160-acre limit, those regulations were to be promulgated.

Later, I also worked on the consequence of the widespread adoption of the second-generation tomato harvesters. The adoption of the new technology led to a major change in the processing tomato industry's labor demand. Crews of 16 to 20 workers were replaced by crews of three to five workers. People who had migrated to the region once again from as far as Texas, expecting to find work as they had in the past got stranded in '75 and '76. I became aware of this through the work in Woodland and the union. In order to help set up a response, I began to work collaboratively with the people who had a long history of collaboration with tomato workers in the region. Part of the response was to set up a Farmworker's Service Center in Woodland that was run by laid-off workers. We mostly raised funds for it in Davis. We raised food. We raised clothing. Thanksgiving, door-to-door—can you give? We raised one ton of food in one day that way. You do all of that stuff and you build relationships.

The 1974 tomato strike (the largest single labor action in the history of Sacramento Valley agriculture) was a recent memory when I began to organize, primarily in Woodland rather than Davis. Early on, I met leaders of the Mexican-American community in Woodland. Then, in the late summer of 1976, the UFW launched its campaign for Proposition 14, to put the recently enacted California Agricultural Labor Relations Act into the California Constitution. If approved by voters in the November 1976 General Election, this would make the ALRA politically invulnerable to changes by actions of the California Legislature. The initiative was deemed necessary because the initial funding for the Agricultural Labor Relations Board (ALRB) had been insufficient for its operations, even for a half a year. When funding ran out and the Legislature refused to approve additional money, the ALRB offices were closed. All of the pending union representation elections were shut down. All of the unfair labor practices cases were suspended because of the lack of ALRB staff. Nothing was happening. It was an impasse. So this initiative was a brilliant move by César. Prop. 14 was defeated overwhelmingly by the voters, but at least [it got] things at the ALRB going again.

After Prop. 14, our focus became the displacement of local workers owing to the widespread adoption of the second-generation tomato harvest machine. The question was, what should be done about it? Then, California Rural Legal Assistance (CRLA) got interested. Ralph Abascal, one of the founders of CRLA, and a guru of that organization, had always been interested in the land-grant university question. The fact that the second-generation tomato harvest machine had been developed with assistance from the University of California Cooperative Extension and faculty on the Davis campus was reflected in signage on many of the machines: UC Blackwelder, a reference to both the University of California and to the company producing the machines.

The Yolo Friends of the Farmworkers (YFF) was an existing organization independent of CIRS, active before CIRS was created, but CIRS was also

Figure 5.2. Don Villarejo, UC Davis rally in support of farmworkers, spring 1978. Courtesy of Don Villarejo.

in our minds. Some of the people who were involved in YFF, such as Dick Johnson and Paul Barnett, saw the wisdom of continuing their work, but in a new way. A 501(c)4 membership organization that would be a non-profit but not tax exempt was needed, a political organization to express the demands that came out of responding to the new situation. You have the tomato strike in '74. In '75, a few growers respond with the first trial of the new generation of tomato harvester. They work, and by '76 they are widespread adopted. By '77, the whole industry up here has them. I don't know how many workers were displaced; some say 10,000, other people say 20,000. We don't know.

The response was already building in terms of what we were doing: first, the Yolo Friends of the Farmworkers, then came the California Agrarian Action Project. The California Agrarian Action Project was created under the 501(c)4 structure—membership, monthly meetings in Spanish and English, with workers, students and other folks, like myself, involved. Then, parallel to that, is the idea of the California Institute for Rural Studies that formally gets incorporated in 1977 as a 501(c)3. The vision was two separate organizations: one a political action organization, the other a think tank.

I was adamant in saying that if we are going to do this in the atmosphere of Reaganomics, and the politics of that time, it had to be totally clean. In other words, there could be paid staff at one organization, but they could not work as paid staff with the other organization. The Boards of Directors had to have no overlap whatsoever. They could not have any cross subsidies of any kind. Paul and I agreed on that. I became the "Executive Director" for the California Institute for Rural Studies, and he became the staff person for the California Agrarian Action Project.

Then two miracles happened. One was an initiative by a woman by the name of Billie Boukas, who happen to be an owner of grazing land near Dunnigan in Yolo County. She gifted CIRS 100 shares of stock in the Wells Fargo Bank and 100 shares of stock in United Technologies: $25,000 appeared just like that, like magic. It just came. Independent of that, Paul had put together a grant proposal to a branch of the Department of Labor (DoL) to study the displacement of workers due to agricultural technology. He put it in a proposal submitted by the California Institute for Rural Studies. What do you know? We got the grant. It was another $12,000. We got the grant to do this work, unlike the Boukas gift, which was "do whatever you want that is consistent with the tax-exempt purpose of CIRS."

We divided the work up and eventually published "Labor's Dwindling Harvest," which was a lengthy document. It was the second publication of CIRS.[1] It's available on my personal website. We did the research and published it.[2]

During these early years, CIRS research was often internally published and directly marketed from its office by mail. Not reliant upon research journals, these "reports" allowed more accessible language and expanded their audience beyond academic disciplines.[3] (Not publicly disclosed, various reports were sent to knowledgeable experts for pre-publication peer review. "Getting Bigger," for example, was sent to five outside experts representing the ag industry, academia, and government. Also, post-reclamation research with Villarejo as first author or co-author was published in peer-reviewed journals.)[4]

A later mission statement illustrates the organization's evolution and unique position, filling a void in the political movements of the era. It described CIRS as the only non-profit organization in California with a mission to conduct

> public interest research that strengthens social justice and increases the sustainability of California's rural communities. Our research informs public policy and action for social change while providing a fact-based foundation for organizations and individuals working to ameliorate rural injustice. While our commitment to the scientific method is at the foundation of our credibility, we recognize the inescapable role that values play in shaping the fundamental questions that researchers pose. Our philosophy of science is therefore based on the principle that scientific inquiry should consciously serve the long-term public interest.[5]

Villarejo patched together the budding organization, often doing so by sacrificing his own compensation while demanding high levels of professional accountability from all staff, including himself.

> I was volunteer staff nearly all of that time. I was earning money teaching physics on a part-time basis at UCD. The CIRS DoL grant money was for Paul and Katherine. Both of them were working for CIRS on the research project. For the period of time that there was money for the (c)4, Paul worked only for the (c)4. After that money ran out, we got the grant from the Department of Labor. Then he went over to CIRS as staff and volunteered at California Agrarian Action Project. Katherine Bertolucci, first hired at CIRS, on the Department of Labor grant, was also a volunteer at the Agrarian Action Project.
>
> During that period, I worked as a volunteer at both places. We all kept timesheets. Every day we had to fill out the timesheet, otherwise no check. Exactly what did you do? When did you start work? When did you end work? How many hours? All very meticulous. That is how CIRS got started. The first time I decided to get paid was for a study of large-scale farming in

California that became the publication "Getting Bigger." I used a third of the Boukas donation, about $8,000, for one year on the payroll to do that research, prepare the report and publish the document.

Around this time Ralph Abascal thought of the research priorities lawsuit. He felt that this was an opportunity to leverage the land-grant university in the direction of serving underserved rural populations: farmworkers, small-scale farmers, organic farmers, and the rural poor. CRLA didn't do the lawsuit by themselves because they saw our organization having the best mix of ideas. We're talking about organic farming. We're talking about sustainable agriculture, though not by that name. We're talking about farm labor. We're talking about rural poverty. We're talking about land ownership.

He said to me, "This is an opportunity to push some levers. Let's see how far we can go."

I said, "We can't do anything in litigation unless our members, some of whom are Spanish- and most are English-speaking, agree. We have monthly meetings. You have to talk about it with them."

CRLA, to their credit, came to the meeting. Ralph with two CRLA lawyers. Ralph is of Hispanic origin himself and speaks Spanish, so the meeting went well. This was probably in '78. At the meeting they presented what they wanted to do, which was a lawsuit against the University of California for failure to serve the needs of small-scale farmers, farm laborers, and the rural poor.

The workers asked, "Are you going to get money?"

I said, "No, there will be no money for me. I will not be getting money from working on this lawsuit." The other people said the same.

Then they said, "Will we get money?"

We said, "No, this is not about money for people. It's about changing the way the government works so that workers will be treated better, so that farmers will be able to continue to farm in a way that is good for everyone." The workers were looking everybody over. Another of the workers' demands was to have the ability to farm themselves. Later, we found some land where they could farm. They eventually got it under a lease agreement with a state agency that we identified. In the end, they agreed.

The lawsuit was filed January 17, 1979 in Alameda County Superior Court. The California Agrarian Action Project was the lead plaintiff. CRLA found 13 individual farmworkers through their own networks of client services who agreed to sign on as individual plaintiffs. Paul Barnett eventually went to work for CRLA as the legal worker to help prepare the lawsuit. The trial was in Alameda Superior Court. We prevailed. It was a great publicized victory. We go to Appeals Court in the State of California, because the University appealed. We won in Appeals Court, which was not hailed as a big victory; it's just the way it went. Then we go to the California State Supreme Court because the University appealed. Meanwhile, and this is a ten-year process, the California State Supreme Court has been packed by Reagan and the conservatives. They throw the lawsuit out, and there was no real basis for appeal beyond that. The lawsuit cost a million dollars.

We had clear demands. These demands were not an end to mechanization, which is how the university characterized it. Rather, it was about the workers sharing in the benefits of the improved technology. We pointed to the ILWU (longshore workers) mechanization agreement. When the longshore industry mechanized, some of the profits were earmarked to serve workers for retraining and for other needs. That's what we wanted. There were patents and royalty income for UC, increased profits for farmers and lower costs. Workers should get a share of that. That's all we asked: not an end to mechanization but a sharing of the benefits. Second, if mechanization research went forward, we wanted the university to serve the actual needs of workers, farmers, the rural poor, and especially the small farmers.

Along the way, in the ten-year period of the litigation, what happened at the university? The Small Farm Center, the Sustainable Agriculture and Education Program, more attention to community needs as the university describes it, and all mechanization research stopped. The university was frightened by what we were doing. And two years later, in 1990, CIRS was invited to become an Investigator with the newly formed Agricultural Health and Safety Center of the University of California, with full participation in the initial five-year federal grant supporting the new center. I submitted a proposal to study California agriculture's increasing reliance on farm labor contractors, and the implications for on-farm safety under these new employment relationships.

Research for Action

Given the University of California's historic reticence—even resistance—toward rural sociology, the emergence of CIRS filled a void in academic scholarship across the state.

An advantage of CIRS's development outside of California's land-grant universities was that it had the political space to align its purpose with the needs of the distressed family farmers and destitute farmworkers. Land reform, small business enterprise, social justice, and the defense of democratic governance were values explicitly called out by the organization.

One of the earliest works produced by Villarejo and CIRS was a booklet published in 1980 titled *Research for Action*. Establishing a primary research method for the organization, the booklet detailed approaches reminiscent of litigating attorneys, private detectives, or investigative journalists. A "guidebook" for activists, it highlighted a method that was time consuming and meticulous, and explicitly sought social change as its goal.

> This guidebook is intended to help activists who are working for social change. Community based organizations often find that they need basic information about the interests of individuals or businesses who are involved in a particular dispute. In many cases, the needed information is available but it is not used because of a lack of familiarity with where to look or what to ask for . . . .
>
> The experience represented in the material presented in this guidebook includes certain general conclusions about how information can be used to promote social change. One of the lessons is that effective action is enhanced by the clear identification of the different, conflicting interests in a particular struggle.
>
> The material presented in this guidebook is designed to acquaint activists with the techniques used in public records investigations.[6]

The intent to create change for social justice in political struggle was explicit, eased perhaps by CIRS's location outside of the nominally neutral political positions of a research university. Villarejo's scholarship was not a product for institutional consumption. It was applied social science that generated tools for citizen action. He did not assume that public institutions like universities, federal bureaucracies, or the court system would alone achieve meaningful research applied to local problems:

> It is vital to realize that information, no matter how accurate, will not, by itself, produce social change. Only the action of hundreds, or thousands,

of informed people acting together has the potential to transform societies. Investigation helps to clarify the real interests of different parties in a particular dispute. But organized groups of people are needed if one hopes to challenge the existing power structure in a community.[7]

Scientific truth alone does not create change; people utilizing and breathing life into findings does.

Similarly, the booklet itself was a product of "collective" political engagement, which Villarejo summarized in this advice:

> First, in every issue that comes up, try to determine who will benefit if each possible outcome were to occur. It is a lesson of experience that behind every controversy there are conflicting interests. One purpose of investigative work is to pinpoint those interests and educate the community about their nature.
>
> Second, document your statements before going public.
>
> Third, try to determine if any of the interests involved in a controversy are among the types of businesses regulated by government agencies. These reports are usually the most complete sources of information.
>
> Fourth, use the information uncovered to organize people.[8]

Still useful, particularly in its set of values and intentions, the method's techniques have been somewhat dated by technology. If MacCannell's macrosocial accounting was subsumed by GIS, so Villarejo's public records investigations have been partially, but not completely, replaced by internet searches.[9] Yet, the critical direction and imperative to interrogate remain. The lessons of "research for action" are best illustrated in the telling of its use and application, particularly in the context of California's system of industrialized agriculture in the Central Valley.

> The structure of California agriculture always interested me. This was conceptually similar to my early work on stock ownership and who owned Cuba.
>
> We really did not have good knowledge of this industry. There was a lot of rhetoric—George Ballis was the master of the rhetoric—some of which was true, but much of it was a stretch.
>
> I realized that there was this gigantic hole—here was an industry, several times bigger than the movie industry, but undocumented in terms of its

structure. I set about trying to craft a more accurate description of the structure of California agriculture, with a focus on large-scale farming.

I found an error in the Census of Ag, which was an opportunity to make a more substantial contribution (see "Getting Bigger," published by CIRS in March 1980). If you read that paper, you will find out about the error and the correction, which really changes our understanding of farm size concentration by demonstrating it to be far greater than Census findings suggest.

I also found something that was a surprise for me and changed some of the discourse about California agriculture. I found that among the two hundred largest farm operations in the state, very few were outside, non-agricultural businesses investing in California agriculture. Most of the large-scale businesses were multi-generational farm families that had settled here and had become successful. They had purchased more land over time or leased land and expanded.

Among the biggest farm in Yolo County, for example, were Heidrick Farms, with about 21,000 irrigated acres. They were descendants of German immigrants. I tracked them in some detail. They started out with relatively small plots of land. They had figured out how to do tomato and rice farming and successfully expanded those businesses here, mostly on leased land. The biggest one was Anderson Farms. John Anderson's dad was from a family that had settled here from Europe. They started out with 80 acres. The son figured out how to put together limited partnerships with investments from urban folk, but for which he or his corporations were the general partner. He leased those lands and used those leases to increase the number of tomato machines he operated. He became the biggest tomato farmer in Yolo County. Real Horatio Alger stories. They were astute business people who were not representative of the Dole Food Company or Conagra, the so-called "big bad guys."

It was a shocker because quite a few of the environmental activists or other folks who had some claim on agricultural policy were just uninformed. What they were throwing out there as rhetoric was not substantiated by the facts. There were some non-agricultural businesses that had owned and operated farming businesses here, but relatively few. Many of those who had come in had gone out because they found that they couldn't do it. In fact, some of them had to change their practices as a result of what they learned about how to do farming here. Tennaco is a good example of that. They just couldn't pull it off.

In conducting primary document research for "Getting Bigger," I went to every county in the state where there is any agriculture at all and spent several days doing public records searches among the local official records. I recorded information about everybody who was participating in the USDA price and income support programs. I wrote on cards that showed how much land was owned and how much was leased. The whole operation—name and address, everything. It was tough data collection. I ended up with 55,000 cards.

When I published it, John Anderson, one of the biggest farmers in this region, thought it was great. He bought fifty copies at face value. The Farm Bureau was pleased. They thought that it contradicted the rhetoric from the critics of Big Agriculture. They had me on their radio and television programs. Farm Bureau also had me speak at various places, which I was happy to do because the work was the first accurate information on the topic. It named names of the 200 biggest farms. Who they were, what kind of structure—corporation, partnership, sole proprietor. All the basics.

These farms were primarily in places like Kern County, the Salinas Valley, some in the Imperial Valley area, but also some surprising ones like up here. Nobody knew about the big farms up here. 21,000 irrigated acres, that's a lot. Anderson, at that time, was up to as much as 56,000 acres, not just in Yolo but in other places. These were very large businesses, and nobody had ever heard about them.

Some funny things happened. Some years later, in conducting a follow-up study, I sent a form out to each of the largest farms asking about whether the newly current information was accurate or not. Most of them never sent anything back, but a few did. I did that for the sake of accuracy. It was important to ask the businesses that I was naming whether the information about them was accurate. I felt that they should have an opportunity to rebut or correct it.

It was a real surprise to me how "Getting Bigger" was received. It was the best-selling CIRS publication in that whole period. We printed 500 copies, and it was gone overnight. It went fast and got a great deal of attention. It clarified some perceptions of agriculture. Now, some of the information in there wasn't quite right, and some of it was dead wrong. But, by and large, the error in the census was a true error, and I figured out how to correct it. And then the identification of the 200 biggest was mostly right. A couple of errors, not many. The full question of who are these businesses got discussed in a whole new way and changed the discourse.

One unanticipated outcome was that Western Growers Association invited me to become an Associate Member. Though somewhat expensive in terms of annual dues, by agreeing to join I got access to their "confidential" farm labor bulletin and to their membership directory.

Two years later, the CIRS report "New Lands for Agriculture" came out in the context of the fight around the peripheral canal—I think it was on the June 1982 ballot as a referendum. It came out because of all this work that I'd been doing on structure of agriculture. Various groups, including church groups, got interested in the California Institute for Rural Studies. Several of them had me speak at their annual meetings. They asked, "Is there something you can do that would be supportive of family farming that would be worthy of some small support?" We aren't talking about major money, just a couple of thousand dollars. I said I'd think about it.

Then I happened to learn, through the investigative work I'd done for "Getting Bigger," about Prudential Insurance setting up this huge tract of olive groves in western Kern County. Five thousand acres of olive groves. I immediately looked at the olive production. They were going to break the market price. Basically, that is what they were going to do. I then looked around for other places where olives were being grown. The main area was up in Corning where there are a lot of small olive producers—two, three, four acres, six acres.

Soon, I heard about this guy, Les Melville, who was speaking about a terrible water deal that was going on. I went up and talked to him at his place. He was Italian with about ten acres of olives. He started telling me all about what was going on, the whole story of the olive business. I said, "Let's figure out who they are getting the water from." We found that they were getting the water in Kern County from the State Water Project for which the Los Angeles Metropolitan Water District subsidized. I knew, "This is it! This is the deal."

A couple of work-study students working at the Institute for Rural Studies, Phyllis White and Jude Crisfield, constructed all of the detailed records of landownership in the water districts that were getting state water. They did all that work and put together great data. Then this student, Jude Crisfield, got seriously interested in it. She turned out to be a filmmaker and put together a film interviewing some of the people we had found. We went down and filmed in front of the big olive groves, then over to the Early California

Industries olive processing plant. Then I discovered a special deal in reading through the SEC filings for the companies. Prudential had made a deal with Early California Industries to be their sole processor. All kinds of detail. It was classic investigative reporting. The "New Lands for Agriculture" piece became the way in which that information got disseminated. Further, I went to Los Angeles to speak at a press conference organized by former New Left colleagues claiming that Los Angeles voters were paying for water they never received; instead, the water went to companies like Prudential Insurance to undermine small farmers.

This scholarship is a different level of investigative reporting. I'm an empiricist. I've got to start with the factual information. Some investigative reporting starts with the discovery that something bad has happened. Then they try to find a cause as to why it happened. In other words, what is the causal relationship? They look for the cause, then develop the investigation around finding more information to support their idea. Sometimes it works, sometimes it doesn't. The reason it sometimes doesn't work is that instead of looking at the entire picture to inductively derive from the available information, they begin with an allegation and pursue that—like an attorney, looking for the evidence that supports that link. That is a shortcoming in some investigative reporting. It leads to mistakes. Probably one of the biggest that we know about in Ag was the allegations that Alar caused illnesses among workers and children. That wasn't happening, certainly not in the way it was represented on national television. There was a misrepresentation, and the environmentalist advocates didn't care. They did horrible damage to apple farmers. It took years to recover.

Being an empiricist means that you look for facts on the ground. You talk to everybody on all sides of an issue. You look for all available evidence on an issue. Then you try to extract from that a version of the truth, what you are able to gather and see. You put that out as a hypothesis to test and see where it leads. That is the only way rigorous science can proceed. The physics training I had as a scientist is what has been the guiding set of rules by which I've done work outside of physics: look at the evidence and move from there. If you look at the study of stock ownership and the control of corporations, that's what that is all about. You look for the piece on Cuba, that's what that's all about. You look at "New Lands for Agriculture," that's what that is all about. If you look at "Getting Bigger," that's what that is all about.

In training activists, I tried to convey this in a publication called "Research for Action." How do you find the evidence? If the evidence is not objective, can you find other evidence that bears on it? It's got to be rigorous. This publication is pre-internet; it's partly obsolete now, but the theory there is exactly the same. Is the evidence objective? One of my labor-organizer friends said it best. He came to me and asked me for help some months ago. I was glad to give it. He said, "We always go to Don because he will do anything for the labor movement except lie." It was a nice compliment, a measure of how I am viewed by people who know that there are skills that they can avail themselves of. They wanted me to do this work because they knew there was a level of credibility that went with it that was important for their purpose.

CIRS methods were based upon empirical social science while maintaining the critical tone of investigative journalism. Knowledge production was not global in scope, but a tool for organizing campaigns around strategic objectives.

New Lands for Agriculture

The premise of the original reclamation law was to increase the number of entrepreneurial businesses by facilitating the access to land for hundreds of new farmers. In retrospect, Villarejo was now able to assess the outcomes and effects resulting from subsidizing agribusiness at the expense of a more equitably diversified economy.

New Lands for Agriculture, written by Villarejo with Jude Crisfield and Phyllis White, detailed the effects of the California State Water Project (SWP) on small farmers.[10] Funded by churches and directly marketed to the community at large, the *New Lands* study compared how SWP water supplies impacted California agriculture. Family farmers such as Les Melville, a small olive farmer with a 48-acre grove, were compared with large-scale agribusiness like the 5,000 acre McCarthy olive ranch owned by Prudential Insurance Company.

SWP water was moved from northern California, near the Sacramento Valley, to the San Joaquin Valley and southern California's cities. This water transfer represented where public subsidy and private investment conspired against family farming to the benefit of corporate agriculture. Inevitably, overproduction by large-scale agribusinesses saturated markets, driving down prices, which inevitably crushed locally oriented, small family businesses.

Only a year after the Supreme Court's *Ivanhoe vs McCracken* decision, the State Water Project was passed by the California legislature in 1959. (Paul Taylor had directly attributed SWP passage to the court decision and the threat it posed to imposing reclamation mandates and principles upon agribusiness.) A general election vote ratified the sale of bonds to fund the project, including construction of the Oroville Dam and the California Aqueduct. The *New Lands* report pointed out that water deliveries started in 1968 with 63% going to the San Joaquin Valley. While only 24% of water deliveries went to Southern California, these urban centers bore 70% of SWP payments. The San Joaquin Valley, where large landowners were again the beneficiaries of public subsidy, made only 13.5% of project payments.

Water from the SWP went to some of the most concentrated, industrialized farms in California. Sixty-two percent of the water deliveries went to five water districts on the west side and southern end of the valley. In these districts, eight landowners owned 59% of the land or 227,545 acres. The "Big Eight" were named:

- Chevron USA, Inc., which was a subsidiary of Standard Oil Co. of California.
- Tejon Ranch Co., whose largest stockholder, with 25% ownership interest, was the Times Mirror Co., owner of the *Los Angeles Times* (a leading proponent of the SWP).
- Getty Oil Co., which leased most of its holdings to independent farm operations.
- Shell Oil Co. (none of its farmland in the area would be productive without SWP water deliveries).
- McCarthy Joint Venture A, a partnership with Prudential Insurance Co. of America, which owned 75% of the company.
- Blackwell Land Co., a company formed by international bankers and owned by multinational companies from England (Midhurst Corp., a subsidiary of S. Pearson and Son), Switzerland (Les Fils Dreyfus), Luxemburg (Unifin, a subsidiary of IFI Int'l), and Japan (Mitsubishi Corp.).
- Tenneco, Inc., with its landholdings owned by its subsidiary, Tennaco West, Inc.

- Southern Pacific Land Co., which was the state's biggest private landowner and leased farmland to independent farming operations.

Of the remaining landowners, besides the eight largest, many were not completely separate enterprises. For example, 35 landowners of 14,000 acres shared the same business address. In essence, the report found, SWP water primarily flowed to the largest agribusinesses in the state.

There were multiple financial dividends to landowners from SWP water deliveries, particularly for these corporations. The most evident was the speculative increase in land values, which went from $50 per acre prior to water deliveries to an average of $2,000 per acre after just eight years of state water deliveries. This water also necessitated on-farm infrastructure that negatively affected small scale producers in the San Joaquin Valley who did not have access to the capital necessary for these improvements. The Department of Water Resources found that smaller producers were forced into "liquidating and disposing of their properties" as lending institutions resisted loaning money to them during this time.[11] The investments needed to farm high value crops remained largely out of reach to smaller farmers.

The report highlighted the olive industry to assess the complex web of effects from SWP water supplies to southern Californian agriculture.

> Prior to the development of the SWP, the California olive industry was dominated by small-scale producers. At the end of the 1960s, the state's olive groves totaled 27,000 acres with an average of 26 acres per farm. As a result of the availability of state supplied water, more than 6,000 acres of new orchards were planted in western Kings and Kern counties during 1970 and 1971. These new plantings had a tree density of 100 trees to the acre as compared with an average of 48 to 50 trees per acre in older established orchards.[12]

The doubling of olive production oversupplied the market, which decreased olive prices and profits. Smaller producers, working from more limited lines of credit and tighter profit margins were squeezed out the agricultural sector. The *New Lands* report found:

... the state of California has used its great power, represented by the State Water Project, to tip the economic scale to the advantage of large-scale agricultural interests. Unlike Federal water projects, there is no acreage limitation on the amount of land that can be irrigated with SWP water.[13]

Through public records and other research, the study uncovered a long-term contract between McCarthy Farming and Prudential with an olive processor named Early California Industries. Under the contract, Early Cal agreed to purchase all McCarthy olives. In exchange, they agreed to defer $1,000,000 in payments for the crop. This amounted to "an interest-free loan of $1,000,000 while McCarthy and Prudential are assured of a market for their olive crop." Since 53% of Early Cal's pack came from McCarthy ranch, they could set a price that would undercut the smaller family farms.

The *New Lands* study illustrated a technique that Villarejo used repeatedly. He named names. More than that, since agribusiness's access to public coffers and the complex bureaucratic mechanisms used in the business partnerships were rarely seen or understood outside of the ag industry itself, Villarejo named these corporations together with the mechanisms that enriched them. He illustrated how deals were orchestrated to benefit the wealthy through the expenditure of public subsidies. He made hidden and obscure relationships transparent and comprehensible.

Reclamation Reform

The 1982 Reclamation Reform Act gutted the democratic principles and progressive values from a longstanding federal law.

After decades of law-breaking and corruption by agribusiness, massive government subsidies continued to flow to the few wealthiest individuals literally at public expense. Goldschmidt's forewarning was now objective reality, and an opportunity for further scientific inquiry.

Following the law's amendment, two CIRS studies were central to understanding its real world outcomes, continuing to pressure compliance with the law, and deepening an understanding of the effects of economic monopoly: *How Much Is Enough?*, and *Missed Opportunities: Squandered Resources.*[14]

A later paper I wrote was "How Much Is Enough?" It is now available on the CIRS website. This paper was supported by the Ford Foundation, published in 1986. It was a study of land ownership, focused primarily on the 1982 reclamation law regulations and whether they were being complied with.

The 1982 Reclamation Reform Act was the undoing of the reformist acreage limitation regulations and a brilliant move by the other side; perhaps it was the J. G. Boswell Company lawyers. You can find out more in the excellent book *The King of California* by Rick Wartzman and Mark Arax.[15] The lawyers figured out that federal environmental laws could be used to require an environmental impact study on the consequences of the proposed regulations. They went to court right after the NLP won the case and invoked this federal act to require that there be an environmental impact statement prepared around the possible implementation of these regulations. It put a hold on the regulations until the environmental impact was completed. It resulted in no action being taken by the federal government for several years.[16]

The regulations were inadequate. The unfortunate environmental impact statement and a decision made by both the big farm interests and the environmental advocates, like the Natural Resources Defense Council, to join together in support of the '82 law resulted in its enactment. The environmentalists wanted higher prices for water to decrease water use. Their other agenda was to take water away from agriculture, accusing agriculture of wasting water. The big farm interests wanted the higher the acreage limit the better. The '82 law was a compromise crafted with the support of Democrats and Republicans.

What did the '82 law do? The '82 law said that you could choose to remain under the original 1902 law or you could elect to go under the new law. If you elect to go under the new law, there were new rules. First, they got the compromise of 960 acres. If you had land ownership in excess of 960 acres, you are going to have to pay full cost for the water on the excess land. You aren't going to be forced to sell it, which had been the rules of the prior law. Second, if you elect to go under the '82 law, then you are absolved from all obligations under prior law, including the residency requirement.

Those obligations, for Boswell and all the other big landowners, included sale of their excess land on a recordable contract to avoid paying full cost for their irrigation water. Prior to the '82 law, they had entered into recordable contracts that obligated them to sell excess land at pre-irrigation prices within 10 years of the date of that contract. This obligation was given away under the '82 law in order to protect the interests of these big landowners. Third, the hammer clause said if you lease more than 160 acres then you have to pay full price on the excess land that you lease, but leasing is unlimited. The lease of land up to 160 acres at subsidized prices was in addition to the 960. So it was possible to get 1,120 acres of fully subsidized water.

But there are other loopholes in the law. If you created a trust—a fiduciary agreement that basically allows for land to be held in parcels of any size—reclamation law would apply only to the proportionate share of each beneficiary. Under the new law, this meant eligibility was allocated not to the trust as a whole but to the individual beneficiaries of the trust. So, if you, Paul Taylor, Trudy, and I form a trust to hold 3,000 acres, then each of us, with a quarter share, would have 750 acres of beneficial interest. The Boswells had the Westhaven Trust, which owned all the land in what was known as the Boston Ranch, 23,000 acres, and guess what, the largest single landholding in terms of the beneficiary ownership was . . . 960 acres! J. G. Boswell II and each of the beneficiaries had 960 acres or less. My goodness! What a coincidence.

How Much Is Enough? was a postmortem of Taylor's reclamation struggle, a generational battle now lost. Villarejo showed how quickly these once clandestine, recalcitrant agribusinesses restructured to become compliant with the new reclamation requirements. The publication focused on how irrigation infrastructure affected land ownership in Californian agriculture with emphasis on the RRA of 1982.

The change in acreage limitation signaled acceptance across all levels of government of industrial scale agriculture as the primary food production system in California. A capitulation with dire consequences, the RRA limited eligible acreage receiving federal water to 960 acres. Villarejo noted:

This report documents the size distribution of farm operators and, separately, of land ownership in ten Central California water districts eligible to receive Federal water. Of the 1,791 farms operating in the ten districts, just 229 (13%) have holdings of 961 acres or more. However, these 229 held at least 62% of the combined 1,020,000 acres eligible to receive Federal water in the ten districts. Farm operators eligible for Federal water deliveries in the districts have substantial holdings in other parts of the state, amounting to an additional 857,000 acres. Farms receiving the Federal water subsidy in California have an average holding of 1,048 irrigable acres. This holding is 7.2 times larger than the average holding of a California irrigated farm. Thus, the Federal water subsidy has preferentially benefited the state's largest farm businesses.[17]

The statewide focus of the report did not limit analysis of agribusiness to a specific farm, town or region. If acreage limitation applied to total acres, how many acres did these large-scale operations own? How were these businesses structured, and were acreage totals accurately counted?

How Much Is Enough? illustrated that water deliveries from public infrastructure projects increased land consolidation and intensified farming practices—precisely the opposite outcome that federal water deliveries were supposed to deliver had occurred. Between 1944 to 1982, California's irrigable land increased by seventy-one percent. The California State Water Project and federal Central Valley Project were responsible for much of this increase. In fact, the three San Joaquin Valley counties of Fresno, Tulare, and Kern accounted for a net addition of 1,377,810 or 37% of the state's total increase. Villarejo noted that "it is not just a coincidence that these three counties are, at present, the top three counties in the nation in terms of annual cash receipts from crop and livestock marketing."[18] Water deliveries also changed farming practices and crop yields, particularly increasing fruit and nut production.

The Reclamation Reform Act of 1982 (RRA) offered a reset for Western agribusiness. Not only did the statute rectify (and finally illustrate in real terms) decades of previous law breaking, it also legitimized continued takings of public resources for private gain. Villarejo calculated the per capita public subsidy going to California's largest agricultural landowners at about $150,000 per year.[19] Ninety percent of land in excess of the new 960-acre limit was also in the state. Of the 415 megafarms in the 17 western states that were above the RRA limit, 399 were in California. Since many of these factory farms leased farmland, Villarejo suggested that the RRA "hammer clause," which stipulated that leased agricultural land in excess of 160 acres must pay full price for federal water, would be applicable to many of these agribusinesses since 49% of California farmland was leased.

Using public records, Villarejo then looked at ten water districts throughout the Central Valley (four in the Sacramento Valley and six in the San Joaquin Valley) to analyze both landownership and farm operator patterns on irrigated farmland.[20] The distribution of farm sizes in these ten districts were presented in a graph.[21]

Farm Size Distribution, Irrigable Lands: Ten California Districts (1985)

Size Class	Number (of farms)	Irrigable Land
80 acres or less	534 farms	20,632 acres
81–160 acres	284 farms	37,042 acres
161–320 acres	317 farms	77,924 acres
321–640 acres	282 farms	133,047 acres
641–960 acres	145 farms	117,207 acres
961–1,280 acres	64 farms	70,611 acres
1,281–2,560 acres	94 farms	167,971 acres
2,561–5,120 acres	44 farms	153,539 acres
5,121 acres or more	27 farms	241,900 acres
Total	**1,797 farms**	**1,019,873 acres**

Villarejo's findings documented a continued failure to achieve the goals of reclamation values for a democratic-scale farm system. Referencing the 160-acre standard, only 57,647 acres or 5.7% of the farmland met the historic criterion. Agribusiness monopolies were so extensive that 62% of landholdings could not even meet the new RRA 960-acre limit. Villarejo also emphasized that the figures were an underestimate of farm concentration because many of the agribusinesses had unaccounted for interlocking relationships and were not truly independent of each other.

In Chapter 3, Villarejo investigated the ten Central Valley water districts in greater detail. Graphs and data were compiled on farm size, farms with more than 960 acres, and landowners with more than 960 acres. The distinction between the last two categories was important because it asked a question: what constituted a farm? Was a farm determined by parcel size or the amount of land owned by a particular agribusiness? Villarejo lined out an argument that the total acreage of particular landowners needed to be assessed cumulatively.

With a tone insistent upon transparency and emphasis on the empirical data, Villarejo bore down into each water district. Questionable public-private relationships were opened up. Names were given. In each district, the mega-farms larger than 5,121 acres were identified, inviting further interrogation and grassroots action. The public records research used business addresses to help determine which farmers were local residents in addition to aiding in identifying farmland in other parts of the state that used the same office location.

Of the ten water districts, the Westlands Water District (WWD) stood out from all others, as it represented its own unique anomaly with the scale of its landholdings. Just as with the other water districts, Villarejo graphed the WWD businesses receiving federal water by farm size in acres.[22]

Farm Size Distribution, Irrigable Lands: Westlands Water District (1985)

Size Class	Number (of farms)	Irrigable Land
80 acres or less	9 farms	375 acres
81–160 acres	33 farms	4,734 acres
161–320 acres	39 farms	10,337 acres
321–640 acres	43 farms	22,072 acres
641–960 acres	50 farms	42,079 acres
961–1,280 acres	20 farms	22,458 acres
1,281–2,560 acres	50 farms	91,397 acres
2,561–5,120 acres	30 farms	104,934 acres
5,121 acres or more	24 farms	215,637 acres
Total	**298 farms**	**514,023 acres**

Eight-five percent of the eligible farmland was above the 960-acre limit. The average farm size, 1,725 acres, was three times larger than any other district in the study.

And this number is a significant underestimate. Since each legal entity was treated as distinct farm operations, multi-entity structures (where, for example, multiple entities share ownership of farmland) were not included. In addition, Villarejo did not include WWD farmland that relied upon private water supplies or was located outside of the district but owned by the same agricultural business entity.

When California-wide landholdings were applied to these 298 WWD farms, the corrections made to the district's farm size graph were even more stark.[23]

Farm Size Distribution, Irrigable Lands: Westlands Water District / California-wide Ownership (1985)

Size Class	Number (of farms)	Irrigable Land
80 acres or less	7 farms	226 acres
81–160 acres	26 farms	3,696 acres
161–320 acres	25 farms	6,510 acres
321–640 acres	34 farms	17,544 acres
641–960 acres	48 farms	40,374 acres
961–1,280 acres	20 farms	22,326 acres
1,281–2,560 acres	67 farms	123,513 acres
2,561–5,120 acres	33 farms	116,216 acres
5,121 acres or more	38 farms	714,880 acres
Total	**298 farms**	**1,045,285 acres**

The revised average WWD farm size was 3,508 acres. Ninety-three and a half percent of the WWD farmland eligible for federal water was above the 960-acre limit. In comparison, the average California irrigated farm was 145 acres.

In order to understand land tenure patterns over the previous four decades, the report shifted geographic focus to the Tulare Lake Basin in Chapter 4. This three-county region (Kern, Kings, and Tulare counties) was well suited for examination because it had gained 1,134,220 acres of irrigated farmland between 1944 and 1982 (the period of time when the Central Valley Project was constructed, drying up Tulare Lake, as water deliveries began to flow to the valley's basin). Villarejo identified every parcel over 20 acres in size within the region. This amounted to 55,000 parcels totaling 5,285,690 acres. Information on each of these parcels (owner's name, land use code, assessor parcel number, acreage, and county) was coded and entered into a database.

Similar to earlier graphs, farm size distribution helped explain land ownership in the three-county region.[24] One quarter of one percent (0.27%) of "farmers" owned 646,785 irrigated acres—over 1,000 square miles—of the region.

Extraordinary land consolidation became apparent as more than half the irrigated farmland was owned by only four percent of the growers. Consistent with his approach of identifying landowners owning more than 5,121 acres, the top five included J. G. Boswell Co. (125,645 acres); Tennaco West, Inc. (94,819 acres); Getty Oil Co. (40,761 acres); Chevron USA, Inc. (40,406 acres); and Southern Pacific Land Co. (38,057 acres).

Forty years of reclamation water had not facilitated the small farm ideal or catalyzed land reform. Rather, it had exacerbated longstanding social and economic inequality due to non-enforcement of federal law.

At the end of the study, Villarejo reiterated the valley's characteristic for economic poverty amid prolific production. What was easy to see by walking through the region's rural communities was also demonstrated in federal statistics. Villarejo noted that in a national comparison, six of the ten cities with the highest percentages of people on welfare were in the Central Valley. He concluded that "multi-billion-dollar public investment" had transformed the valley into the world's most agriculturally productive region, while simultaneously making it into the most impoverished place in the United States.

> I talked to Dan Beard, who became the guy who was responsible for enforcement. He told me—these are not his exact words, but it is pretty close— "We got snookered by a bunch of country lawyers. We never knew." George Miller, the California Congressman at the time, said the same thing to me. When I talked to Rick Wartzman, for his book on the Boswell Company, he said "It was a done deal. The people who were at the table, negotiating for 'the good guys,' were not George Ballis. It was not the people who really knew how it worked. It was people who didn't know anything about agriculture and who had not had much direct experience with the way in which agriculture really works."

In 1988, Villarejo and Redmond's *Missed Opportunities: Squandered Resources* studied changes in the structure of Westlands agribusinesses after the RRA in 1982. Had the Westlands Water District (WWD), the region most indicative of subsidies to large-scale industrial agriculture, complied with the regulations? If so, how had the final implementation of federal law affected the structure of agriculture in this water district? Villarejo and Redmond framed the report's findings in the study's abstract:

> This study found that large landholders have been representing them-selves as several smaller units even though their land was being managed as one operation. In fact, comparison of documents from different agen-cies showed that large farm operations often told WWD that they were many small units, while registering at other agencies as one farm. These schemes involved 49% of the land in the WWD operated under the RRA by only 50 different operations.
>
> This research uncovered a pervasive pattern involving considerable effort on the part of large operations to comply with the technical require-ments of RRA in order to receive low-cost water while circumventing the RRA goal of assisting family-scale farms . . . . Although these schemes may appear unscrupulous, and indeed do not reflect the intent of Congress, it is the current policy of the Bureau of Reclamation to encour-age them. Ultimately, it is the Bureau, not the farmers, that must be held accountable for these massive violations of its legal mandate and of the public interest.[25]

Nominally the representation of Westlands agribusiness adjusted under the RRA, but the social and economic structure of the region remained undemocratic and polarized.

Missed Opportunities restated and affirmed previous research by Goldschmidt and MacCannell connecting farm structure to regional social conditions.

The RRA stipulated that full water costs must be paid for by farms larger than 960 acres in the 17 western states receiving water from fed-eral irrigation projects (previously the law had applied per water dis-trict). Corporations were held to 640 acres if they had more than 25 stockholders. The 960-acre limit included all landholdings as a single farm regardless of the number of people or legal entities on the title. Villarejo and Redmond recognized that the RRA's acreage limitation identification shifted from "land ownership" to "landholding" thereby including lease agreements.[26] Due to this new distinction between land ownership and landholding, Villarejo began to use the term "ownership unit" to describe the extended and non-local nature of land subject to these regulations. The residency requirement was eliminated under the RRA.

Questionable political processes occurred in the drafting of the law as loopholes were placed into the RRA. Villarejo and Redmond found that there were substantial changes made between the drafts distributed for public comment and those that were passed into law. The worst of these involved the 960-acre limit:

> No restriction was placed on the number of 960-acre tracts that could be farmed together as one unit by a management company; no provision prohibited members of a farm's controlling body from acting as manager of a farm operation. Thus, a few individuals could retain control over a large farming operation simply by "restructuring" it into 960-acre pieces, and then forming a management company to farm the entire operation as one piece.[27]

The report observed that many agribusinesses formed into trusts which "broke" the farm up into 960-acre parcels or less. The new farms could be placed in a trust where a child or other confidant controlled the property on paper, but the original owner was trustee.

For the Westlands Water District, the change in reclamation law created restructuring on paper but not in actual business operations. Villarejo and Redmond referred to these new business entities "water user clusters" or "clusters" that often shared the same phone number, address, and contact information. They found instances where separate clusters were listed together on loan applications, agricultural permits or registration under USDA programs. Since the federal definition of a farm involved an entity that puts capital at risk, Villarejo and Redmond determined that the water user clusters fit this definition and therefore should not have multiple 960-acre parcels eligible for subsidized federal water.

After years of non-compliance, Villarejo and Redmond also found that while WWD landowners reorganized under the RRA, irregular regulatory oversight at the Bureau of Reclamation allowed landholders to escape the 960-acre limitation:

> The Bureau of Reclamation is now allowing landholders who had entered into contracts to sell excess land irrigated with project water to redistribute their holdings in order to retain ownership and control. **Sales of large tracts of excess land, as approved by the Bureau, are being made to persons who are already owners of large amounts of land receiving project water.** In some instances, the total holdings are now in excess of the new ownership limit.[28]

These practices were consistent with a history connecting industry interests with the manipulation of laws, lax bureaucratic oversight, and slack regulatory implementation.

As a central component of dissemination of the CIRS research on reclamation policy, Villarejo was invited to present evidence as an expert witness to the U.S. Senate Committee on Energy and Natural Resources. His testimony concerned new research findings about land ownership and farm operators in ten irrigation or water districts of California's Central Valley Project. The findings, reported in the CIRS publication "How Much Is Enough?," indicated conflicts with the Bureau of Reclamation's acreage limitation provisions.

A second appearance as an invited expert witness was before the U.S. Senate Committee on Water and Power. This testimony described how some of the largest farms in the Westlands Water District had undertaken a legal restructuring. Each of these large farms created subdivided, separate 960-acre farms that were operated by a single, newly formed management company. The total land area was unchanged, the same equipment was used, and the workers and managers were as before. But the changed operation claimed to be simply managing the group of newly formed entities with separate ownerships and bookkeeping.

A Life's Work

The leverage and opportunity of implementing existing federal reclamation law had eroded. The terrain continued to shift, problems persisted, and CIRS nimbly evolved to meet them.

In the years following the reclamation fight, CIRS thrived by responding to funding proposals, requests of partners, and the needs of rural communities. A new advocacy frame was built up around community-based research, community organizing, and adult education. Filling community needs was balanced with keeping the doors open, staff paid, programs running. Numerous grants sustained the organization, which spurred diversified programs and added capacity.

One project was the "Farm Labor and Rural Poverty Project," funded by the Ford Foundation and The Aspen Institute to bring together scholars with community-based advocates. The initiative examined the generally unrecognized insertion of indigenous Mexican migrants from southern Mexico into the California farm labor force. The project also looked into the growing influence of farm labor contractors in California. Its interface with farmworker communities was "El Proyecto Laboral Agrícola en California," headed by Luis Magaña and based in the San Joaquin Valley with an office in Modesto. In addition, the 1986 Immigration Reform and Control Act (IRCA) created the need for research into its new opportunities for immigrant workers to regularize their immigration status and obtain a green card.

CIRS was still responsive to calls from labor unions for assistance. During the 1989 lettuce strike by over 3,000 workers at Dole Fresh Vegetables near Huron, CIRS staff and Villarejo played an instrumental role in assisting Teamsters Local 890. A lawsuit was filed by Dole's growers claiming damages for lost revenues and property damage. Teamsters Local 890's attorneys contracted with CIRS for consulting services and for expert witness testimony. The union prevailed in the lawsuit, setting the stage for later state labor legislation.

In these years, the California Agrarian Action Project also remained active. Immediately after the filing of the research priorities lawsuit, at CAAP's very next meeting, a new activist-oriented focus was taken up on pesticide policy. The "Rural Toxics Project" brought a corresponding shift to CIRS research priorities. The pesticide industry claimed

Figure 5.3. Don Villarejo, at a farmworker strike in Huron, California on October 31, 1989. Courtesy of Don Villarejo.

that loss of registration of some of the most dangerous chemicals would result in major economic losses for the industry, so CIRS embarked on a two-fold strategy: producing new informative resources, such as *Pesticides: A Guide for Farmworkers* in English-language and Spanish-language slide shows, and directly engaging at the community level in organizer training and support for sustainable agriculture alternatives.

Continuing to grow, by 1990, CIRS was funded through the University of California to conduct a large-scale survey of California labor contractors together with a smaller sample of grower clients and their employees. The "Farm Labor Contractors and Agricultural Worker Health & Safety" project was then launched as a five-year effort to identify the extent of increased penetration of labor contractors into the California farm labor market, and to examine how responsibility for farm safety was being divided between growers and contractors.

During the early and mid-1990s, in four successive years, CIRS sponsored an annual Spanish-language health fair, *Festival de la Salud*, held in the Yolo County Fairgrounds in Woodland. About 200 volunteer health professionals (nurses, physicians, medical students, dentists, and health educators) provided one-day, free health screenings for hundreds of community members. With funding provided by the Sierra Health Foundation and the first-ever California award by the U.S. EPA Environmental Justice Community Grants program, an intensive, Spanish-language, promotore/a training course was developed. Volunteer promotores developed a modest health survey instrument that yielded new information about access to health care services.

From this grew the "California Agricultural Worker Health Survey," an outgrowth from a request from a newly formed foundation, The California Endowment. CIRS proposed to conduct a statewide survey of the current farmworker population that would include lengthy in-person, face-to-face interviews as well as a comprehensive physical examination. Based on a household survey design in seven representative communities, the survey was conducted during a fourteen-month period in 1999–2000 and eventually included 970 participants, of whom about 680 completed all components of the survey. The findings were striking: untreated health conditions, abysmal lack of access to care, and high-risk behavior at work and at home. Eventually, The California Endowment allocated $50 million to address health concerns highlighted by the research, plus another $25 million for improving farmworker housing.

An additional dozen important, short-term projects were carried out by CIRS staff and colleagues during this same period. These included the Agricultural & Community Project, led by Trudy Wischemann, and funded by the state's Humanities Grant Program; a study of Childhood

Agricultural Worker Injuries, funded by the National Institute for Occupational Safety and Health; participation in the Central Valley Partnership for Citizenship, funded by the James Irvine Foundation; and a study of the community-level impact of reduced irrigation water to regions of the western San Joaquin Valley that were required by the Central Valley Project Improvement Act, funded by the U.S. Department of Agriculture.

During his tenure as CIRS Executive Director, Villarejo also served as a consultant under contracts that paid CIRS directly, not Villarejo, for numerous non-profit services requested by agencies, labor unions, government agencies, and private foundations. Villarejo also presented more than 210 speeches, seminars, college or university or law school classes, policy briefings, and other presentations during his 22-year career as CIRS Executive Director.

Following Villarejo's retirement from CIRS on June 30, 1999, the organization continued its work. Meanwhile, post-retirement from CIRS, Villarejo was appointed to serve on Expert Panels by the National Academies (Institute of Medicine); the National Institute for Occupational Safety; and the U.S. Department of Agriculture.

Until May 2018, Villarejo also served as a consultant to various agencies, including CIRS and the California Agricultural Labor Relations Board. While he no longer accepts invitations to speak or consult, he continues to write.

Politically Engaged Scholarship

When we listen to Don Villarejo, we remember Ernesto Galarza. Not that their paths were identical, but they faced similar constraints and worked from similar positions.

Neither was settled on university campuses, and both affiliated with farm labor movements that failed to fully recognize their contributions. Most compelling, they worked from the margins, in precarious and insecure spaces between formal institutions and the struggling workers in the fields. They improvised, bridging research, education, and organizing within campaigns that fully integrated workers—especially farmworkers—and frontline immigrant communities.

But rather than work within an existing framework, like a labor union, Villarejo built an organization from the ground up to do his scholarly work. The California Institute for Rural Studies, unrestrained by institutional boundaries, blended rural sociological research with farm labor advocacy and community-based education. Its mission and work were not constrained by any particular academic discipline. With this freedom, CIRS set out to bring hidden truths to the public, and to organize communities to solve their own problems.

Here is Villarejo describing his craft as a politically engaged scholar. His goal was empowerment. His approach, fostering social change through political power.

> Change is brought about by social organization of people who are affected by a problem. Only through the organization of those folks is real change going to come about that benefits them.
>
> Power is based on effective people standing up for what it is that they see as the need to have changed to fix their problem. Unless you have that, I don't see how change happens. Change does not happen by information alone. We're talking about a political process. A political process is about power. And power is based on political or social organization that pushes for change.
>
> My life has really been about trying to link what I do with those forces in the society that I think represent the political or social organization that is pushing for change. I've worked for the United Farm Workers union. I've worked for California Rural Legal Assistance. When the Teamsters came to me about the food processing industry and wanted me to do some work for them, yeah, I'm there to help. I'm there to do it right, to make sure that it's done accurately and scientifically.

The type of accuracy and scientific scholarship Villarejo pursued often wasn't possible in the UC system, and the limitations of just why this was the case came through after years of his interaction and collaboration (sometimes unsuccessful) with the University.

> The Kellogg Foundation approached us about Coop Extension in '91. The first Hispanic program officer at the Kellogg Foundation wanted to change the University by serving Spanish-speaking people in the Southwest, which they should have been doing all along. He came to me asking advice.

I said, "We should make sure that the University of California puts into place Extension officers who are labor advisors—not farm advisors, *labor* advisors."

He said, "Where would you like to do that?"

"Let's start with the San Joaquin Valley, maybe the Salinas Valley and other places. How about five? Let's shoot for five."

And he says, "Okay, if you can get the University of California to agree to that. We will make a grant of—I won't say the number, but it was very large, really huge—we'll make a grant of X million dollars to the California Institute for Rural Studies. You will get the University of California to be a contractor of the California Institute for Rural Studies for a five-year period to implement this program.

I spent eight months of my life traveling around talking to most of the local county Coop Extension Directors and the four statewide Regional Directors, the latter of whom I got on board early on. I talked to all of the San Joaquin Valley, Salinas Valley and Imperial Valley directors. Some were on board and some were not. I got a whole bunch of UC faculty on board as well.

We were going to hire five folks to become labor advisors. Each of them in one of the Coop Extension offices. They would have a salary paid for by this grant. They would have their overhead at U.C. Coop Extension covered, including insurance, travel expenses, and all of the goodies that come to a Coop Extension farm advisor. The program would collaborate with the farm advisors and the UC Agricultural Personnel Management Program so that they could become integrated into the whole system. The funding would come from Kellogg, but through CIRS under contract, but the people to be hired would be employees of the University of California. The Kellogg guy once said to me, "If you can get them by their short hairs, their hearts and minds may follow soon after."

We would not play any direct role in the hiring process other than to outline what the criteria should be for a labor advisor. There had to be agreement with Coop Extension that they would use the criteria in the hiring process. They could hire anybody they wanted just so long as they were a native Spanish speaker, they had extensive experience either as an employee or as a supervisor working in farm labor in California, and a few other things. They had to be not only bilingual but also biliterate.

So I spent eight months, not funded by Kellogg, going around talking to all these people, then a meeting gets pulled together in Oakland at the University of California headquarters. Lowell Lewis, who was the Chief Assistant to the Vice President for Agricultural Science, chaired the meeting. All these faculty, Coop Extension people and me are in the room. Before anything else in the room happened, Lowell Lewis looks straight at me, and says, "Don, you have to understand that the University of California is not a democracy."

I knew right away that it wasn't going to happen, and that's what happened. He said, "You have all these people supporting you but we're unclear whether this is a good move for the University at this time. There would be a lot of antagonism to trying to do this. We are especially concerned about the focus on labor. Now, we would be supportive of people doing community development work. We would be supportive of work associated with social services, teaching people how to access social services better. But this is too close to labor organizing."

The meaningful statement that the university "is not a democracy" was an interesting admission. The University of California is a public institution and the land-grant college of the state, so its purpose and mission are directly linked to public resources and, arguably, the support and advance of democratic principles and ideals.

As Emmett Fiske argued in his University of California doctoral dissertation in 1979, the state's land-grant system has actively participated in the industrialization of agriculture.[29] Yet in this case, they were reticent to accept five labor advisors at no cost ostensibly to balance the systems past unequal support of agribusiness interests above those of rural workers.[30]

At the same time, historically, the University of California and other colleges avoided and refrained from even allowing farmworker problems to be identified, let alone proposing solutions like promoting worker rights and sustainable agriculture practices. Recently, this has begun to change, but too slowly to adequately respond to the economic devastation and ecological damage from the forewarned development of factory farming and industrial agriculture.

If politically engaged scholars choose to remain outside of academic institutions, they will likely have more latitude but less financial security and economic resources to accomplish their objectives. Still, there are steps to bridge the gaps between scholarship and organizing.

Change organizations have a different agenda than the world of scholarship.

Being outside of the academic system has a number of advantages in terms of your ability to choose what it is you want to do and how you're going to do it. It even offers the opportunity to do things that the system would find difficult to tolerate, including working in a collaborative fashion with other change organizations.

I remember talking to a farm labor union, and I asked them what kind of research would help them in their work. They said, "Nothing." I didn't share that view, but it reflected the distance, the gap, between scholarship and the world of organizing. It is hard to overcome that gap from our side of the table. At the same time, I could have done things differently that would have been conducive to sustaining a larger scale scholarship enterprise outside of the system. For example, I did very little publishing in the peer reviewed, academic literature.

It was an inadvertent choice. My responsibility for fundraising to keep 13 people fed was just too demanding. I also had to have a certain kind of visibility in the media and in the world of scholarship and in the world of organizing, and at the community level which entails a whole lot of travel. Part of this is responding to requests from folks that want you to appear and sanction their thing. Though there were talented people at CIRS who made commitments to publish, they failed to publish even when pushed on it. I didn't push hard enough in retrospect.

My wife, who is a scholar, pointed out that there is important and valuable material that was developed during that California Institute for Rural Studies time that will be lost and needs to be available more widely.

The educational and organizing components of politically engaged scholarship are relational and communicative. The distance between scholar and subject is diminished, as are differences in status. Perhaps because of this, the space separating the social problem and creation of a solution is also narrowed. Learning and engagement become increasingly linked and interwoven.

There is a mantra in community organizing that Tom Hayden explained when we were both at La Paz, the UFW headquarters, doing organizer training. It went like this: When you're born, you're neutral; then you discover there is injustice.

So you become a liberal and you try to fix things through liberal mechanisms. You find that that doesn't work, and you become a radical. Then the question is, what kind of a radical should you be? Should you be a Marxist, anarchist, progressive labor, social democrat?

Pretty soon you are in a group of two ready to split over some fine point of doctrine. You think you are really getting somewhere, refining your ideas and zeroing in on the real problem. Whereas, in fact, you have become more distant from people, from the "folk."

There are two ways to go about clarifying your understanding of the world and clarifying your thinking, either go into academia or go take a bath among the people. If you really want to purify yourself, you take a bath among the people. That's how to purify yourself. You talk to everybody. You listen. You learn. That's how you learn what the real world is all about.

Trudy does that. As intellectuals, as scholars, as people with knowledge that often folks in the community don't have, I've always felt that part of our obligation in the community setting is to figure out how to connect with folks to make at least some of that available without charge, without any preconditions, without any agenda.

Trudy did this when she put together a series of community poetry and narrative readings. One of them was in Parlier with Mas Masumoto, Gerry Haslam, and Luis Omar Salinas. We put up the photo essay with photographs from Bill Gillette and some narrative. Here in the middle of winter, Saturday night in Parlier, the library was packed with people listening to the readings from these three valley writers. All of that was free. No charge. She saw that as part of her mission, in the context of the folk, to be able to bring those resources into the community.

In another setting, with the leaders of the Oaxacan self-help groups in Bakersfield, the whole question of non-profit organizations and philanthropy arose. These folks were initially against incorporating as a 501(c)3 because that would limit their ability to do politics. We talked at length about how, at the California Institute for Rural Studies, we created both structures. We started the (c)3 but also (c)4, the Californian Agrarian Action Project, where you can engage in any kind of grassroots lobbying and political work, except work for a candidate for election to a partisan position. Similar models have been used by every sophisticated progressive organization in the country, like Planned Parenthood. Fifteen years later, the self-help groups all have (c)3's. They get foundation money.

We know about these things that many people in the community don't know and don't even know what they don't know. If they are thinking about building organization in this country, these are things they have to know. These communities are deprived in terms of intellectual resources concerning how U.S. non-profit law works. They don't even know how much they are missing.

In community-based research, I want to put together a representative body of what I call "the folks." I don't want professional advocates. I don't want labor union leaders. I don't want people who are experienced speakers with an agenda. I want *folks*.

The advocates are valuable and crucial. They really sharpen what it is all about, and bring forth valuable information on the one hand. But on the other hand, if you think about what you need to say when you knock on somebody's door, someone who is just trying to get through this life by doing farm work, they are not as helpful as folks who are actually living that life.

The advocates play a critical role. You've got to have them, but in terms of trying to design scholarship to understand how to bring indigenous people together, I don't want the advocates in the room. I felt that the non-advocate folks had to speak. Otherwise, the advocacy agenda could take over the meeting and distort an accurate reflection of what the folks themselves are saying. It is a subtle thing, and sometimes people are offended by it, particularly my friends at CRLA and the unions. But my experience tells me that this is the only way.

My lasting contribution to the struggle for democracy and justice is my personal website, where copies of everything I've written is being posted. No registration required, no cost at all, any paper or report I wrote or contributed to can be downloaded by anyone. There are also a few videos that can be viewed online, including one developed by Daniel and his colleagues at the Reedley Peace Center on October 7, 2016.[31]

Emerging from an era of reaction, after the reclamation fight and intensity of the farmworker movement in the fields, a scholarship of political engagement evolved that combined action research, adult education, and community organizing. New approaches, reminiscent of Galarza, were developed in spite of—and possibly as a result of—institutional opposition from the University of California to critical research.

As problems worsened, the roles and methods of engaged scholars evolved and adapted. Blurring distinctions, hybridizing methods, and innovating at the edge of customary approaches, these scholars closed the distance between scientific study and on-the-ground problem solving.

In some respects, their work shifted away from proving the negative—that there were social costs associated with industrial agriculture—as they entered into relationship with local communities to proactively mobilize for change. A university without walls welcomed all. Union halls became classrooms; the fields, laboratories.

If Villarejo represented an educational organizer working outside of formal academic institutions, Isao Fujimoto took on the task from within, at the University at California's flagship agricultural institution at Davis.

6

War Stories

ISAO FUJIMOTO

In numerous ways, I am a student of Isao Fujimoto.

Both Orville Thompson and Isao were emeritus professors in my department while I studied for my master's degree in International Agricultural Development at UC Davis.

As part of the Human and Community Development Department (the historical descendent of Applied Behavior Sciences), all of our offices were clustered together on a wing of the second floor of Hart Hall. Doors always open, I visited them often.

In the decades since, I continually returned to commune with Isao when I passed through town. On each visit, he always inquisitively peppered me with questions. What was I doing? Who was I collaborating with? Isao even typed notes during these debriefs. He cared, like a mentor, a father of sorts, a colleague.

The organization I came to lead—the Central Valley Partnership—was explicitly named after a previous Irvine Foundation-funded effort that Isao had coordinated and facilitated a decade earlier, and which eventually was the topic of his own doctoral dissertation. When we incorporated the nonprofit, I had suggested that name. Each time I hear it, I smile remembering Isao and his previous work, which I aimed to carry on.

There are many weighty spirits who animate this book, but for me, Isao's stands particularly tall. It is impossible to know how many others, like myself, are busy with our work in the world because of him.

Isao launched a thousand ships, and I was one of them.

The Reaping of Societal Consequence

Like the voice of a persistent conscience, Isao Fujimoto's life and work were a refrain of injustices he personally experienced.

His ask: for the University of California "to be accountable to the larger public" rather than serve groups "selected by nature of their manipulative advantages and concentrating of power and money."[1] In this respect, the land-grant university itself represented a structure to be investigated, challenged, and transformed as well as an institution from which to educate students, conduct scientific studies, and partner with California communities.

On June 22, 1973, five years after arriving at UC Davis, Fujimoto organized a one-day conference "to initiate the redirection of the priorities for University research."[2] Along with faculty and administrators, the event also drew the nucleus of the emerging sustainable agriculture movement, including small farmers, organic producers, consumer groups, and environmental organizations. In his speech at the end of the conference, Fujimoto said:

> The over-riding concern is that the University cannot continue to allocate such a high proportion of its resources in the name of growth and efficiency, to tackle priorities for the benefits of limited audiences as those involved in production and corporate agriculture—without eventually reaping serious societal consequences.[3]

Just as Goldschmidt had warned of the consequences to rural Californian society if the agricultural system was economically consolidated, Fujimoto later cautioned the state's foremost land-grant university about those same industrial forces and the negative effects of agribusiness manipulation and influence on its scientific inquiry.

In subsequent years, Fujimoto personally experienced the pressure applied by these forces due to his prominent role as a movement leader.

Persistence over Adversity

On April 13, 2007, Fujimoto gave a lecture to UC Davis graduate students and faculty. He titled it "War Stories I Have Lived to Tell: 40 Years of Encounters with Community Development and Sustainable Agriculture at UCD."[4]

During this lecture, he discussed his upbringing and education:

I will briefly mention my own background. I grew up on an Indian reservation. The reason I was on that Indian reservation was because of the Alien Land Laws. The Alien Land Laws were passed in 17 states.

They were directed against Japanese farmers who were very efficient. The law denied Asians citizenship and the right to lease or buy land. No Asian could become a citizen of this country until 1952. That meant Chinese, Filipinos, East Asians and others.

The Indian lands were under federal jurisdiction and the Alien Land Laws were state laws, so the Yakima Indians rented land to the 125 Japanese immigrants on their reservation. That is where I was born. I grew up there. I learned insights into isolation there.

We got yanked out of the reservation when the war started. We were sent to the concentration camps. My introduction to California was the Tule Lake concentration camp in Modok County. People came to California for a lot of different reasons. I came via the camp.

When we got out of camp, people started to scratch for a living again. One of the common routes was to be a share farmer, and that is what we ended up doing. We became share farmers and grew strawberries. After about four years, we were ready to become independent. We started renting our own land.

Then I left to go to Cal. The town that I was living in was called Coyote, population 150. All I had to do was go out on the road and wave to stop the Greyhound bus. When I got to Berkeley, I tried doing the same thing. It didn't work—I didn't even know about bus stops. My first class was Chem 1A. 350 people. It was double the number of people in Coyote! So that is the background that I came out of.

Two other things were important. I got drafted and sent to Korea, where I was a US Army correspondent. When I was there, Russia sent up Sputnik into space. The people in this country were scared. They were saying, "What are we going to do to beat the Russians?" The answer was to beef up our high school science programs. I was teaching chemistry in high school at that time and got all of these pamphlets encouraging high school teachers to go back to college. You could go to all kinds of places.

It was 1960, only six years since Brown vs the Board of Education said segregated schools were illegal. The Montgomery boycott was just a few years before. People from minority backgrounds could sense something going on. I said, "That's a wakeup call. There is this science revolution going

Figure 6.1. Isao Fujimoto, as a student at UC Berkeley in the 1950s. Courtesy of Isao Fujimoto.

on, but there is also a civil rights movement. I can learn both!" So I went to Howard, a black school. Howard is one of a hundred black colleges in the country. All of my classmates were black, except for two nuns from Chicago. I learned about what challenges we were up against talking to these people.

Later, when I left teaching in San Jose, I went to Cornell where I did work in biology for a year. After I took a group of people down to Honduras on a literacy project, I decided to stick it out at Cornell as T.A. for biology. Then I started my rural sociology program and did my field work in the Philippines. Before I finished, my chairman said, "Look, the Davis people are interested in having you come." So I came here.

This is the story.[5]

War Stories

It is said that if we are going to make any sense of what we are doing, we have to know what story are we in. I am going to talk about stories and the story that we are all in together, because we have a lot in common.

I came here and started teaching about 40 years ago, in the Spring of 1967. I was brought here from Cornell to help start a department from what was called Agricultural Education. One of my first instructions was to change some of the courses. UC Davis had been a place where people came to become agricultural teachers for vocational education in high school, but introductory courses like Agricultural Education 10 were getting less and less people. We needed to turn it around.

I looked around campus and found many departments that were split. The Psych Department in Young Hall was split and not communicating. The first floor was bare, but the second had all of these psychedelic drawings. I thought, "Maybe that is what we should teach students. What are the biases in every discipline? What are the revolutions going on?" So instead of Ag. Education 10, I started a course called "Scientific Bias and Social Myth." The course just took off! We put it in the Experimental College at first.

The first year we had 18 students, the second year we had 118, and the third year we had 325 students. I was also brought here to teach a rural society course. The rural society course was not in the College of Agriculture; it was in Arts and Science, in Sociology. I had a joint appointment there. They said to boost the course enrollment, so the first year I had 11 students, second year 55, and the third year 125. I did that. But instead of getting credit, I started getting negative feedback. It had to do with another assignment.

The Department changed its name from Ag Education to Applied Behavioral Science. They then got some money to look at farm labor. The department had never gotten this kind money. They were going to look at the real-life situation instead of the supply and demand side. I put two people out in the fields as workers. They went out from Day Hall at 4 o'clock in the morning to record everything they saw. They found out things from the point of view of the worker. How they are getting scammed. The sheriff's department arrested people, put them in jail, and then had them work for free for people. We realized that something wasn't right here, and it's not just a matter of getting at the truth.

Let me get you going with the double decker bus story. When I first came to Davis, I went to see my friends Juanita and Jerry Brown. They were finishing up their Ph.D.s in Anthropology and were working with the United Farm Workers. Jerry was the research director for the UFW.

I went down there to a strike going on at Giumarra Farms. Right away Dolores Huerta gave me a sign. So I start picketing, going around and talking to Jerry and Juanita. Word got out. When I came back, I got a call from a union organizer up in the Marysville area named Pancho Botelho.

He said, "Hey, perhaps you can help us out?"

"What is the situation?"

"The county has stopped the bus services from the migrant labor camp. Our kids have to walk to school. It's dangerous. Can you do something?"

I said, "Give me some time, I will look around."

In 1967 and '68, Bob Black was the student-body president, and the vice president was Richard Kleker. These guys came up with an idea to start a public transport system here. They wrote to London to get some used double-decker buses and got ten of them! They were sitting out in the garage.

So I asked, "Hey, Bob, what is the chance of getting a bus to help some kids get to school?"

He said, "Sure."

There was a guy named Glen Burch from University Extension who was interested in rural community development. He gave me some money and I hired Molly Freedman as a research assistant. I knew the bus driver too, a guy named Bud Johnson.

Bud said, "Look, I need some help because these buses are high. I don't want to go on the highway and I don't want to go anyplace there may be high wires. Can somebody come with me?"

I said, "OK, Molly will go with you." So Molly went with Bud and they drove that double-decker bus. Can you imagine going 50 miles up the backroads to Marysville, Yuba City, and Live Oak? It attracted a lot of attention! They took the kids to school.

People started to ask, "What is going on?" They started calling into a talk show in Yuba City, and the talk show host located Molly.

He said, "Can you come on the show and answer some questions?"

Molly got on the talk show and talked about why they were there. "We respond to somebody needing help, so we are here. We got the buses for free."

People started calling in who were critical. Word got back to Mrak Hall. It wasn't called Mrak, because Mrak was still alive. It was the administration building.

Mrak really got upset. He said, "Who is responsible for all of that?" He found out that Molly was hired with money given by Glen Burch, and told him to get rid of her.

Glen had no choice. He called me up, "I've got to fire Molly."

Molly didn't take it laying down. She started firing back. She got her friends and started picketing the administration building. They attracted a lot of attention. They were saying, "What is the administration doing? Picking on farmworker kids! Why aren't we helping them out?"

I told Molly, "Maybe there is a cooler way to handle this. Why don't we organize a discussion?" So we had a big debate at Wyatt Pavilion on the social responsibilities of research in the College of Agriculture. About 200 Ag College professors were there. It had Roy Bainer, the Chairman of Ag Engineering, Molly, and myself. (Bainer has a building named after him. All of these people have buildings named after them. Mrak has a building named after him, too.)

The ag press picked up on this debate and the next thing you know, I start getting feedback. The classic one was a letter from the Director of Extension in San Joaquin County saying, "You are persona non grata. Do not come here!"

I figured, "This is going to be kinda tough working here."

A Fujimoto lecture was a performance. Over the years, I have seen many, and most offered similar information, like a stump speech. Yet, each was differently inspiring because no matter how the world had beat me up (and I was always aware that Isao's journey had been rougher than most), I left feeling uplifted.

When Fujimoto taught (a more appropriate word may be "shared"), he emanated optimistic energy. I marveled that he could consistently deliver tales of injustice and challenge, yet constantly smile and laugh throughout his talks. Though we have not included most of them in this profile translation, Fujimoto often says, "All right" and "Okay" in his lectures, sometimes tinged as questions: "All right?" and "Okay?" As if saying, "Are you with me?"

Figure 6.2. Isao Fujimoto. Courtesy of Isao Fujimoto.

He offered affirmations, always uplift, as he sent us, his students, off to do what the Black Freedom Movement organizer Ella Baker referred to as "spadework."[6]

If you think I am exaggerating, and these are not war stories, you tell me later on. But I call them war stories because I felt I was in a real battle here.

One of the reasons is that this area, the Central Valley of California, is unique. The Central Valley is very special. It is the richest agricultural area not just in California, not just in America, not just in the world. It is the richest agricultural region in the history of the world!

The public image of the Central Valley is that the wealth is in agricultural productivity. But I would say that the wealth is really in all of the people that are here. Tremendously diverse. We don't have time to talk about the diversity, but you could go around the world by just staying in the Central Valley. There are Hmong, Mixtec, Zapotec . . .

Now take a look at this map. I plotted the median income of the wealth of the top 50 and the bottom 50 out of the 480 cities in California. Look where 430 to 480 are. Where are one to 50? Look where they are! All the wealth is on the coast: San Francisco, the Bay Area, L.A., San Diego, Orange County. And where are the poor ones? They are in the interior of California, pretty much all in the Central Valley. And the poorest ones? The bottom five are all in Fresno and Tulare counties.

There are about 3,000 counties in the country. If you ranked them according to agricultural productivity, the top ten usually have almost all the San Joaquin Valley counties. Numbers 1, 2, 3 for the last fifty years has been Fresno, Tulare, and Kern County. Yet you have on the map towns like Huron and Mendota in Fresno County, the richest agricultural county in the whole country. The poorest cities in California are also there. That's called a contradiction, to have poverty and wealth in one place. This is why it is very important to really start examining these kinds of questions.

Usually this work is done by rural sociologists, because they raise questions about the humanistic side of any issue. I found out that there were no other rural sociologists in California at all, not just at UC Davis. The UC System has three ag schools—Berkeley, Riverside, and Davis. But there were no rural sociologists. I discovered I was alone, and said, "Where are the other rural sociologists?"

After the debate at Wyatt Pavilion, I started doing some digging. I said, "God, what constitutes this climate?" Then I came across this article by Richard Kirkendall, published in 1964, in the *California Historical Society Quarterly*. It was called "Social Science in the Central Valley of California."[7] Hot dog! I read it and what it was about. It was a story of the Goldschmidt study. What Kirkendall did was to analyze the study. All of this communication between the Bureau of Agricultural Economics, Walter Goldschmidt, and Paul Taylor.

I read through all of the footnotes and found one footnote that said, "The California Farm Bureau passed a resolution saying there should be no rural sociology taught in California." Ah, ha! So, as a result, here's California, the largest agricultural state in the country, and no rural sociology. You go to places like Cornell, Wisconsin, Missouri, Illinois, they are all land-grant schools, big ag schools that have big rural sociology departments.

I came across some other articles. One was by Gregor, who taught geography here. He wrote an article called "The Plantation System of Farming in California." Zounds, I realized he was right. He pointed out the contrasts between the west side and the east side of the valley and how you can tell the difference between family farm operations and large corporate scale operations. Earlier, I had read another amazing book by Thomas Kuhn called *The Structure of Scientific Revolutions*, because I was thinking what it was going to take to change the mentality and atmosphere here. The book commented on the major changes in science and what it took to change them. For instance, Galileo was a guy that said the Sun doesn't go around the Earth, the Earth was only one of its satellites. We are going around the Sun. Boy the people in Church attacked him. He got blasted. So the question was, "What did it take for the people to come around and say Galileo was right?" Kuhn analyzed all of this. I read that and got more of a sense of the reality of working here.

I felt like I better get some advice. I went to see three people who had been identified with doing work to improve the quality of life in rural areas, especially rural California. These were Paul Taylor, Henry Anderson, and Ernesto Galarza. Paul Taylor was on the faculty at UC Berkeley. Then, Henry Anderson had been working on one of the first union efforts in 1960 before Chávez started moving on UFOC and UFW. He had a regular program on KPFA on farm labor. The third guy was Ernesto Galarza. Ernesto Galarza was a historian with a Ph.D. I went to see these people. I told them, "I'm new to UC Davis. I'm doing work on rural poverty, but I am getting a lot of flack. Could you give me some advice on how to approach this? What is the best way to do work here?" They were very kind. They all talked to me. Ernesto was in San Jose. Henry and Paul Taylor were both in Berkeley.

They all gave me the same advice! Everyone said the same thing summarized in two words: Get tenure! Everybody said, "You better figure out how to survive." They told me the reality I was up against. It was a real education.

All of this was happening very fast. The whole thing about the debate and Wyatt Pavilion, that all happened within the first year that I was here. I wondered to myself, "God, how are you going to move on this?"

Applied Behavioral Science

After the Wyatt debate, Alex McCalla became the Dean of the College of Agriculture.[8] He was sympathetic. He said, "I'll get money and we'll put in three positions to get the Community Development Program going." I started bringing people together and had these courses for undergraduates.

It was a three-course series. 151 was *Research*. I taught people how to go to any town and look at a plot of land, like a gas station, and find out who they bought it from, who they owed money to, if they had any lawsuits against them, etc., and do that without talking to anybody. You do that by going to county offices. You go to the assessor's office, the recorder's office, look at fictitious names, and all that. You can find all this out. When you do this, you can start learning about ownership, power, corporate control, which was the whole purpose of that. The second course was *Community Development*, to learn how you do things. Alright. What kind of things are going on? How do you solve problems? The third one was *Internship*. Go out in the field—don't stay in Davis. Go away for a quarter. I put people out in Appalachia. I put people out on the Navaho reservation. They struck out into the Central Valley. They did great stuff! Here they are undergraduates doing all kinds of stuff about who owns what.

Eventually we started a graduate program here. Alex really came through. We were able to hire three people: Wilbur Sheen, Dean MacCannell, and Miriam Wells. They came on board and we started the graduate program. Before they came, I designed courses. Here is what I did. Rather than say, "Here is a course on research or theory." I asked, "What kind of questions do we want people to be able to answer by the time they get out of here?"

These were the questions behind each of the courses:

1. How can I make sense of the world and explain what is going on around me? You do that by studying theory, but also learning research methodology. Good theory helps you to make sense of what is going on.
2. Another was, "How can I get people to work together to solve problems?" That is the essence of community development.
3. The third one was, "How do I find out what works? Where and how?" You do that by going out in the field, by being an intern with both grasstips and grassroots. There is a big difference between those two, as well as different agencies.

4. We also wanted everyone to be confident about their skills and their passions. We encouraged people to pick courses that would help them pursue their own interests. You could specialize through doing a thesis. The question was, "What can I contribute that draws on my particular skills, passions and interests?"

5. The last one was about skills. Any work with people needs more than knowledge. It is also, how to get along; how to inspire people; how to conduct meetings. The other thing was, how do you keep your sanity? You are going to be under a lot of pressure. I know a lot about that stuff after my first several years here. How do you do work that allows you go home energized? A lot of people go home from work and they are pooped out. This other work is where you feel high.

If you can answer these questions, you can get your degree next week. This was the idea behind the graduate courses in community development.

Another war story was later, after setting up the department and courses, when I was about to get fired in my tenth year. As things started picking up, I was getting even more flack. They were trying to redo the different units at Davis. The Applied Behavioral Science Department had a reputation of having two kinds of students: the most creative on campus, and the most lost. We had all these courses that used to attract a lot of people. Ethnic, Native American, and Asian American Studies were in the department also. The move was on to get rid of these programs. They were going to axe about four people. I was also with Asian American Studies, so I was getting the double whammy.

I wasn't going to stick around trying to save my own skin when I could be doing other good things. So I went to NCAT in 1977. NCAT stands for the National Center for Appropriate Technology. Get this: it was an effort to figure out how this country could save on energy. Get alternative sources of energy. Use solar power. Use geothermal. You hear that today? Right. But that was 30 years ago! We started the program in Butte, Montana. So, in 1977 I became Associate Director at NCAT. I was in touch with all the CAAs, the Community Action Agencies. There were a thousand of them in the country. I was in communication with them all. One of the things I worked on was farming and agriculture. There is a lot of energy use there. I found people in Missouri that were interested in energy conservation and stopping the use of pesticides. I began to communicate with them. That eventually became ATTRA.

At the same time, instead of people in the university, we got a group in the community raising questions about social responsibility called the California Agrarian Action Project. It's now called CAFF, located out on Road 31. They started working on the health problems related to the use of pesticides. Then they found that a Chairman of the Regents, who was a lawyer, was helping a foreign corporation located in one of those ABC islands in South America. This company was incorporated there, and he was helping them buy land in the Delta—a couple thousand acres. CAFF said, "Hey, what's wrong here? How come the university, including the Regents, are willing to help out large entities but they are doing so little for family farmers or workers?" They sued the university. It brought about more change.

At this time, I was still getting all this flack. We had a retreat and I asked Glen Hawkes, who was in Child Development, but also an Associate Dean for the College of Ag, "Hey, Glen, maybe you can help me out. Why have I been getting all this flack all these years?"

You know what he says to me? He was very frank. He says, "Well, first of all, you are a social scientist. The College of Agriculture doesn't have social scientists (usually it's in a rural sociology department). Secondly, you're a minority."

I should tell you something about the climate in Davis. When I first came here in '67, there were very few minority professors here. There were a number of Asians. Some Mexican-American students came up to me and asked if I could be the advisor for their club. There were no Latino professors here at all. No black students could get a haircut in Davis. They had to go to Sacramento. This is 1967.

When he said I was a minority, he meant that people don't like the idea that a small minority guy is asking questions about social responsibility. That didn't go over too well.

Mobilize Networks

I found myself working more and more with groups outside the campus. I got involved with many grassroots organizations.

My home became a headquarters for five of them. The person who started the Farmer's Market, who built the Food Coop, and became mayor later on was Martin Barnes. He was also instrumental in starting the EcoFarm

Conference. The first EcoFarm Conference in Winters had about 75 farmers. It grows every year. Today, 1,000 people interested in ecological and organic farming come to Asilomar. These are the people who had their offices in my house. My house had all the records of the Farmer's Market.

We were trying to put into practice doing appropriate technology. I had people living in the house and they had a workshop making a solar-attached greenhouse. We were raising bees and chickens in the backyard. I dug up the front lawn and we were planting herbs there. The classic one was the rooster cock-a-doodle at 6 o'clock in the morning. We also had a grand opening for the Alternative Resource Center with a bluegrass band in the front yard at the same time. We invited the neighbors, but some got concerned that not only was their property value going to go down because the lawn was dug up. We had all this noise and traffic. So I got invited to the Planning Commission. When I walked into the Planning Commission meeting, I thought, "Hey, this isn't going to be bad at all." Four of the seven Planning Commissioners were my former students. There's a lesson there about the network.

At that time, other people in the world start coming to Davis because of this work. I remember meeting with Bill Mollison from Tazmania. He started permaculture. A person with IFOAM (International Federation of Organic Agriculture Movement) came to meet with me. Henry Esbenshade stayed with me. While he was living with me, he started the Davis Farmers Market. Here are all of these people coming and visiting. We had Schumacher, who wrote "Small is Beautiful," come. He completely filled Freeborn Hall. They propelled appropriate technology, sustainable agriculture and all these movements.

I wanted to mention the importance of connecting up with other people. If you are going to do things in the community, get to know your community. Let them in on it. You can't just go ahead and do things. Community development seems like you are stuck in one place. It's not that way at all. If you do work with community, you are working with all kinds of people.

One of the things we do in this department is sponsor the Rural Development Leadership Institute. We have been doing it since 1985. The RDLI recognizes that there are lots of people working in rural areas with minority backgrounds who never got a chance to finish their education. They stopped or wanted to do grad work and they couldn't do it. So the Institute developed a three-way partnership. The institute starts at UC

Davis. People then go home and find a mentor in a nearby university to sponsor their research project or other project that will help in the community. Antioch College grants them their degrees. That was the three-way deal.

I have a map that shows where these fellows live. It is color coded by ethnicity. Red are Native Americans. Purple are African Americans. Light blue are Latinos, and so on. This is a good way to get a sense of what is going on in rural areas all over the country. They come here every couple of years. The Institute is also a chance for grad students to meet these people. They are board members and fellows. Middle age people of minority backgrounds who are doing a lot of very good work. They are sponsored by groups like the Federation of Southern Coops or the Appalachian Collective. They come here and get a chance to finish their Bachelor's or Master's degree, then go back and work in their community. They work on projects that are helpful to the community where they came from. This is one important network that's right here.

Another network I have been working with is the Central Valley Partnership for Citizenship. We work with emerging immigrant organizations. The valley is rich with diverse peoples. We follow up with the "Civic Action Network" of 150 emerging groups from all kinds of ethnic backgrounds. We bring together people so they can network.

Here is a GIS map referring to all of the 18 Central Valley counties. It is really an organizing tool because if you look at the map, it is colored but it also has a lot of different symbols. By looking at it you encourage people to connect with other people. You can find people with the same ethnicity or the same language. For example, a star represents people working on preserving the traditions of a culture or the arts. Blue is Spanish speaking. Yellow is the Hmong speaking. Orange is other southeast Asians.

There is a real diversity. We take these to a meeting and say, "Look, see if you can find people to hook up with and name some of these groups. This is another kind of network."

Build Community

When you are at the university, you are really busy studying, but don't neglect your avocations and your interests because a lot of those may pay off just as much as your degree. I got my first job after finishing at Berkeley as a

San Mateo County Probation Officer, because I had been on the judo and wrestling teams. Many of the things you do in addition to your studies are important.

I also want to mention something about what we are doing here. You are involved in work called building community. What does that involve? Max Lerner, who wrote *America as a Civilization*, was once asked, "Can you summarize your book in one word? What is American in one word?" He said, "Access." That is the job of community developers, too. You want to improve access for everybody. You don't want to split community. You want all people to have opportunity and be able to fulfill their skills and their talents. You are trying to bridge communication.

How do you do this? One of the things that I learned was from my wrestling coach, Henry Stone, at Berkeley. He was the U.S. Olympic coach at the 1932 games in Los Angeles. He started the season saying, "There are three kinds of people. There are those who work with their hands; they are called laborers. Others work with their hands and their head; they are called a craftsmen. Another person works with their hands, their head, and their heart; that is the artist." I want all of you to be artists. I think that applies no matter what you do, and especially if you are in community development. That is how you want to operate.

So I told you a bunch of stories. It is important to put yourself in the context of stories we come from. That is why I think that it is important to see all of this here.

Near the end of his "War Stories" presentation, in a PowerPoint slide reading "Lessons for Action," Fujimoto offered parting advice in everyday language to the students and faculty in the seminar:

- Don't let three strikes stop you—the catcher might drop the ball—so keep moving, keep going.
- Reflect on what you do: Experience is not what you did or what happened to you. Experience is what you do with what you did or what happened to you.
- If you're looking for something, look in your own backyard.
- Test question for any project: Does it build community?
- Give it your all.

After the lecture, Isao took some questions from the graduate students and faculty. Professor Frank Hirtz came up and thanked him. The department video operator kept recording as the audience bustled out of the room.

With the microphone still on, the camera focused on Fujimoto before his PowerPoint and lecture materials.

He says to himself, "*All right . . . okay.*"

Getting the Straight Dope

The University of California promoted Fujimoto to a Lecturer, valuing him as a teacher.

How did he structure and teach his courses? His ABS Community Development courses and internship were examples of his pedagogy and its purpose. These classes integrated rural sociology, community development, and adult education with applied, experiential learning. An education based upon praxis.

When Fujimoto arrived at Davis, the university asked him to get the students (who were demanding "relevant" instruction and education from the administration), back into the classrooms during the turbulence of the late 1960s. The university relied upon Fujimoto to design curriculum and courses in response to student demands, but also to salvage the legitimacy of their institution in the eyes of their most valued "customers": the students. He accomplished that task, however, at personal cost and sacrifice.

The ABS course series that Fujimoto built was similar to courses that both Galarza and Villarejo taught in the 1960s and 70s at other University of California campuses. These courses emphasized direct engagement and applied learning in community-based settings over extended periods of time.

Internship and fieldwork experiences were supported by classroom instruction in social science methods and academic theory. Undergraduate students learned to be politically engaged as they directly witnessed and confronted social injustices and economic inequalities.

Two course readers written by Fujimoto and his students during this era illustrated the purpose and values taught in his ABS community development courses. The first was titled *Perspectives on Community*. Its first edition was compiled in 1970, with Fujimoto as the sole author. It was followed by a second edition in 1977 by "The Perspectives Collective." The third edition in 1978, which we quote from in this chapter, was by Fujimoto and David Benaroya Helfant. The other reader was called *Getting the Straight Dope*, a collaborative project by Fujimoto and undergraduate students returning fresh from internships in the Central Valley.

In describing an "activist, grass-roots approach," *Perspectives on Community* combined many facets of applied community development theory and practice with demands for social change. It included articles by Mao Tse-tung, Bobby Seale, César Chávez, Walter Goldschmidt, and George Ballis' National Land for People. It also included lessons and reflections directly from ABS 151 students. As a whole, the reader was a compact toolbox emphasizing the theory of applied research in community.

The *Perspectives* reader prepared undergraduate students for community-based internships with underserved communities. In the introduction, Fujimoto and Helfant describe how its purpose and design was different than other community development material:

> This reader is different from most current textbooks on community development because of our activist, grass-roots approach. We believe that a better society will be created only through the efforts of ordinary people working for change in their own communities. This contrasts with the planning model in community development, in which the emphasis is on the power of the professional instead of on the community members. Social change must be accomplished by the people, not for the people.
>
> An important message to pick up is that information is power, and that no research, especially community research, exists in a political vacuum. We can choose to study oppressed people—and either directly, or indirectly, help maintain their oppression. Or we can study the "power structure," those powerful corporations, institutions, and families that have great impact on community welfare. Through information and organizing, we can take power from these narrow interests and assert control to improve our lives.
>
> Another message here is an emphasis on actual experience in the community. Education is a process in which we participate in the community,

not just study it as if it existed in a textbook or in a test tube for student experimentation. We are the community, and our education comes from our action. By doing we learn and as we learn we gain confidence. As we gain confidence, we build strength and power!

One of the reasons this collection is called Perspectives on Community is in recognition that we each bring our unique point of view to a community situation. This is beneficial because it provides a variety of ideas when we work together, but it also makes it necessary to be aware of racist, sexist, ageist, or class biases within each of us.[9]

The reader was built on the idea that ordinary people will create the popular movements for social change. Education, therefore, was needed to empower people through participatory methods. A praxis for change. Through action, informed by scientific information, both learning and social change fed each other.

The biases and assumptions of social science were highlighted in Fujimoto's instruction. He warned that research was imbued with power, which could facilitate community building, but also held the potential to be destructive and unethical. His one-page "How Do We Relate Our Research to the Community?" in the *Perspectives* reader discussed the values and purposes that related "one's inquiry to the needs and sensitivities of the community" while also protecting the community from "being exploited." Fujimoto pointed out that exploitation had resulted from scientific study as he warned that "ethnic communities have become increasingly sensitive to exploitation—both commercial and intellectual." The issue of who benefits from the research was central to Fujimoto's lesson and the basis for determining a study's relevance for both "the researcher and the resident."[10]

The reader acknowledged tensions between the "neutral" position of scientists and the unavoidable intrusion of values into their research. Fujimoto suggested a research approach that bridged some of the seemingly contradictory roles in applied social science:

Objectivity need not mean sacrificing of sensitivity. If the researcher has a commitment to a community as well as to his scholarship, then being objective and sensitive need not be polar opposites. In working in a community, the key word is "with"—to work with rather than on the community. Knowledge, if meaningful, is best shared. The test of its relevance comes in the form of its use to the community as well as in the generating of new knowledge on how people, communities, and society can change constructively.[11]

The scholarship necessitated a balance, feeling one's way into a community-based research setting. Fujimoto's lesson here involved concepts of space and distance, distinguished by the prepositions "with" and "on" to teach the importance of positionality in research. The preposition "with" evoked inclusiveness and togetherness with community partners; conversely, "on" suggested hierarchy and distance above an object of study.

Fujimoto emphasized the sharing of applicable research findings in ways that were useful to the community. He often co-authored academic papers and published informal booklets and accessible pamphlets with his undergraduate students without personal attribution. Instead of promoting himself through singular authorship, he engaged his students in the shared production of classroom learning materials. His self-effacing approach strayed from an academic culture that rewards self-promotion. While Fujimoto's collaborative character led to low formal measures of his academic productivity, it was extraordinarily successful in mentoring and recruiting generation after generation of politically engaged citizen-scholars who applied the lessons he taught over their entire lifetimes. His students changed the landscape of California.

Another part of Fujimoto's educational approach was to construct applied research and experiential learning that cultivated student capabilities over time through reflexive assignments and group interaction. These tasks helped them build identities as social scientists. One example, included in the *Perspectives* reader, was a paper titled "Journal Critique of ABS 151" from an anonymous Native American student. This student had been a community activist before coming to UC Davis:

Many of the Indian students have had a great deal of experience in the community. I am twenty-five and have been active in my own community, as well as in other Indian communities. I have been to jail with two hundred other Indians, watched my friends get kicked to death by the police, had guns pointed at me and had experience with county records. So I don't feel that I need the awareness of problems of the community.[12]

Due in part to her/his/their background, the student had not been comfortable with the group of primarily white middle class students she/he/they was assigned to work with who had not been exposed to the life experiences they had endured. These economic and ethnic tensions were brought into the class through group work, which from this student's perspective, detracted from her/his/their ability to learn.

Student feedback and input was crucial to the development of course content and refining an evolving student-centered research method of community learning and engagement. In this case, Fujimoto put the journal entry into a later edition of the reader. This Native American student's journal concluded:

> I know my community does not need people like my group members to solve problems. We need people with knowledge and a feeling for the problems, not do-gooders. I don't recommend this class for anyone with a background similar to mine, as he will be wasting his time. This class is fine for the beginner. It is geared to make white kids feel good.[13]

What does including this entry say about Fujimoto? What does it tell future students? Many instructors would refrain from using critiques of their own class in later course readers of that same class; yet pedagogically, by doing so here, the problem is confronted and turned into a learning opportunity.

Future Native American students would perhaps see that their experiences were going to be valued, while white students were introduced into the critical perspectives of their own class and racial bias in classroom and community interactions. In his next reader, Fujimoto went even further in incorporating his student's learning as a central component of course material and pedagogy.

The 1973 action research handbook *Getting the Straight Dope* was a collective project between Fujimoto and his students, developed from their ABS 159 internship experiences. Mostly written by students, it was accessible to them. The handbook was copyrighted by the "Davis Motion of the Ocean Super Collective," and as the name implied, the booklet integrated youth culture and humor, even using cartoons, to illustrate some of its themes. Its title page was a handwritten drawing with cursive writing rather than formally designed and typed. Its table of contents framed fieldwork preparation considered most useful by students who had just completed assignments in Central Valley towns.

Getting the Straight Dope was a how-to manual for community-based researchers. It advised and taught undergraduates how to enter the field, view the purpose of their work, interact with community groups, encounter research subjects, and literally how to survive in difficult settings. The advice in the handbook was like getting the low-down from someone between a returned Peace Corps volunteer and a SNCC organizer; for example, there were "survival" tips for "living in a car," finding food, depression and isolation, and "making money." Compared with the *Perspectives* reader, which was mostly theoretical, *Getting the Straight Dope* was practical advice straight from seasoned activist student scholars.

The introductory chapter, "Why This Handbook?," distinguished differences between the roles of "action researchers" and "organizers." The role of the action researcher was to build usable knowledge, whereas the organizer applied the information to make change.

> We are university students involved in community development emphasizing social action research. We received academic credit for our field work and hope this type of program can be instituted in other colleges as well. Thus, this book is intended for other college students who want to broaden their experiences and work for change in society. This type of experience is specifically for students who can devote a limited amount of time with community groups. This philosophy coincides with the intention of the university to extend itself into the community and aid those populations which, in the past, have been disenfranchised.
>
> This is a set of guidelines for action researchers, not an organizer's manual. The researcher's role is less visible, but vital to the whole organizing process. Researching an issue yields information to base action. An organizer needs accurate and useful information on an issue to build a group and to formulate solutions. This handbook comes from the research experiences of eight of us in varied California Valley towns.

Although the particular circumstances of our work in communities will differ from others, we hope to share some ideas for doing effective action research and living day-to-day in a new community.[14]

These scholars were not claiming neutral research positions as they described their "less visible, but vital" roles played through participatory research. They were interested agents trying to change society.

In a one-page piece titled "Some Guiding Assumptions," included in *Getting the Straight Dope*, Fujimoto framed undergraduate field research. This matter-of-fact instruction bounded the difficult field work of ABS internships. His message to the often idealistic student scholars was to be critical, strategic, and reflexive in their fieldwork. His first assumption was that anger by itself won't produce constructive change:

It is not enough to recognize the situation and get angry. Getting something done means expressing anger intelligently and also being conscious of why the homework is being done. This means being alert to asking questions that do not stop at doing something about the flaws we see, but get at systemic causes for the existence of these flaws. It is one thing to be angered by the use of child labor in the fields and to direct energies to developing summer schools and day care centers and another to ask questions about the nature of agribusiness—the corporate welfare system, tax policies and subsidy programs—that are the sources of the manifested flaws.[15]

Fujimoto's concept of "homework" framed this applied research as an assignment like any other, though internships lasted months, required living in unfamiliar settings and enduring hardships. The young scholars were then instructed through a sociological frame to examine, understand, and communicate the "systemic causes" of economic control under agribusiness and systems of monopolized property ownership.

Fujimoto's second assumption emphasized a critical research orientation, the politics of scholarship, and the concept of power:

Another assumption is that information is power and this means being acquainted with every resource around. Knowing and using the system is therefore a must. By itself, information is a neutral resource, but as with all resources in a competitive, materialistic society, the decisions concerning how information is generated, how it is used, and for whom, are very political. Academics and scholars who profess value-neutrality and refuse to recognize the social context out of which they work too often become "part of the problem rather than part of the solution."[16]

Fujimoto engaged the students in a political project. He was clear: they were in a "social context" and could not claim neutrality within their research without ethical dilemmas.

In laying out his third assumption, Fujimoto discussed the purpose of scholarship, maintaining a sustained critical tone reminiscent of Laura Nadar's concept of "studying up."[17] He critiqued conventional social science research and offered the possibility of agency to scholars involved in the "study of change" for those in the most need of assistance.

> Thirdly, we assume that those involved in doing community research, or any kind of social research for that matter, must be able to answer the question, "Whose side am I on?" Community research does not mean mindlessly getting information or doing surveys and getting information on people, who often become the very victims of the information they gave out unwillingly or unwittingly. We have too many examples of research being done on people rather than for them. Considering the nature of power in the society and the role of the University as a closed corporation, this outcome should not be surprising. Invariably, information is gathered on those who are powerless or who challenge the power structure. Such information becomes a very important arsenal in the maintenance of the status quo. What compounds this is that American social science stresses the study of structure and functions of things as they are. Under this orientation, the study of change becomes one of examining flaws rather than the structural and institutional context out of which flaws originate.[18]

To help his students' avoid the danger of exploiting their research participants in their applied research, Fujimoto directed students' gaze to a horizon beyond the immediate setting, with its given assumptions and simple narratives.

If knowledge was power, then how it was produced needed to be interrogated, including the conditions of the university and the processes of scientific inquiry. This instruction centered on being reflexive. Students were to reflect upon their experience and analyze their own conduct and presuppositions within their studies. In turn, this awareness should affect future action and position.

The last assumption began with a point that Fujimoto mentioned at the conclusion of his third assumption: choose significant problems to study by focusing on structural, not psychological, explanations. Rather than being the subjects of a study, many of the working class and immigrant groups that the undergraduates worked with needed social scientists who could help them orient, engage, and counter oppressive aspects of California's socioeconomic system:

> And fourth, we assume that community-oriented research groups need to select priorities. Not every question, interesting and exotic as it may seem, has an equal amount of payoff. It is those questions that will provide further insights into the structural constraints as to why things are so screwed up that demand attention. Work on attitudes, individual problems or psychological explanations that put the attention on the flaws, do not contribute much to pointing out the contradictions and places in the structure that need changing. The role of grassroots research and analysis is to point out systemic causes and to put the results together in a way that is understandable and usable to enable social change groups to move ahead. It is in attention to problems pointed out by community groups rather than what the establishment wants done, to structural problems, rather than psychological ones, that we see as the major area of work.[19]

If community groups were to access scientific data and analysis, scholars' texts needed to be "understandable and usable." Politically engaged scholars needed to coherently translate social science to the community-based groups on their own terms, and for their own needs.

Keep Moving Ahead

From 2000 to 2002, I completed an M.S. thesis at Davis. My study sought to understand why and how white parents had removed their children from a rural California small town's only elementary school. It examined how segregation operated and functioned.

While doing the research, I learned of Goldschmidt's study and the history of the Human and Community Development Department (previously Applied Behavioral Sciences). Orville Thompson (an emeritus professor who had originally founded the department) had an office down the hall from me in Hart Hall. I would stop by to hear stories of the department's beginnings. Isao, though retired, still worked with students, including helping to advise me on my thesis research. Without realizing it, at this early stage, I was being introduced to my dissertation topic.

Doing ethnographic research in Knights Landing, about 20 miles north of Davis, I asked Isao if he had information from previous research in the community. We scheduled a meeting, and he brought me into the attic of Hart Hall. Up there he had saved his undergraduate student's ABS 151 research papers. I remember the space in seeming disarray filled with filing cabinets. He walked straight over to one particular cabinet, opened it and immediately found earlier student papers from Knights Landing. I spent a day going through them, seeing the community I had come to know well through these young idealistic eyes from the past.

Reading the student reports, I felt their exhilaration at their branching out. Off campus. Interviews. Analysis. Entering an expanding world. Who knows where they went and how they made their way, but here was an introduction Isao provided them. I couldn't use their information for my research at the time, but I still have the reports because they were meaningful in other ways, perhaps simply to reference in this book.

A few years later, I returned to graduate school at Cornell for a doctoral degree, influenced by what I had learned at UC Davis. The problems in the valley had persisted, if not worsened. If previous approaches had not resolved the region's problems, what would? What should be the next steps to continue the struggle?

As my dissertation project developed, I once again turned to Isao for advice. On May 27, 2006, I emailed him before my first site visit to the San Joaquin Valley:

Isao,
Hope all has been well. Since I saw you last at the Sust. Ag and Higher Ed. Conference in California, I have been working with Mark Van Horn and

others to try to start a national organization and perhaps co-host a second conference with Penn St. and Cornell. (I am in a doctoral program at Cornell, just finishing my first year.)

I received enough money to fly out to California and head down to the southern San Joaquin Valley this summer. I am exploring the idea of revisiting Goldschmidt some 70 years later—in addition to your work, MacCannell's . . . I will be coming through Davis in the first week of July and likely staying at the Domes. Will you be around?

It would be nice to catch up and get some advice on how to move forward. I am considering doing a public records search, a power structure analysis of sorts, similar to the work you used to have students do for your class. I have been looking at Don Villarejo's "Research for Action" guidebook for advice.

Are you in town around July 7 through 11th? Could you spare some time?

Hope to see you,

Daniel O'Connell

We were not able to meet that summer as Isao was teaching in Japan. I emailed back to say I planned to move to Visalia the following year and network through American Friends Service Committee projects. I also asked about "Getting the Straight Dope" as a research approach.

Later the same day, Isao responded:

Hi Daniel,

Visalia has a small but very fine Friends Meeting. People associated with that meeting have made major contributions to improving the quality of life in the south San Joaquin Valley—from organizing Self-Help Housing to helping kick off the United Farm Workers to preserving Allensworth. Proyecto Campesino started out over 50 years ago and some of the key people are still alive.

The booklet you mention came out of a class that I taught which put undergraduates out in the community for the entire quarter interning in Appalachia, the Navajo reservation, the United Farm Workers, etc. It got revived as Rural Research Access Project which organized the first Eco Ag conference with 75 people in the Winters firehouse but now brings in 1000+ to Asilomar. Martin Barnes revived it in the late 70s and

with it came a number of spin offs such as the Alternative Agricultural
Resources Project, Winds of Change newspaper featuring the drawings
of R Crumb (who used to live in Winters and now is in France along with
Martin Barnes). Barnes was here on Wednesday for the 30th anniversary
of the Farmer's Market which had its records kept in the back room of
my house.
Isao

Many of Isao's emails, like this one, were about networks and connections, introductions and suggestions. He laid out multiple potential
paths of inquiry and encouraged me as I felt my way forward.

On January 15, 2008, I emailed news of my family's arrival in the San
Joaquin Valley. At that time, I continued to explore doing an ethnographic, community-based study:

Hi Isao,
We moved into a home in Visalia this weekend. Good to be back. I am situating myself. Much of the time I have found the AFSC/Proyecto Campesino
office as the best fit. I really enjoy working and commiserating with Graciela Martinez, the director.

There are so many community efforts going on, it feels like Peace Corps
with a bit more resources. I honestly feel more at home here than in academic settings. My time at Davis and Cornell was important and refresh-
ing, but I like getting my hands dirty a little bit more often.

I am considering looking at the intersection of rural governance and
community organizing particularly in unincorporated areas.

I hope all is well and we can meet up soon.
Best,
Dan

Hours later, Isao replied:

Hi Dan,
Welcome back to California! I was in on a conference call with Graciela this
morning.

I just completed the draft of a manuscript on the work of the Central
Valley Partnership. Tom Lyson was my chair and after he died, Charles

Geisler took over. David Holmberg in Anthropology and Ron Mize are the other two on my committee.

I have some material you can look at as you search for a focus on the Valley.

Isao

Unknown to Isao, while at Cornell I had been nudging Tom Lyson (who was also on my dissertation committee) to push through and finalize Isao's doctoral degree.

I told Tom that it was "unfinished business" that should not be left incomplete. Isao had done the work of dozens of dissertations. We needed to honor him for his choice to propel a movement rather than finish his degree when he first arrived in Davis.

Back to the issue at hand, the next day, I emailed:

Hi Isao,

I was in the adjoining office when Graciela was on the conference call. I think the world of her and am so pleased to be able to spend time with her.

I am glad to hear that Chuck took over for Tom on the committee. Chuck was very helpful with me my first year at Cornell (He had kept all of the newsletters of George "Elfie" Ballis' National Land For the People—an interesting journey through history for me).

By the way, I don't know if I previously mentioned it, but I met with Walter Goldschmidt a couple of months ago. Feisty as ever. He is now in an assisted living center in Los Angeles but doing well. I am going to try to meet up with him again soon to hear some of his stories about Paul Taylor and Dorothea Lange. (Last time we talked about As You Sow).

Hope to see you in a couple of weeks.

Best,

Dan

Isao replied the following day:

Hi Dan,

Good to get an update on your plans and interests. George Ballis is still very active. He's made lots of short documentaries on all kinds of social

justice issues as you may have seen on his web site. Good to know you are
in Visalia and focusing on the movements in the Valley. This is an important topic with a long trail of events and sporadic writing so pulling it
together with a current analysis would be a great contribution. Many of
the post WWII players are still around.

Good to know about Walter. One of the books from his library
that he passed on to me to keep or donate to UC Davis is a gem
called *Labor Unionism in American Agriculture*. It details all the
movements in California and especially in the Central Valley prior
to WWII. It was written by Stuart Jamison and published by the US
Dept of Labor when Frances Perkins was Secretary of Labor in
Roosevelt's cabinet.

Last spring I gave a talk to the CD grad students titled: "War Stories
I lived to tell from 40 years of encounters with community development
and sustainable agriculture at UC Davis." I don't recall mentioning this
to you. If you're interested, I can send you a powerpoint that outlines
the talk. The talk is available on a CD.

The time period you are considering for a visit to Davis fits in with my
being here. So let me know when your plans firm up.
Isao

By 2008, I was considering writing a history comparing the valley's
traditions of social science scholarship to the region's community organizing as a dissertation project. I had previously discussed with Isao the
six scholars (including himself) for the study.

Perhaps idealistic, I entered the valley without a firm research project identified and in hand. I wanted the ground to speak it to me, just
like an ethnographer may look for patterns or a topic of resonance after
being immersed in a place. In the evenings I would attend community
meetings of groups like Quaker Oaks Farm, Tulare County Citizens for
Responsible Growth and the Community Water Center. In the historic
African American community of Allensworth, I helped the community
plan for the town's 100th anniversary celebration.

All of the groups were ones that I had close affinity with, so if I could
conduct research and further their objectives, all the better. But no project hooked me.

That spring I emailed:

Hi Isao,
I wanted to check in with you since I will be coming though Davis on
Saturday, April 5th. I hope to discuss your work and experience as a
scholar working within the context of the Central Valley. There appears
to be a history of political pressure in which social research has been
conducted in the region; a history that belies the narrative of scholars
being able to do their work from neutral positions and without outside
pressure.
    Are there other scholars I should be thinking of by the way? Perhaps
Angus Wright or William Friedland?
    Look forward to hopefully seeing you.
Best,
Dan

In his March 19, 2008 response, Fujimoto suggested what would become a central facet of my study. He also continued to connect me with
literature and contacts:

Hi Dan,
Looks like you're on to a topic "the politics of academic research in the
Central Valley of California," or if you go on to something else, at least
you'll have the realistic foundation on which to proceed. The title I gave is
a take-off on the Kirkendall article about Goldschmidt's experience. This is
mentioned in the powerpoint I sent you. I would recommend all the items
there. The Hardin book recommended by Larry Busch has a lot about the
battles researchers had to wage (and lost) taking on issues in Land-Grant
colleges of agriculture.
    Yes, talk to both Angus and Bill Friedland. They can tell you plenty.
Another person to see is Bill Lacy, now Vice Provost for outreach and Intl
Affairs for UC Davis. [...]
    I finished the dissertation on the Central Valley Partnership and
just sent it to Chuck Geisler for his review. I'm attaching the front
pages, title sheet, table of contents, figures and the preface to give
you an idea of what I worked on. If you're interested in reading the 7

chapters I can send you a CD which you can drag the icons on to your computer and use the tracking system on Microsoft Word to inject any questions or comments you want to make. Send me a snail mail address if you want to see it or if you prefer to pick it up when you get here in April.
Isao

A short time later, Isao passed his B exams at Cornell earning his dissertation almost a half a century after leaving to work at UC Davis. In November 2009, I emailed Isao before Thanksgiving:

Hi Isao,
I am finally trying to finish my dissertation after working for a year and a half as Farmland Conservation Director for the southern San Joaquin Valley.
    The focus of the study is the historical scholarship that has occurred in the valley by highlighting the social science and educational practice of Paul Taylor, Walter Goldschmidt, Ernesto Galarza, Dean MacCannell, Don Villarejo, and yourself. In the next week I will visit Stanford's and Berkeley's libraries to research Taylor's and Galarza's papers.
    I had wanted to compare how Quakers and scholars have organized and worked in the valley, but my committee suggested that I focus on the scholars only.
    Hope all is well and I look forward to catching up.
Best regards,
Dan

Late November, Isao emailed news that had already ricocheted crossed the valley: Elfie Ballis was dying.

Hi Dan,
There's been a number of events that relate to the topic of your disserta-tion. Last week, there was a farewell gathering for George Ballis at his home at Sun Mountain in Prather. All the movement people going back to SNCC and UFW organizing days that Ballis documented with his photographs plus current activists arrived to enliven Ballis' final days. He hasn't long to live and expressed a desire to see everyone while he was still alive. George got trained

in photo documentation from Dorothea Lange and carried forth Paul Taylor's work in land reform in California through National Land for People.

Keep me posted on how things are developing for you.

Isao

In March 2010, I had fully engaged in writing my dissertation. Isao continued to receive recognition for completing his own dissertation:

Hello Isao,

It is great that your achievement is receiving the public recognition it deserves. Recently I have turned toward completing my dissertation as well. For the last two years I have been deeply engaged in various community development, non-violence and non-profit projects in the southern San Joaquin Valley. Now, I am putting those on hold in order to finish my research.

My committee recently signed off on my proposal. As you know, I will be looking at the work of scholars in the valley. I am currently outlining and framing this history. For your work, I thought about focusing on your organizing and educating students. Pamphlets like "Perspectives on Community" and "Getting the Straight Dope" will be ideal for understanding this work. [...]

How does this sound to you? Since my dissertation will be examining what I call "pedagogies of scholarship" to look at the intersection of knowledge production and its dissemination, your work and educational practice may be some of the strongest examples of this in the valley.

Again, I am so happy that you have completed the degree as are many others. Hopefully I will be finishing mine soon too.

Best regards,

Dan

Later that day, Isao emailed:

Hi Dan,

Good to hear from you. I'll be glad to discuss and respond to any questions you have regarding your dissertation topic. In addition to the materials you mentioned, I set up a 12 unit field course (formerly ABS 159) which was the third leg of the Community Research (ABS 151) and Community

Development (ABS 152) classes. The 12 unit placement (no longer offered) placed students as research interns with various community organizations to apply what they learned. The three courses mentioned are still on the books but not in the research for action approach they originally took.

An example is the research done on who owns the land in the Central Valley. The posters summarizing all the landowners were used by National Land for People calling for the enforcement of the 160 acre limitation law that would encourage the development of family farms on the westside of the Valley (but never happened due to the continuing control of corporate land ownership and water use).

In addition to working with students at UC Davis, a team of us—George Ballis, Chuck Gardiner from the Visalia AFSC office and I—ran workshops on how to research community power and use it for community organizing. We did this through University Extension training hundreds of War on Poverty workers over a four year period in the early 70s. In the UC Davis faculty archives, there's an interview I conducted with Jim Grieshop that comments on some of these projects. Emmitt Fiske's dissertation can also be applicable to your dissertation.

I'm planning to come to Ithaca for the graduation ceremonies in late May and again in Mid June for a reunion of Cornell students who were part of the CURW sponsored Cornell-Honduras projects that ran from 1961–65.

Isao

On March 24, 2010, I emailed Isao after watching the "War Stories" video. I asked him about the ABS 159 student interns who went to work for NLP and George Ballis.

Later that day, Isao emailed me back. His message illustrated the long-term outcomes of his networking approach to education and community development. The ABS undergraduates went on to continue his work in many different ways:

Hi Dan,
Among the students who worked on land ownership issues in the Central Valley via the full quarter internship included Judy Whalley, Garrett Starmer and Marie Jobling. Judy went on to law school and work with the US Dept of Justice that broke up the AT&T monopoly. Gary became a

Figure 6.3. Isao Fujimoto, at Cornell University commencement ceremony, May 2010. Courtesy of Isao Fujimoto.

minister and Marie was a full time community organizer in San Francisco. She was an associate of Mike Miller, director of the Organizer Training Center and author of A Community Organizer's Tale: People and Power in San Francisco, a story of the rise and fall of people power in San Francisco's Mission District. Garrett and another intern spent an entire quarter working with George Ballis, documenting who owned what land in the westside of the San Joaquin Valley. This was used to push for the enforcement of the 160 acre limitation law which was meant to open up the Valley to small scale farming and build communities on the West side of the San Joaquin Valley owned mainly by corporations and huge landowners. George made a slide show that included the detailed work showing who owned what. This was used as an organizing tool for public meetings. Judy Whalley did something similar, showing corporate interlocks on the power brokers in Shasta County where corporations like PG&E took the land belonging to the Pit River Indians for 12 cents an acre. This became the subject of an earlier Ballis film called "The Dispossessed." Marie worked with the Filipino community in Stockton, turning the at large voting system to one [based upon] districts. This enabled

minority communities to have candidates represented on the school
board and city governments. If you have a copy of Getting the Straight
Dope, look at the authors who contributed to the various sections. Most
are still around.

I'm coming to Cornell for the commencement. I've been asked to be the
Degree Marshall leading the procession from the Arts quad to Schoellkopf
stadium.

Isao

As I wrote my dissertation, I emailed chapters to Isao to review as he
continued offering advice and encouragement through the process.

Nearing the end of my research in early March 2011, I stopped by UC
Davis. I walked over to Hart Hall to meet Isao. The hallway was dark.
Most doors shut and the offices empty. Budget cuts had prevented the
replacement of retiring professors.

It was the usual visit with Isao. Like a reverse interview, he was asking
what I had been doing. What have my interests been lately? What projects am I doing? He typed the information straight into his computer
along with the names of people and organizations I mentioned. We also
caught up on campus news and old friends.

At one point, he mentioned a lesson from his experience working as
a professor. *"Most people wait until they get tenure [to become politically
active]. But when they do that, they get sandpapered. They learn to be cau-
tious and can't get back to their roots."*

Later, he described what the disposition of a scholar should be: *"Play
down the ego. Develop contacts in the community."* Simple advice that was
hard to follow.

Meetings with Isao were always educational; he was teaching, always
teaching.

7

The River

TRUDY WISCHEMANN

"Go talk to the farmers!"

Feeling shy, like an outsider at a party with strangers, I am prodded by Trudy to mingle.

The gathering is an odd mix of Spanish-speaking farmworkers and small-scale family farmers invited into dialogue in an attempt to bridge interests.

Chairs in a circle, we go around sharing our experiences. A lot lost, literally, in translation; progress is going to be a slog. Still, it's a start, and I am introduced to people who will become close friends in future years.

It's the summer of 2005. I am starting my research. Much of my time is spent with the network of Quakers based around Visalia. They are the beachhead from which I move forward. One family is particularly welcoming—Bill and Beth Lovett. They own Quaker Oaks Farm and invited me to stay on the property. Situated in the Kaweah river delta, the farm is on about twenty-five acres adjacent to the Kaweah Oaks Nature Preserve. Stands of enormous valley oak speak to the fertility of the land.

The Visalia Friends Meetinghouse is also on the farm. It is here, on most Sundays, that I see Trudy at Quaker meetings. One afternoon she asks me to stay late and shows me a treasure trove assortment of books, photographs, and memorabilia. These are her heroes—Paul Taylor, Dorothea Lange, Walter Goldschmidt. Over the next few years I learn just how intimately Trudy has been involved with almost every subject in my study.

Their legacy is her work.

* * *

Now more than a decade later, my dissertation completed, Scott and I are doing interviews for this book.

Figure 7.1. Trudy Wischemann's assembly of remembrances, United Methodist Church, Lindsay, California, April 1, 2019. Author's photo.

We arrive at the pristine and manicured, slowly dying, United Methodist Church in downtown Lindsay.

Old churches hold ghosts beyond their graveyards. And so these grounds and buildings, proud and dignified, slumber quietly, nurturing memories of children's voices and the presence of past generations. The lawns are still mowed, edged with precision, dutifully managed by the care of some remaining church elder or diligent groundskeeper.

The community room we enter has been choreographed. One of Dorothea Lange's cameras is on the table. A photograph of Paul Taylor with Trudy. A copy of *American Exodus*, first edition.

Laid out like museum pieces across the room, they are a preface before her story, markers locating Wischemann in the arc of remembrance.

Getting into College

I'm fourth generation failed family farmer.

Grew up working class in western Washington where it's soggy and cold and hard to make a living. My father and family were Republican—working class Republican.

My family moved to Hawaii my senior year of high school, which was an inopportune time. I lost my residency at Washington's state universities, and my dad was not about to let me go to the University of Hawaii because the president of the college was a communist. I'm the oldest child and a daughter. My parents wanted me to go to the community college on Maui where I could stay home and work to pay for my own tuition and books.

From before kindergarten, I had been prepared to pay for my own college education. My parents started a college education fund, a savings account, with my great Aunt Agnes's Christmas check for $5 in 1955. I didn't know what college was, but we started my college education fund then because my dad was sure he wasn't gonna pay for it. From that time on, I was saving for college, not having a clue what that was all about.

I graduated seventh in my class. The school counselors didn't want me to go to community college. So, they started shuffling scholarship opportunities and college applications to me. I filled those out and got a scholarship to Willamette University in Oregon. I went over my father's objections, but I only was able to pay my way a short time. After the first semester the money was gone, and I was working more than I was supposed to work. I gave up after two years.

I was in Salem, Oregon and got involved in environmental work. A Catholic nun befriended me and took me to a writing workshop one day. Together, we got involved with planning processes in town. One evening I went to this public hearing on emissions from the Boise Cascade paper plant on the Willamette River. It was in the high school gym, full of people protesting the emissions.

Every day at 4:00 p.m. the plant emits plumes of sulfur gases that would put old people on the ground. The capital and the Willamette campus are there. Some mornings you get a special deal when it hangs in the fog and just penetrates you. Protestors were demanding the plant's gases be stopped, and a panel moderator wanted them to shut up, referring to us as "agitation." We weren't even people. We weren't agitators, we were agitation.

Only one person made a difference. There was a man who had facts on stack scrubbers and where they had been used in other places. He showed it was possible for Boise Cascade to do something. In the end, we won, but it was only because of that man. I saw him do that and I said, "I want to be able to collect facts." I learned that you could question the world and do something about it, but to do that you needed an education.

That's what sent me back to school. By 1975, I was in Berkeley looking to take courses through Extension as a non-resident. At first it wasn't easy being there with my Oregon habits. Walking down Euclid Avenue I would meet people's eyes. And people said, "You don't do that in Berkeley—look down, look away. You're gonna get in trouble doing that." But I was from Oregon. I met people's gaze.

I wanted to make a difference in the way we live in the world but had no idea what to do. Finally, I found a new interdisciplinary program called Conservation of Natural Resources, where I could make up my own program, take the courses I felt I needed to do something in the world, and they took my previous credits.

I was loose. It was magic.

Meeting Paul Taylor

I met Paul for the first time at a talk he gave on water.

Still trying to figure out where I was and what to do, I was still taking classes through Extension. I thought about being a hydrologist. I wanted to go out and free rivers—to make dams not happen. I went to his talk on water to see how things fit together.

Here's this old man. He's got his eyelids taped up. They don't work because of his Parkinson's. He's talking, and it's absolutely riveting. His framework is based on the common good. All of the illegal and immoral impacts of what is being done with the water behind the dams. He's standing there, this ancient man, trying to tell us they've broken the law. I'm blown away.

Nobody on the Berkeley campus knew him anymore. This is the mid seventies, and people have shifted from being hippies to being dressed for success. They're there for career goals—pre-engineering or pre-med. It's in that transition where we go back, and Berkeley goes back, to being the conservative bastion of business that it was.

As soon as that talk was over, I stood in line to shake his hand. Thanked him for his lifetime of work. Then I literally ran to the Ag library on campus and found *American Exodus*. I sat down and read it the whole night. It was the only book they had with his name on it. I didn't know who this Dorothea Lange was. Who the hell was she? I already didn't think he needed a co-author!

It was the first edition with the words of the people in the endpapers and the beautiful captions below each photograph. Every word and every picture attempt to help the people who were then being swept off the land. It shows how the government's attempts to help people through the Agricultural Adjustment Act actually resulted in sweeping more people off the land. It's a story of America.

The book cemented me. I recognized that these were the people my aunt lived around on her ranch in Centralia, Washington: Okies that went north, and not to California.

The next summer, I'm sitting on a bench. It's on the north side of the campus where the extension of Euclid Avenue comes down and goes across Strawberry Creek below the Earth Sciences Building. I'm in the sunshine studying for a meteorology midterm. It's June, and I'm happy. Feeling good about the exam.

Then I see Paul coming down the walk. He's walking really slowly with his briefcase in his left hand and his cane in the right.

I think about it, and I think about it.

"Should I go up to him? He won't notice me. He won't see me."

I'm sitting there, and then I think, "Yes." I just left everything on the bench.

"Professor Taylor, you don't know me, but I saw your talk back in November, and I just wanna thank you again for everything you did."

"Come with me to my office," he says.

I jammed everything into my little blue cheap backpack, grabbed it up, and turned toward him. He offered me his arm, and we walked that way to his office at 380 Barrows.

He put his things down, turned around to me, and says, "Do you know my wife Dorothea Lange?" As if she's still alive though she had been dead for several years. "Do you know." It wasn't "did you"; it was "do you know my wife Dorothea Lange?"

"No," I said.

He started showing me pictures. He got things out of the file cabinet. He got things down off the wall and showed me. And I'm just going, "Whoa, whoa," because reading the book I had no idea she was his wife. I thought she was some working colleague.

All of a sudden I realize my midterm had started already, and we're on the south side of campus! The Earth Sciences Building is on the north side of campus. I said, "I'm sorry, but I have to go." I ran and aced the midterm because I was high. I was off the ground and didn't have any feet.

I started going back. Once in a while I'd drop in on him hoping it was okay.

At that time I had a job doing housework and kid-watching a few hours every afternoon for a freelance couple, Ted and Shirley Streshinsky. Ted took the photos for the book *Delano*, by John Gregory Dunne. A giant picture of California fields was over their fireplace. Shirley was a writer. And here I am by accident in Ted and Shirley's house looking after their two beautiful children, ironing once in a while, and just doing odd jobs so they can work in their respective corners of the house.

One day Shirley came back from doing an interview with Paul for an article she's working on. She tells me, "I just met the most amazing man."

"Oh, I met him. I've gone to his office a couple times."

"You should go work with him." She was absolutely adamant.

"I don't know what that means."

"Just go, you will find out."

I started going to Paul's office more frequently. Pretty soon, he said, "We need to get you some money for doing this." I had work-study money, so he

Figure 7.2. Trudy Wischemann and Paul Taylor, February 1978.
Courtesy of *The Daily Californian*. Photo by L. C. Valdes.

arranged with his department to pay me for my hours. That's how I ended up becoming an assistant to him. It was never an RA like in graduate school, but he thought of me as his research assistant.

I helped him think; I helped him find things. I typed (he typed beautifully with two fingers, but I had 10 to use). I'd run down to the department office to make photocopies. It was still one of those photocopiers where it was a round surface, so I'd put the books over it. It took some physical ability, and it was hard for him to do that. He was always sending copies of news articles or quotes to politicians or to other scholars. He was part of a big network. I was just helping him send out his stuff.

He was in weekly contact with George Ballis in Fresno, organizer of National Land for People. They were sending things back and forth. He was also in constant contact with Ben Yellen down in the Imperial Valley. So there was correspondence, and I helped him get copies ready to send off. He was active in that network by mail, which we now do by email.

One day he got a call from Paul Wallace Gates, the historian from Cornell, who said, "We need to collect your law journal articles in one place. All we need from you is an introduction." So we started to write the introduction. He would write on that yellow photocopy paper, scratch it off, rewrite, and then hand it to me. I typed it up.

The first paragraph took three days.

When we began, sitting there thinking over the blank paper, he looked up to the top shelf of books behind me and said, "Where's my Bible?"

"Why would there be a Bible there?" I thought.

The next day he came back with a little 2 x 2 yellow Post-it. It had the words of Isaiah 5:8 written on it: "Woe unto them that join house to house, that lay field to field, till there be no place, that they may be placed alone in the midst of the earth!"

I didn't know what it meant, so he explained it to me. "Well, they're just talking about the land concentration. Like we have in California."

What scholar do you know who starts with a quote from the Bible? We've got this whole separation where you don't want to mention the spiritual or religious if you're an academic. It would ruin your reputation.

Turns out, 20 years later, I discover this whole field of land theology that looks at the prophets, including Isaiah, that were screaming about the impacts of land concentration.

Arvin and Dinuba Revisited

I have a Bachelor's degree in Natural Resources Conservation, and all-but-thesis for a Master's in Environmental Planning. For my thesis at Berkeley, I decided to update the Arvin-Dinuba study, devising my own methodology using the camera.

The roots of my study came to me when Paul and I were in Fresno for a hearing on Westlands. George Ballis is there in his overalls. So was Willoughby Houk, a field crop farmer from Firebaugh who was there to challenge the non-enforcement of the acreage limitation, even though he had 2000 acres. He was there against his personal interests. He knew it was wrong. Paul was in absolute admiration.

This was probably 1977. I was sitting there with Paul. Listening to George and Willoughby. Listening to people talk about the Arvin and Dinuba study, I thought, "If people could only see the differences between Arvin and Dinuba, that would break it open. It would take care of everything. Just like the bear went over the mountain to see what he could see, I'll just go with my camera to see what I could see."

Not having seen Arvin and Dinuba myself, I thought I better go look. My mother was coming to visit my brother in prison at Tehachapi, so I rode with her. We went through Arvin on our way down. It was a Saturday afternoon. Bleak. I took a roll or two of pictures, got in the car, and continued to Tehachapi to see my brother. Spent the night. Went to see my brother again. As we're leaving on our way home, I said, "I'm sorry mom. I have to go to Dinuba." My mother was congenial about it, so we re-routed ourselves and stayed overnight in this crazy hotel at Tagus Ranch, where in the middle of the night, there was a fight and the police came. Sunday morning we went to Dinuba. Took another couple rolls of film.

It was real. No question you can see the difference between Arvin and Dinuba. You can see it. You don't have to have scores of numbers. I wrote it down. Got maps. A year later, I did a deliberate documentation with the camera. I took a picture of every church, school, and park. All the neighborhoods. Every business downtown. Every business outside of the downtown. I mapped them. I had them ID'd and located.

Then I moved to New York with a mate. For three years I lived on Long Island trying to make sense of my notebook full of negatives. I'd watch the picture come up in the tray and see what detail I'd caught. I'd write, and when I'd get lost in the words, I'd go back to the negatives to tell me what to do next. It was a really iterative and wonderful process. Eventually I had a large, totally unwieldy manuscript.

I took my big manuscript back to my primary professor at Berkeley. He looked at it and said, "I don't see any difference between the two towns. And you don't have any data on farm size. How can you say that farm size is still affecting the development of the towns?" He essentially sent me back to the drawing board. I knew he was right, but the implication was enormous.

I went back home and said, "Well, it's clear to me. I can see the difference. Maybe I haven't explained it or found the key things that express that well enough. Obviously, I have to get numbers on farm size."

So I contacted both Dean MacCannell and CIRS (the California Institute for Rural Studies).

Researching Agribusiness

I had heard about the Agribusiness Accountability Project that Dean, Isao, Don, and other people were part of. They'd been doing it since the seventies.

Years before I left for New York, I had gone up to talk to Dean about doing some work with them. We sat down in the grass. I didn't know all the right words to say, and he was totally unimpressed. It was a very short interview. I don't think he spent 15 minutes with me. I tried to use Paul as my entrée, and it didn't do any good.

Later, when I was in New York, I contacted Dean again about a possibility of coming back to work with him. I had an interview with him then, and he was very embracing. He said, "Come. Come. Come. We'll find a place for you. We'll find some money. Don't worry about it. Just come."

So, I packed up my stuff and my old dog. I put us in this 1974 Datsun station wagon that had a rusted-through frame rail on the driver side, and drove back across the country to be in Davis. I had nothing, but it was an opening. I squatted in a one-room shack for a year just to make it.

That's when I met Isao for real. The first thing Isao says to me is, "It's very interesting what you're here for, but why are you wanting to do research? Why aren't you organizing?"

I didn't tell him this, but my brain is saying, "I'm not brave enough to organize. I'm doing research because I want that ivory castle, I want that tower around me. I want the protection. I do not wanna go out there," I thought.

I have always respected Isao. The first time I laid eyes on him was at a hearing on the Westlands Water District. I drove Paul from Berkeley to Sacramento in his little Volkswagen bug. Isao presented preliminary findings from his study at that hearing. Paul asked me to get a copy from him. Isao just gave me the copy in his hands. That was Isao. Paul was interested in it, especially since Wally had never finished his research after the Arvin-Dinuba study was completed. What Wally called the third phase of the study, which was to go and look at a large sampling of San Joaquin Valley towns.

Wally's argument was that because the Bureau of Agricultural Economics was disbanded, and the money went away, there wasn't any support for it. He said he was prevented from doing the third phase, which would have eliminated all doubt about the findings. Wally always said it that way until the day he died.

But Isao goes and does it. And I don't think he had any support. He was working out of Davis though, and as part of the larger research group working together from the seventies, so Isao had some collegial support.

Paul was excited by Isao's testimony. He understood it as the emergence of a cohort of scholars. But it was Paul's testimony at that hearing that I will never forget. I've written about it in my paper "Paul Taylor: A Love Song" that I read at our "In the Struggle" conference a few years ago.

We're in this giant room at the California state resource agency. It's full of agribusiness giants. Full of their lawyers walking around in their tailored, three-piece suits jingling coins in their pockets. The room is full of these people who are there to talk about the Westlands Water District. There are US senators up in front.

And Paul's there, in his little dark blue corduroy zip-up bomber-type jacket. He has dandruff on his collar. He's got his eyelids taped up as usual. Three sheets of typed yellow paper are in his lap—his testimony, which we have spent five days preparing. I typed them.

All he has is me. I'm twenty-eight. I don't look good. I'm terrified. A wimp.

When his name is called, it takes a long time for him to walk up and sit down. Then he gives his testimony. After it's over, the hearing chair says, "We thank you very much for your testimony, Dr. Taylor, but I have to ask you this one question. How are we going to compensate all these landowners if we sell the land at pre-project prices like we were supposed to? How are we going to compensate all these large landowners for their tremendous losses?"

The whole room goes dead quiet. Paul answers, "How are you going to compensate all those people who are unable to buy land and become farmers?"

I will never forget seeing him do that, because it doesn't matter what you have on. It doesn't matter how old you are. That truth just came out. The balloon was broken.

They covered it up. They went back to being important people with their three-piece suits, and their coins jingling in their pockets.

Later, I remember watching Dean get ready to go give testimony at another hearing, around 1986. It was in Sacramento in a university setting, like a conference, with people on both sides of the issue presenting. His studies showed that the large farms were detrimental to the rural communities. Juliet was in the room, too.

I was watching him, and his hands were shaking. One of the reasons I was in Dean's sphere was because he was so sure of himself. "At least I know somebody's brave enough to keep doing this. If he's safe, then I'm safe. If he's fine, then I'm fine," I thought. And Dean's shaking!

That was a revelation, because Dean has this wonderful way of presenting—he told the truth, like "I'm going to tell you whether you want to hear it or not." I'm so grateful I saw that moment of Dean being frightened, because I'm frightened every time, whether it's a hostile audience or a safe audience. I'm still frightened.

When I arrived at Davis in October of '85 to work with Dean, they found me a space where I could work. I just started hanging around in his office and helping. Other students were coming in, and I was a part of that group.

When I started, he said, "Finish your thesis." I was sitting there holding all this qualitative information, all those photographs printed from the negatives, laid out on maps, with hand-counted statistics, documented observations that I then analyzed verbally. When I showed him the draft I had written, it was apparent that I was not a scientist. He was discouraged by my writing. "You can't say that," he said, over and over. I didn't finish it under him, though that was the intent.

The Macrosocial Accounting Project was alive but in its last days. They were still building databases for Dean to work with, even though Dean's real love was semiotics. I started by getting variables I needed from the macrosocial database. I helped develop some of the variables, too, because they didn't have good assessments of the size of land holdings. Together with Jerry White, who was a geographer, Dean had said, "Just do a three-mile donut around every town." But the picture that their data told of land holding patterns around each town wasn't adequate to show the influence of the larger farms.

It was skewed because any small-scale farmers that exist in a large farm area are going to be right around the town. It was downplaying the influence of the large landowners. I suggested a new data set that became available at the zip code level. I convinced them that we needed to do the data at the zip code level instead of the CDP level—Community Designated Place, a census designation for data on towns—instead of these donuts. The census data didn't include the agricultural land holdings. The zip code data was a better measure of communities, but had some difficulties too. The biggest problem with doing a statistical examination was getting the land holding data because nobody collects information on the size of farms, and much less information still on ownership versus operating leased land. Nobody was doing that.

I found some data within US Population and Housing census that was measuring households with income from farm self-employment and individuals with income from agriculture. I worked out a way to make a ratio of those.

We started recalculating some of the numbers that Dean had done with the donuts at the zip code level, and compared what we were seeing with those data sets. That gave us the best numbers we had. It gave us a social measure of farm size. It gave us a strong variable.

Around that time, Don Villarejo at CIRS had been trying to make a database about farmers who actually owned land versus the large businesses leasing it. He had a farm structure database. I was starting to get to know CIRS better. I'd heard Don talk about their database on farm ownership and knew it was what we needed to do. Ours was underestimating. We weren't getting good numbers. (Later, CIRS gave me the operational base for my Humanities project called, "Seeing the Invisible: Mega-Farms and the Rural Communities of California.")

I tried to get Dean and Don to work together, but merging them was impossible. I couldn't get those two thrusts moving towards the same thing. I couldn't get them to work together. Each one had enough trouble staying on top of their databases.

In the files that Goldschmidt had given me were correspondence letters between him and Wischemann. The main thrust of them was to try to get Goldschmidt to collaborate with MacCannell on a journal article.

Like other female scholars in that era of male-dominated academic disciplines, Wischemann felt compelled to act as a facilitator or go-between. Over time, frustrated by efforts at fostering collaborative research projects, she eventually found a place doing community-based projects in the region outside of research institutions that were inhospitable.

While busy with the work of fighting for racial and economic justice, even delineating these mechanisms of oppression occurring within institutions and social structures, gender-based bias and discrimination was active, from the start and in systemic ways, within academic research in the valley.

I couldn't get Dean and Wally to work together, either. When I first moved back in '85, two ag economists at Davis had published a paper in *Science* saying the whole farm size thing was a bunch of hooey. The Arvin-Dinuba study was full of shit, and these were the reasons why. So I'd contacted Wally before I left New York and said, you know, we need to answer this *Science* article.

Once I got to Davis, Wally came up for a three-day weekend and Dean and Juliet hosted him. It was all very pleasant, but there was nothing that came out of it. It was difficult for them to collaborate. I understood, they had criticized me for being territorial about the Arvin Dinuba study, but it might be that it takes one to know one.

Wally was unhappy with Dean for using the term "Goldschmidt Hypothesis." Wally said, "It's not a hypothesis: I proved it!" Dean found great utility in calling it a hypothesis, though. He was still presenting it to people who didn't want to think about it at all by saying, "Here's the hypothesis. Do large farms make better towns or worse ones? Here's what we got to show, prove us wrong." He was working in the science realm trying not to get killed.

I think the retests sort of undermined Wally's excuse for not going on. I believe Wally felt guilty. This is from a woman's point of view, and I loved every single person in this story. I didn't know Ernesto Galarza, but I loved every single person. I tried to understand who they were, and on some (understandably human) level, I don't think Wally wanted to see things progress. It undermined his reason for not having gone on to do the third phase. I think he felt guilty all his life for not having gone ahead and done the study anyway, with or without government support. I don't think he really wanted Isao going out and doing his third phase of the study either.

Everybody has their part to play. Ben Yellen used to criticize Paul Taylor for not being in the valley. "You sit up there in your ivory tower office," he'd say. What if Paul hadn't? What if Dean hadn't kept himself safe enough to get that stuff done? In truth, the semiotic stuff is actually more useful to me as we're de-mythologizing agriculture. That's what I'm doing from the pulpit.

What if Isao had stayed in research and not gone into his real love, which is organizing people? That's the river, that's the current. It will pick you up, and it will take you.

What if we weren't doing what we're called to do? The spiritual harvest out of all of this is, if you don't do what you're called to do, then you have to limp along on the sidelines. I'm really sorry Wally felt guilty, especially when he couldn't have ended it. The restoration of the family farm is not going to happen in my lifetime. But I have to push. I have to nudge my fellow congregants and say, "You do care about your neighbor that's going out of business, don't you? You do."

These scholars—Wally and Dean and Don and Isao—they're part of a great cloud of witnesses. Ted Streshinsky who took those pictures of the grape strike, also took one of Saul Alinsky. Alinsky hired Fred Ross. Fred Ross found César Chavez.

All part of a network. The river. A fountain.

The River

This thing keeps moving in this sinuous river.

The river is this subject that has found every one of us. Paul didn't grow up to challenge agribusiness. He stumbled onto this through his affection for smaller farms, and understanding the value of rural life being from Iowa.

Even though he was from a town family, he also had family out on a farm. He worked there growing up. He understood the value of it. When Paul stumbled into that topic and started to look at it, it swept him into the current. He gave his life to it.

The current is a moral part of our country's existence. It's equality. It's justice. To get spiritual, it's the work of God. It will always be there. We pretend we are for truth, justice, the American way. We pretend we're doing great things while we harvest the resources of others for ourselves. God doesn't want this. We should share. That's the current.

It's no accident Paul started with Isaiah in his book. When I saw those things together, I became convinced that the river has a spiritual dimension. It's there whether we pay attention to it or not.

I just preached on Luke at church. It's the moment where Jesus is riding the donkey colt into Jerusalem. It's Palm Sunday and everyone is triumphant.

The Pharisees tell him, "Shut those people up." And he says, "If they were silenced, even the stones would cry out." That's the river.

The reason I set these out on the table—these books, the photograph of Paul and myself working, Dorothea's camera—every single piece has been a guide. They explain what I'm doing through a spiritual frame, not just a rational or intellectual one.

Let me tell you the miracle that happened while I was doing my Humanities project. I had applied and got a grant with the California Council for the Humanities (CCH). It had me running up and down Highway 99, getting hooked down here.

I was contacted by a man named John Pitney, a Methodist minister from Corvallis, Oregon. Grew up a dairy kid. Became a minister. His vocation became applying Christianity to the rural situation, to the land and environment. He introduced me to land theology.

He'd heard something about the study. Somebody had recommended me to him. He wanted to have this Forum on Church and Land in Fresno in '91, but by the time we got all the people together and did all the planning it was February of '92.

Pitney was working primarily through songs he wrote. He tapped the power of music, which brought up my roots. All of a sudden there was also a place to be a musician, where songs hold all the power there is. He's singing the truth. Doing it in funny, different ways, cracking people open with music.

At that point, I was still secular. I was not going to waste my chips on religious people. But it was a chance to put up my photo exhibit, fulfill the requirements of my grant, and talk about the Arvin-Dinuba study, which I still did really badly.

During that four-day event, I saw what he was talking about, the potential of working with churches. The valley has all of these religious people who are hard. But in the forties the churches got behind the support of the acreage limitation and against the chambers of commerce. Back then the churches joined in on our side, maybe they would again.

That was the beginning. I felt a need for some kind of faith, and after I moved down here in the summer of 1993, I began searching for a place to find it. I went slow at first. It takes time to find a place to be in a small town. Then one Christmas Eve, I went to the Methodist church because I knew the pastor, Dick Pitcher, from planning the church and land conference.

Figure 7.3. Trudy Wischemann, at the second Kaweah Land and
Arts Festival, November 2010. Photo taken by John Greening.

Later I attended the Presbyterian church. The minister there was Tom
Elson. He responded to my questions. I learned from him. It hit me that my
work has been handicapped by my faithlessness. By thinking I have to do it
all myself, I was too afraid to go forward. I start things but can't finish them.
Understanding of the power in that river, that I had been trying to do without, but that I need.

I was raised to be absolutely and unfailingly suspicious of religious people. That's only reinforced in the university. I had a lot to overcome, and was
worried about drinking the Kool-Aid.

Through these years, the Quakers became a refuge, an anchor for me, just as the Reedley Mennonites are an anchor. The Quaker faith is really where I find a faith home and a religious community that I feel part of. I'm a little uneasy with Methodists simply because I don't buy all the theology. I expect to be pointed at as a heretic and thrown out at some point. But this is also where there's a possibility of rebuilding within a structure.

The mainline churches in the valley are almost dead as faith communities. This Methodist church is almost dead, and the Presbyterian church is almost dead. But this is where the work has to happen, out here with these communities. I came back to the Lindsay Methodist church because they had no pastor at the time. There was an opening.

One of my goals right now is to have another Forum on Church and Land in California. Some of the people are still alive who participated in the first one, and I want other people to have a chance to experience where their faith and their existence comes together.

The churches are part of that river, but also a venue to do work through. Not a paying venue, but they are a venue. That's why I'm preaching right now, and working to get credentialed enough that they'll let me talk.

The Sunday before yesterday I was preaching in church. My sermon was on "Giving Up Silence for Lent." The silence of being afraid to talk. Afraid to speak out. We see our neighbors disappearing to immigration raids. We see the olive growers got no contracts from Bell-Carter. The dairies are going down. The groves are getting pushed out, and we sit here silent. We need to give up silence for Lent.

The month before, I preached on epiphanies. The epiphany of the Arvin-Dinuba study was smack dab in the middle of that. I preached it, baby! And the month before, the first one in January, was on remnants. How God uses remnants. We feel like we are leftover scraps. We feel like we are dying, pieces too weak to get up.

Remember, Nehemiah rebuilt Jerusalem with remnants that were left over from the exile.

Building Up Remnants

People down here are afraid. They're afraid to speak. But there are people who have spoken, and shown you can do it and still survive.

One of the reasons that I write a local newspaper column is to show that you can write what you think and not get killed. There's a terrible temerity that is actually part of a respect package. People are afraid it won't be respectful if you speak up.

In the book that I'm working on now, I'm trying to present the great cloud. I want to show people who believe that academics do not give a flying you-know-what about us that in fact, people in the ivory tower, and in other places, have sacrificed to care about us. And maybe we haven't cared about ourselves enough.

We're trying to contradict and demythologize these misperceptions. To show the great cloud of witnesses who came from academia. Scholars who crossed over out of their comfort zone, out of their fields, into other places. People who have written about agribusiness and community, and who write about it today.

Phil Leveen is part of that cloud. He paid the price for working on this. He lost his bid for tenure at Berkeley in the Department of Agricultural Economics. Paul told Phil, "Get tenure first." But the times wouldn't wait. It was the Carter Administration, the time when we were trying to see if we could write rules for the enforcement of the acreage limitation. Phil went ahead with his research, produced critiques of the economies-of-scale argument, gave testimony, and lost his bid for tenure. He deserves a place. He's got a berth in the great cloud. He ended up working as a consultant, then a home builder.

Merrill Goodall is definitely part of this. Merrill served on the California Water Commission. He sat on boards with these people. He was there. He was giving his wisdom. Merrill is a hero. He did advocate, but it was easy to miss. Merrill was quiet. He was generous. He was spiritual. He was Ruth Bader Ginsberg.

There are women in this story. Martha Chase was Paul's legal researcher. She tried to get a state job after she graduated from law school. She's a full-fledged lawyer. They wouldn't touch her with a ten-foot pole in Sacramento. She ended up, I believe, working as a hospital attorney. When she was having trouble finding a position, Paul was afraid that working with him had put a limitation on her. Her research was central to one or two of his law journal articles.

A troubling part of this story is the recognition that women were often institutionally barred from formally credentialing into positions as scholars and professors during the early twentieth century.

Even as much as Paul Taylor recognized the extraordinary talent of his partner Dorothea Lange, he had to do somersaults to even hire her as a "typist" in order for her to produce photographs for their research. Walter Goldschmidt's wife was instrumental in assisting his valley research, yet was not fully recognized for her contributions.

Later, Juliet MacCannell and Merna Villarejo, both renown scholars in their own right, undoubtedly experienced the pressures and burdens of their partner's work while substantially supporting their spouses.

Wischemann recognizes the gender bias in the story because she lived it, and negotiated within its limitations.

She chooses to speak as a woman back to the men, including us.

Anne Loftis wrote *Witnesses to the Struggle*. She is the daughter of a respected historian, and a historian in her own right. A labor historian. She was assisting Paul, but she didn't go out into the field. As I disappeared to go to Long Island, she came in and helped him pull together that volume of his labor articles. She helped him pack up his office and get the stuff to the Bancroft. Can you imagine doing that? I can't imagine doing it!

I saw Anne after I came back from Long Island, at a conference with Dean in Stockton. I saw her sitting at a table, and I went over to her. I squatted down next to her, and I said, "Anne, I don't know if you remember me." She says "Oh, Trudy." I said something about being in Paul's office, and she said, "Not a day goes by I don't think of him." And tears welled up in her eyes.

Thinking back about Paul, one of the most important things I got from working with him was the sense that I am not inferior. I had problems with feeling inferior with every other man I worked with. Never with Paul. There was never a sense of his superiority. It had nothing to with him. His passion had nothing to do with being Paul Taylor. It had to do with the subject. It had to do with getting the information out. As long as he could get the information out, he would do it. It was the subject. It was the cause of rightness.

That's why whenever I work on my book, I don't sense my inferiority, I don't sense my weakness. I don't sense the fact that I didn't finish my thesis. I don't sense that! I sense my wholeness. My proper place, that I'm still doing what I'm supposed to be doing. That I'm working on this thing. I'm keeping my part of the river moving. I'm doing my part in the river. That was really the magic of being with Paul. And I think that's why the river continues.

This story has been constructed as a fight, and Paul was a soldier. You see that from his experiences in World War I. I saw that in the way he always told me about being gassed. It's David and Goliath, which I think has something to do with my inability to work in it. It leaves out the nurturing, organic, development for and of the small farms and their communities. The whole question about what kind of community we live in is really a female thing.

What kind of community do we live in? The guys' concern is, "Do they have a job for me?" There's the old divide. Everybody's worrying about getting a job, and we're all becoming placeless. The whole idea is that a place matters, though it seems like it no longer pertains. The church you worship in matters. The building matters. Things matter. The visceral physical community wasn't really in the purview of any of the scholars, except Isao. And frankly, I think that was the reason that Wally, Dean, and Don looked at Isao's work and said, "Well, it's nice, but it's not usable," because you need numbers to do the fighting.

But if you're trying to organize people, or encourage people to see the importance of what we're building, or what organically works, you need qualities! You need to be able to talk about why it's better for kids to stay here, to verbalize the positive. That's where women are drawn. Louise Fortmann at Berkeley worked on the communities in forest regions. She looked mostly at what happened when the forestry industry went from smaller mills to giant corporations. It's looking at the destruction of communities still, but it's the change from the positive to the negative. Louise Fortmann's the only person I know at Berkeley who works on what produces real community.

I don't know if the academy has a place for this thinking, or if it might have a place for it in the future. I don't think the politicians have a place for it. I don't think the young people have a place for it. They're busy with their screens. What possible difference can it make if you've got a place to go, when you're happy looking at your virtual reality. That's an assumption, but you see where the culture is going.

My concern is about the person that gets up and goes out on his tractor in the morning. It's about our need for a connection to place, our food. We have that need, both politically and economically, because when we lose control of our food supply it's over!

In California, the land and water are the connection to place and food. If we lose control over the land and water, we're screwed! So we have to fight.

Really Live in It

Years ago I felt some calling, some instruction that I should be here.

For a year and a half I had been doing the humanities project out of CIRS. I had devised a program around how to look at the negative consequences of agribusiness. What was missing? What could you not see because of this agribusiness frame?

I had a photo exhibit done by an Iowa photographer named Bill Gillette, primarily on farmworkers. I held little events, or I'd just put up the photo exhibit in a library, maybe have a one-day event. Sometimes I'd attach the photo exhibit to a conference that was already ongoing.

As I traveled up and down the valley out of Davis on this project, it got harder and harder to leave Tulare County. I would break down and cry every time I crossed the Kings River. I got so I'd stop at the Kingsburg rest stop and call Bill Preston. He's a geographer at Cal-Poly San Luis Obispo, and co-editor on my book now. Back then, he was a friend. Born and raised in Tulare. I'd call him and say, "Bill, I can't go home." And he'd say, "You'll be all right, you'll be back." It'd get me across the Kings River and back to Davis.

I felt pulled geographically. It's the Tulare Lake Basin. It's the Kings River. The Kaweah River. All words I first heard in Paul Taylor's office. It was a visceral connection. Words that I'd heard that were just words now started having physical properties to them.

One day I was wandering around on the Kings River fan near Centerville. I had gotten out to take a photograph of a sign that said, "No Eggs Today." As I put my foot on the pavement, I heard myself say, "I'm supposed to be here." And I started looking for where I was supposed to live.

A few months later, I was in Lindsay to shoot a burial of their "griefs" from the 1990 freeze. This was November of '92, and I realized that Lindsay is a town that's in transition from once having been like Dinuba to becoming like Arvin. It was another one of those flashes. I looked in the paper, and I found a house for sale.

Lindsay lies between Arvin and Dinuba in two ways. It was in transition from one to the other, and it was also about an hour's drive to each one. I could keep going on my Arvin-Dinuba study. It was the combination—to do something that will teach us about this relationship by being planted in Lindsay, and to continue my research on Arvin and Dinuba.

There's a third thing that brought me here. I thought, "If I'm gonna go and spread this word about land, about small farms, I should be here to reap the consequences, which are most likely gonna be negative. When I was doing that humanities project out in Davis, I had this constant sense of inauthenticity. That I would be down here, spread my little seeds of dissension about the way things are, and then go home. It felt absolutely inauthentic and without integrity.

Here was a chance to really live in it, and know if those things that I saw from a distance were true. Is a small town really a better place than a large city? Do small farms offer a better social structure than large farms?

It was a way to test my own hypotheses.

Welcome to the Water

Saying goodbye, we walk into the sunshine.

A funeral is passing by on the street. The casket pulled by horse-drawn carriage. Crawling by, cars follow in a procession that stretches east toward the foothills.

As we say goodbye, Wischemann placed us in her river.

"It picked you up, Dan. I don't know Scott well enough yet to know where you are in the current, but I suspect the boat left the dock with you a long time ago. Welcome to the water, brothers."

We get in the car and head south across the citrus belt toward Porterville, humbled by the sweep of her story and its current.

8

Cultivate Diversity

JANAKI JAGANNATH

Driving north on the 99 freeway, it feels like Scott and I are leaving the valley.

We weave past big rigs along the commercial corridor. Freight trains, fallowed farms, gas stations, warehouses, and billboards pass by the window along the highway.

We have completed the archival searches and almost all of our interviews for the book. Now we arrive in Davis, an insulated sanctuary, its protected spaces of inquiry and study. Skirting the north edge of the university, we drive down Russell Boulevard to an upscale neighborhood a block from campus.

Arriving early, we wait in the car expectantly. The neighborhood is quiet, it's easy to envision university administrators and old professors safely burrowed within these sedate homes beneath the canopy of mature trees.

Janaki arrives and welcomes us into the large home she rents with other students. A year earlier she left Fresno for law school at UC Davis. She's entering her second year.

Sitting in the living room, we have tea, start the recorder, and listen to her stories.

Back to School

I made the choice to go to law school, and to come to UC Davis, on Inauguration Day, aware we're in a time where respect for the sciences has declined dramatically.

My undergraduate degree is in International Agricultural Development, with a focus on plant sciences. I thought that I wanted to go back to school for an advanced soil science degree. Having minored in plant sciences, I thought about going back to school to study soil since my political frame is rooted in ecology.

But I came to a point where I realized I was already engaged in a lot of legal strategy in the work that I was doing. There's a big divide between people in the Valley who are activists, advocates who don't have legal training, and the people who are lawyers who work with them, who are in the Bay Area and Sacramento. I wanted to shift that for myself and for the people that I was working with, then apply it back in the valley.

The Messy Fertility of Diversity

My upbringing is a muddled immigration mess. My parents came from south India, and they immigrated to the American South.

My father immigrated to rural Louisiana. He then went back to India, got an arranged marriage to my mother, and brought her back to the United States. My father worked in paper mills, so they moved around from little town to little town across the Atlantic coast and in the South during a time when International Paper was building a lot of new boilers across the region.

I was born in Mobile, Alabama, and my brother was born in Paris, Texas, because there was no hospital in Idabel, Oklahoma, a tiny rural town where they were living at the time. When my parents divorced, we moved to San Diego where my mother raised my brother and I as a single mom. I grew up in Encinitas, a little hippie surf town where my uncle was living at the time. The move was a dramatic life transition. If my mom hadn't made that choice, I might still be in South Carolina or Memphis, Tennessee, where my dad lives.

I grew up working for this idyllic farm in North County San Diego where I fell in love with agriculture. Our family friends were a Japanese American farming family, and I grew up running around their farm. I also got politicized around agriculture at that farm because the crew was Oaxacan. I would go back to Oaxaca with them for Christmas posada festivals. I was often in between the Japanese family that owned the farm and the field workers. I grew up in this super multicultural and multi-class community and came to understand how agriculture truly relies on farmworkers. Without them, the farm doesn't operate. That led me into getting interested in social justice in agriculture rather than just wanting to go back and be a farm operator.

I had a political consciousness about agriculture before going to university from life on the farm. One moment that sticks out in my mind was having to give a pesticide handling training to the farm crew members because I was one of the people that spoke Spanish at the farm. Granted, the field workers speak moderate Spanish. They mostly speak Mixteco because they're from this rural part of Oaxaca. So already, the language barrier was bad. Here's me, an Indian girl, giving a Spanish language training to a bunch of Oaxacan field workers that barely speak Spanish. It's just like, wow, this is a mess.

But the moment for me was when I was doing this training. Normally, we were never inside doing anything sitting down with the field workers. It was always—you get to work and everybody assembles behind the packing shed. Tom, the farm owner, would give you a harvest list and you just get out in the fields. So it was awkward. I was standing in front of these guys who are much older than me, and I have a certain father-daughter relationship with these dudes. I was a little squirt that they would tell, "Do this and this thing." Suddenly I'm in front of them, having to give this presentation.

It was 7:00 in the morning, and one of the guys was falling asleep. Poor dude. I asked him, "Que paso, dormilon?," like, "What happened, sleepy-head?" He answers, "Yeah, I had to get up at 3:00 in the morning in order to drive across the border, because I live in Tijuana." I had known this man for six years, and I never knew he lived in Tijuana. He drove every morning across the border to get to work, worked all day in the fields, and then would drive back home. You know how hard it is to get across the border. It can take two hours.

That is how it is for a lot of field workers working in San Diego. The rent is so much cheaper for them to live in Mexico. It even makes up for the fact that they basically get no sleep, work all day, drive back and forth, and have to pay for gas.

International Agricultural Development

My brother and many members of the farm family had gone to UC schools, so everybody pushed me into doing ag at UC Davis. It was a big deal.

I graduated early from high school and started undergrad a little late to spend some time in India with my grandmother. So I didn't start with everyone, but just slipped in mid-semester. I immediately became a part of the cooperative community. I helped start the bike collective. Without that, I probably would have hated school. A lot of students don't get that exposure, and I never felt societal pressures that a lot of adolescent girls feel. I was just a wild bike punk weirdo. I had a lot of fun in college.

My time at UC Davis was great. I went to school for International Agricultural Development (IAD) as an undergrad from 2007 to 2011. The IAD program was questionably an ag science program. It was a makeshift degree, a blend of economics and development ideology. They teach how modern systems of capital are working to alleviate rural poverty in the world. It was questionable material but that program at Davis is blessed with a few amazing faculty that come from a deep tradition of countering those ideas.

I was lucky to be involved in some research by a professor named Ryan Galt, who started the year before I arrived. A lot of us students, we're like, "Where did this guy come from?" He just dropped out of heaven from Wisconsin. He had this amazing vision for a food systems degree. He taught a food systems class where the whole first third had nothing to do with learning about the food system, it was all self-analysis and trying to understand, "What is my lens when I view the world?" Is it through a feminist lens or through a political economy lens or something else? Where is my internal compass leading me to engage politically?

More than an influence, Ryan invited me to be a collaborator. I worked with him on a paper that was published with Damian Parr about competency development as a form of gauging educational attainment, a pedagogy looking at competencies in sustainable agriculture education rather than conventional grading. I'd been terrible at school basically my whole life, so that was really nice for me. I thought to myself, "Not only can I challenge this whole grading notion, but we can also publish a paper about it."

During my undergraduate years I was steeped in white counterculture in formative ways that I never expected to be useful later on in life. It strangely armed me with this ability to view western society, and find a way to engage it, thoughtfully and artistically, rather than to simply feel the need to protest all the time. I say that with some caution, because so many people from communities of color don't necessarily get that privilege. They don't get the ability to step into activism from a place of feeling accepted and rooted.

I was given that privilege. It's helped me navigate a lot of political systems, the university system, society in general, and not corner myself off with a bunch of other brown people and to have our own party, which I think is also really important, and I do that 80% of the time. But I allow myself a lot of other latitude, thanks to my exposure to white counterculture.

Intercultural Movement Building

After my undergraduate degree, I went home. My stepdad was in the hospital, and my mom was alone. I wanted to be there for her. I also wanted to farm and ended up doing that full time for two years working at Chino Farm, slinging vegetables to wealthy chefs.

I also worked for a couple of nonprofits on the side for other income. I did refugee ag training for the International Rescue Committee in San Diego. And then worked for COFED, the Co-Operative Food and Empowerment Directive, doing cooperative business training with university students. I was doing a mix of stuff for money, but primarily went home to be with my family and to farm.

After my stepdad passed away, I went to India with my mom so we could take care of the last rites. Then I applied and got a scholarship for the UC Santa Cruz agroecology program at the Center for Agroecology and Sustainable Food Systems (CASFS). It's a six-month program that I saw as a little vacation. It's like a paradise. There's a strange aura about CASFS as a place. It's on this hill at UC Santa Cruz, overlooking the Monterey Bay. It doesn't lend itself to a lot of engagement with the rest of the world, which was part of my critique of it. You don't really learn anything about farming, but you live in cool tent cabins and get to interact with all these people from around the world. I'm not sure if the program was useful for me, but I appreciated the time that I got to spend at it. After CASFS, I ended up working as a botanist for eight months at the San Francisco zoo. It was a strange year of my life that was spent doing nonsense.

From there, I decided to apply to work at California Rural Legal Assistance (CRLA) in Fresno. When I was in San Diego, there was this judge named Claudia Smith who came to the farm all the time to buy produce, and specifically figs. I would always go out and harvest her specific basket, and she would talk to me. She had started numerous CRLA offices across the San Diego-Mexico border doing work with Guatemalan immigrants. I didn't have to have a law degree to work in legal services, she told me, "You just have to have your head on straight and have your heart in the right place, and you can do it." I also knew of CRLA through Martha Guzman Aceves. When I was an undergrad, I was a student rep on the Ag Sustainability Institute board. It was in its first year, and Martha was on the board with me. We were the only two women of color there. Both Martha and Claudia told me how important CRLA was.

So, I decided to take a leap into a whole new area of work, out of agriculture, botany, and production. I hadn't spent a bunch of time in Fresno. Obviously, I had studied the valley. I had read the Goldschmidt study. Ryan had introduced it to me. He doesn't make you read the whole study, but he goes over the results of it in his class. I had learned a lot about disparity in the Valley through Ryan and the community of people who were in that space at Davis. I have diary entries from my early twenties of these impressions.

Isao was the major influence, though, his legacy of intercultural movement building in the Valley. That was the thing that really drove me into wanting to do work in the region. Layers of immigration stories that have resulted in this incredible confluence of cultures. I wanted so much to experience it. If you ask me what period in time I want to go back to witness, it's early 1900s in Fresno's Chinatown! Can you imagine? Even today, when you go down there, there's Central Fish, with fish smells and the masjid calling prayers. Chinese herbal markets are open, the Oaxacan bakery right there, and you wonder, "What world am I in right now, all these people are here together?"

That's the stuff that really set me off. I wanted so much to experience that when I first moved to Fresno, thanks to Isao's writings. My curiosity was so sparked by the things that he had written, the weaving of intercultural movement as a response to industrial agriculture. I was doing independent research, reading everything that he had written.

I'm not even sure if Isao would remember my name if he saw me, but we've had multiple interactions. I can tell you that if I do see him again and I tell him my name, he'll ask me the same question that he asked me every time. He always asks me what region of India I am from, he always wants to associate my last name with a place in India. He knows geography so well that he can pinpoint where in India my family is from, which is Chennai on the Bay of Bengal, based on my last name.

Arriving in Fresno, I rented a little house in the Tower District. I immediately made a group of friends. I was part of a small group of nonprofits because of my work with CRLA. Mostly young people in nonprofits and environmental justice groups. Regardless of whether you're in environmental justice or immigration or socioeconomic development, everybody comes to these same convenings all the time. It was really fun, and I was so excited to be there.

I had no problem adjusting in terms of my friend group. Historically, I've told myself, "I'm gonna go do my own thing." A lot of people that age think, "Maybe I should think about where I'm gonna set down roots?" Or maybe, "I should stay in my hometown." I never did that. For me, it was, "I'm gonna pursue this political curiosity that I have to the foremost." I went to Fresno and did that.

It was this need to understand the Valley as a place. This backbone of California and of the country. This old forgotten sacrificial landscape. This space that has brought people of every shade together. And a place where the climate crisis is happening. I wanted to be on the ground for these things. I thought, "I can't miss this. I need to see this." I just went right into it and started observing things.

Community Legal Worker

Quickly, I realized how shitty legal aid in rural places is. It's so underfunded. I was hired as a community worker at CRLA, but changed the title to "community legal worker." It is like a minion position in this huge organization. But the community workers are the eyes and ears on the ground for the legal services that are provided by the organization.

As a community worker, we patrol the fields. I'd drive down the 99 and get off on these dusty roads, take binoculars out, and check to see if there's shade cover and if people have enough water to drink. Sometimes you get a call from somebody with a violation, then you go and stand outside the gate to the farm and wait for somebody to come to the gate to talk to you. If you can gain entry, you go in, and basically deal with whatever the situation is.

I did this with the migrant unit in Fresno, which is CRLA's largest office. It's the one that provides the most legal services for things like wage theft, sexual harassment, pesticide exposures, all of the day-to-day hazards of being a field worker, which are tremendous. I witnessed people my age frothing at the mouth from heat stroke, waiting for an ambulance to arrive while somebody's on a table surrounded by cantaloupes that she was harvesting. A big bag of them that's her own weight.

Seeing female farmworkers. I remember Avenal in 110-degree weather, sitting on the phone waiting for OSHA to route a violation to a farm. Out of a crew of 60 farm workers, 30 of them are women. They don't have access to a bathroom, because they'd only bring a men's porta potty out. I'd have them bring a porta potty out for these women. This was something that recurred 10 or 15 times, clearly malicious.

I was doing that maybe 30% of the time, and working on the Community Equity Initiative the other 70%. The Community Equity Initiative was the predecessor to Leadership Counsel for Justice and Accountability. It was a project started by a wonderful attorney named Phoebe Seaton and another community worker at the time, Veronica Garibay. They started the initiative at California Rural Legal Assistance specifically focused on bringing legal services to underrepresented, disadvantaged, unincorporated communities.

These un-annexed towns are not incorporated by their local cities for a variety of reasons. Sometimes outright racism, sometimes ecological problems, and sometimes the community hasn't wanted to be annexed. Regardless of the reason, those towns lack local governance while dealing with some of the worst outcomes of pesticide exposures, groundwater pollution, lack of affordable housing, no sidewalks and streetlights, and other basic elements of a safe and healthy life.

Phoebe recognized that disparity early on in her legal career. She actually studied the way that those outcomes impact communities on the entire southern border of the United States in Texas and Arizona. These little towns exist everywhere across the rest of the country. They're called "colonias" in Spanish. We don't need a translation to know what that means. They're colonies. These are places that are extracted for their labor. They are places that have been historically neglected by government in spite of their importance to local economies. Even though they pay taxes, they suffer these outcomes.

Phoebe worked to develop this initiative at CRLA for these towns that were oftentimes created during the Dust Bowl migration into California. Today, they are predominantly Latino communities populated by farmworkers or people that have been farmworkers for most of their lives. When I arrived, Phoebe and Veronica had just left, to take that project out and start Leadership Counsel apart from CRLA. So, when I started, they had moved right across the hall.

I had the vestige of the project that was still there at CRLA. It was strange time, I was in this office by myself, with no legal support, and I would hop across the hall to Leadership Counsel's office and ask Veronica for downloads about policies and learn all this stuff from them. They were still in the process of pulling their old documents out of the office. I was just a random girl from San Diego. They didn't know who I was. Nobody knew who I was. They were very helpful and kind at that time. Lacking legal direction, I had to carve my own path at CRLA. I was frustrated, making close to nothing and working my ass off.

I developed a large case load because I was committed to organizing. Without legal experience, I was doing so much research, so much travel. Yet, CRLA was not allowed to call me an organizer, and if I had said that I was organizing, I would have gotten fired. But I was definitely organizing in the sense that I was going out to little towns, talking to the postman, going to the gas station. Just wandering around, going to the park if there was one and chatting people up, asking, "What's going on in this place?"

One of the communities that I started working in immediately was Del Rey. You all may know of it because Masumoto Family Farm is there, and the town itself is the site of the biggest packing house for Pom pomegranates, one of the commodities produced by the Resnicks. I had gone to a board of supervisors meeting related to some other land use issue, and one of the agenda items was about approving expansion of Pom's wastewater facility in Del Rey.

"Sounds weird," I thought, "Maybe I'm just gonna drive and see what's happening over there." I went, talked to some people, and I got a call from one of the residents to come over and review some financials for the Del Rey Community Service District. I went over to this resident's house, who later became a client of CRLA, so I'm not going to disclose their name.

She was serving as a financial advisor, an accountant for the community, even though she was not paid. There was basically no accounting infrastructure in place in this town. This one woman had been collecting this information for seven years, and here it is. She looked to me, a completely unqualified 23-year-old legal service worker, and asks, "Does this look good to you or not?" She was showing me a history of the packing house wastewater facility co-mingling their wastewater with the residential wastewater services of this town. There was the first red flag.

Figure 8.1. Janaki Jagannath, during lunch break with farmworkers at Chino Farm in San Diego, California. Courtesy of Janaki Jagannath.

Then, she told me about how the community had sued Dow and Shell chemical companies in the early nineties for DBCP infiltration in the local drinking water system. They had seven wells in the town, and two of them had been completely saturated with contaminants. They had received a little settlement from that suit that she had never seen the results of, and basically wanted to start an investigation into whether there had been embezzlement of that settlement fund.

In the end, we find out that the attorney of that community service district had embezzled that entire $120,000 fund. Once this was figured out, he promptly retired and was never to be seen again, which was actually something that you see often in these little towns. The attorney will just take a bunch of money and then disappear.

Cantua Creek and El Porvenir

After my first assignment, I started working in Cantua Creek and El Porvenir during the peak drought period of September and October of 2014.

It was utter pandemonium across the Valley. People's wells were completely running dry. They were calling our different offices, saying, "I live on the corner of this and this street, and I don't have water." Yet, there was no local or state response. We put together a response group with legal services organizations, Self Help Enterprises, and the USDA. We documented the calls we were receiving on a spreadsheet, coordinated our response, and sent the information over to the governor's office. The governor soon announced a state of emergency.

Cantua Creek and El Porvenir started out as shanty towns. A Quaker construction project—Self Help Enterprises—helped turn them into full-on towns with actual houses, pavement, a park, and access to water. They are not farmworker housing on private land but unincorporated communities of Fresno County, so they don't have a city council.

They're on the register of Fresno County as Community Service Areas. There's maybe 140 CSAs in the County of Fresno. For these places, the county deals with the delivery of basic services like municipal waste, lighting, electricity, gas, and water. For the people of these communities, it's a fifty-minute drive to get to the Federal County offices that control these services, including the delivery of water.

The drought brought me there as part of a larger survey of the west side that I was doing with Ephraim Camacho, another community worker who has been at CRLA for 40 years, since the early days. Ephraim said, "The west side is terrible, and people are suffering. Nobody ever pays attention, so let's go take a drive out there." We did, through the farmworker communities of Cantua Creek, El Porvenir, and some incorporated cities like Huron and Avenal.

The landscape of the west side of Fresno County is vast and flat and hot in a way that the east side is not. The east side has smaller irrigation infrastructure. There are central aqueducts, but there's also canals into people's smaller land holdings. On the east side, these canals provide water to much smaller acreage farms. People are there, actually living in the community. When you drive through the east side, you'll see the communities of Del Rey, Sanger, and Selma, and also little pockets of neighborhoods. But when you drive to the west, you just don't see anything for miles and miles and miles.

Occasionally, you do see farmworker housing, which looks like military barracks, that are located on these huge farm properties. Farmworker settlements, like Cantua Creek and El Porvenir, are tiny housing communities in the middle of these vast farmlands growing commodity crops. Almonds, pistachios, cantaloupes, processing tomatoes, grapes, pomegranates, onions, the kinds of onions that get dried into onion powder that goes on Fritos, stuff like that. It's big commodity agriculture, and it feels like you're on Mars.

Our west side survey targeted farmworker communities. It is basically impossible to get information about their lived reality unless you knock on their door and talk to them. There's no government oversight of what's happening. Ephraim knew this from 40 years of doing community work for CRLA. This is especially true for people living on other people's land. It's a step below the governance of an unincorporated community. The basics are lacking. No one regulates the housing standards or drinking water quality. It lacks government.

Most startling is that all of those people are still using propane to heat their homes and have to buy it themselves. On top of that, there are people living out there who don't drink the water that comes out of their tap. They said, "I wash my clothes in it and it smells like sulfur, and all my clothes smell terrible because of this. The water coming out of the tap is brown. It's likely untreated irrigation water that they're getting. So they buy bottled water. They buy those big blue, garrafones (five-gallon jugs) of water. I don't even know how far away they go to fill those up. These were the people who Ephraim and I went out to talk to.

We interviewed around 200 people. It didn't matter if it was anecdotal. We compiled as much data as we could and sent it over to the Office of Planning and Research at the Governor's office. They needed to hear about what's going on here. People were losing labor hours due to the drought in tandem with not having access to clean drinking water and basic elements for a safe and healthy life. The drought was severely impacting these people, more than anyone else.

In our research, Ephraim did Cantua Creek, and I did El Porvenir. After dropping me off, I walked around in the community, and somebody came out of their house with a piece of paper and showed it to me. It was in English, and he asked me, "What does this say? Does this have something to do with child support?"

I said, "No, this doesn't have anything to do with child support. What this says is that the County of Fresno is adding a surcharge for your drinking water every time you pay with a bank card. This notice is saying, 'We're gonna be charging you another two hundred dollars every time you call and make your payment over the phone with a bank card.'"

So, he's like, "Well, my water's already so expensive. What is this about?"

I asked, "What's the deal with the water price?" He goes in and he shows me his water bill, and it's $210 a month for water that he can't even drink.

He's living in one little trailer house, and I think, "There's no way in hell that this person's even close to using the amount of water that this says."

Knock on Every Door

The County of Fresno has a contract with Westlands Water District (the biggest irrigation district in the United States) to purchase water that is then piped into a treatment facility in El Porvenir next to the aqueduct. That treatment facility treats the water to almost drinkability quality but not quite.

The residents, who are rate payers, pay service charges for the treatment and provision of that water in their water bill. In addition, they pay the raw cost of that water, charged by Westlands Water District, to the county. Is this making sense? This is difficult to understand a lot of the time.

What ended up being the case for El Porvenir, of why that water rate was so high, was that during the drought, Westlands went about engaging in contractual purchasing of water to provide to their customers, their members. And in times of drought, obviously, when the federal Bureau of Reclamation is not providing an allocation, Westlands goes shopping for water in other places.

In 2014, they went shopping for water in the peak of this drought. It jacked up their price of water so high that it also increased the water rate for these residents. This then poses a question to all of us as members of civil society: Should residents who are farmworkers in this area, one of the most impoverished regions in California, be paying for the "drought suffering" of Westlands Water District? Especially when those residents can't even vote or run in elections for this water district where they have no decision-making power whatsoever.

The voting structure of Westlands Water District is such that in order to vote or run for the board you have to be a landowner. Each landowner is allowed one vote for each dollar's worth of land to which they hold title. So, if a landowner has a million dollars' worth of land, they get a million votes. This may be why Westlands barely even knows that these communities are there. On top of that, it is Fresno County who purchases water from Westlands. The county is the district's customer. So Westlands never sees El Porvenir or Cantua Creek. They don't know them in their books.

If I remember correctly, land acreage in the Westlands service area takes up a third of Fresno County. Essentially the district's water is used for irrigation, to some of the biggest landholders in California. They are allocated water yearly from the federal Bureau of Reclamation and from a number of other sources. All of these farmers growing commodities out there could and do drill down 2,500 feet for water that they can draw up and irrigate with also.

The problem is, the Westlands is an ecological disaster. The land there is saturated with salts—selenium, all kinds of different contaminants due to agricultural irrigation and the natural geology. A primary barrier to added production in that region is salt. Yields are going down. Their soils are so crappy that they're unable to continue growing their commodities. So, they need clean water from the federal government coming from an aqueduct— clean, cold, sweet, federally subsidized, melted snow. It's what everybody wants to irrigate with to flush out the pollutants.

So, Westlands sells the sweet stuff. That's why you see all of these billboards everywhere that say, "Congress Created Dust Bowl," those Tea Party slogans begging the federal government for water. It's not that they don't have it; they can keep drilling and causing land subsidence. And they're doing that, too, when they don't get the federal subsidy. But those aqueducts provide clean, regular, and predictable (at least what they had thought would be an easily predictable) source of sweet water to irrigate their lands.

The easy story would be Westlands is just price-gouging farmworkers. That they are buying water super cheap and selling it super expensive and keeping the profit, which might be the case. The question we have to ask is, should farmworkers, the people that are working in the fields, be paying the same rates as the huge landowners who have the ability to vote and run in board elections?

Before I went to any meetings, I put in a request for their public records. I said, "Show me your purchase agreements. I want to see how much you're buying water for versus how much it's being sold to Fresno County, so that I can compare that to what rate payers are paying in their towns." This was scarier than going to their meetings, but important because the information tells you exactly what is going on. I asked for a ton of records and set up a time to go to their office.

When I arrived, a robotic Stepford-wife lady brings me into a huge board-room where they hold their meetings. I wondered, "Why would they put me in here?" The table is covered in documents. She says, "Whenever you're done, I'll be waiting outside," and closes the door. They just left me alone in this dim, cavernous room where some of their most important and confidential decisions are made, with all of these papers stacked on a huge table. It was like something out of a bizarre film. And as if to say, "Look as hard as you want, you won't find anything here." This is after driving out into the west side. There's nobody out there, just Ford F-150s everywhere. It's scary, like if something happens to you, there will be no witnesses. Alone in this huge room, rifling through papers, I'm thinking, "Where do I even start with this?"

So, I start by looking into the water pricing situation. This is the part where the local governance law gets really dry and boring. People's eyes glaze over. I never know how to quite explain this in an exciting way. But here in California, Prop. 218 says that any time there is a utility rate increase, if 50% or more of the community bearing the increased rates protests, then the rate increase will not be allowed to continue.

In El Porvenir, there had been a big rate hike, and another rate hike was being proposed. So that guy who was already paying $210 was going to experience another rate hike due to Westlands continuing to raise their rates. Turns out, the Prop. 218 deadline was just around the corner. Coincidentally, I had found out about this situation from that guy only days away from the Prop. 218 deadline—this 90-day statute of limitations period from when the rate increase gets announced and notification letters are sent out to everybody saying there's going to be a rate increase. If you have anything to say about it, then you have 90 days to submit letters or petitions.

I found out around 80 days after the announcement being out, then hustled to educate the community. It wasn't only me. Veronica and Phoebe helped. They didn't come out to the community at this time, but they helped teach me and gave me a presentation to give. I told people about Prop. 218, and its time limitation provisions, "You have this much time if you want to do something." Then it was hands-off for me. A couple residents in the community canvassed and collected signatures. We got letters from as many people as possible.

On the day of the hearing they showed up with more than half the community having protested this rate hike. People wrote their information— name, address, and I don't agree with this rate hike—on pieces of paper. I brought them in a stack to a Fresno County Board of Supervisors meeting where they counted the protest letters. During the agenda item, the clerk went to the back room, counted the votes, and returned announcing that the rates could not be raised because of the successful protest.

Cantua Creek was the first community to deal with this. I think it was 2014. The supervisors looked and said to each other, "Should we just shut off water to the community then, if we can't pay this?" In the end their decision was to "send the item back to staff," unresolved and open. I was like, "That's your solution? You are either going to turn water off or what? You have to give me something else." They were basically saying if we can't pay this money to Westlands, we're just going have to shut water off to these communities.

This is in front of a whole audience. In front of all of these residents! In my mind I thought, "If this was anywhere else in the country, anywhere else in California, can you imagine the public outcry?" I mean shutting off water to at least 500 or 600 people that live in Cantua Creek in the off-season; during harvest season it's more like 800.

When that took place, in that moment, I decided, "All right, this is madness. I'm gonna knock on every door in Sacramento." I determined to speak to each policy maker to see what was possible in terms of getting money from the state government to give to Fresno County so they can pay Westlands Water District to keep the water on in these communities. Because it was peak drought year, we were able to get the state water board to use funds from the state revolving fund to write a $120,000 check and figuratively slip it under the table to Fresno County to pass on to Westlands Water District.

To make this happen, I basically sent a lot of emails and texts to staff at the state water board, telling them, "This is the situation. We have literally no understanding of how this rate setting is happening, because it's not transparent to anybody." I also got on the phone with the federal Bureau of Reclamation and the Department of the Interior to try to figure out if they had any information on how the rates are set. In the end, it appears that Fresno County was blindly accepting whatever rate Westlands was charging them, and passing on the charge to the community. This helps us understand why Buddy Mendes, the Fresno County Supervisor, acted like his family was being attacked when I brought this up, which occurred a year later.

Cantua Creek was the first community to deal with this. Then, a year later, the same issue happens a second time in El Porvenir: rate hike, Prop. 218, protest letters on scraps of paper come in, and rates can't be raised anymore. And this was the iteration with the Buddy Mendes fiasco, after it had already happened once before. What was caught on tape was Buddy Mendes flipping out. It makes sense when you realize he has some connections out there. I don't know if he's on the Westlands board or used to be on it, or he's a landowner out there.

Can we look into what Mendes' connection is to Westlands? I can't believe I don't know this. But I called out this opacity. The fact that we can't understand, and nobody at the federal government level, state government level, or apparently the local government level, has any understanding of why this rate was so high at this time. Why do residents in these poor places have to pay for those costs?

When I called that out, it didn't matter that I was actually pointing out the holes in Fresno County's pocket. His allegiance to Westlands Water District took over. Something in him snapped. He barely contained himself, and almost got out of his seat to yell me down, saying, "Don't come here in front of me and lie like you are doing right now! I cannot stand that and will not hear that!" He lost it. Something came loose and started rattling around. His deep emotional connection to Westlands Water District took over. He stopped being a politician representing people in his district who are the rate payers. You know, the people who pay for this water.

What ended up being the main problem was not having clear information on how the specific rate is set for farmworkers, the people living in these little towns. Ultimately, we did actually get the attorney general involved to call the federal Bureau of Reclamation to call Westlands and say, "You guys need to set up a committee meeting and talk about your rate-setting structure." More information began to come forward, which we broke down by line item.

An important piece of information was listed under municipal and industrial rates. That's because Westlands primarily sells water to a bunch of farms, which is irrigation water. The water they sell to other guys: cotton gins, a tomato seed company, a processing and packinghouse, the City of Huron, Lemoore Naval Air Base, and Fresno County. Those are not irrigators and are listed as municipal and industrial users. They are the entities whose rates we could not understand.

That's what I brought up in that meeting when Buddy Mendes flipped out. He yelled, "Do you know why the water rates are so high? Because your leftist buddies up there in Northern California won't let them run the pumps. That's why that water is so expensive."

I answered, "Supervisor Mendes, I'm talking about the municipal and industrial rate, not the irrigation rate." Like I could give two shits about the irrigation rate. I'm talking about what people who use this water for drinking and bathing and washing their clothes and, you know, giving baths to their kids, are paying. Not the guys using this water to grow almonds and tomatoes.

That was what our breakdown of communication was about, if that's what you call it. And that happened to be caught on tape. He didn't like me questioning him at all. Moreover, he just didn't even know or pretend to care that there are people using that water for survival, not profit, in the fringes of the county.

During this second time around, a new guy named Brian Pacheco was elected as a supervisor from the west side of Fresno. The issues were still there with the county supervisors threatening to shut off the water as I was scratching on doors in Sacramento to get money to Westlands. I have a voice recording of Pacheco on my iPhone where he looks over to the rest of the board members and asks, "Can we just turn water off to the town? Is that within our privilege to just shut the water off to these communities?" He was a complete and utter moron.

After that, the county's Department of Public Works held the meeting at an assembly hall on the west side. Everybody came out after receiving a notice saying, "You're gonna have your water shut off by Cinco de Mayo unless we figure something out." The county public works presented different scenarios to the community: "We can either raise your rate by this much, or we're gonna have to shut the water off. Would you guys be okay with that?"

Brian Pacheco came to that meeting, and the fury against him in the room was palpable. He literally had nothing to say. He was like, "Sorry, we just don't have any discretionary funds, and this is how it is. You guys need to just accept the water rate hike." His rationale, if you could call it that, was that these towns in community service areas are going to continually be in deficit forever. He refused to look at the structural issue of Westlands holding these communities by the throat. Instead he was like, "Well, the tax base is too small." Basically, you guys are so poor that there's no way we're ever going to be able to give you treated water unless you accept this rate hike now, so that we can get the treatment facility up to working order. He was basically saying, maybe it'll stabilize over time if you suck it up and pay for it now.

I remember a resident at one of these meetings stood up and said, "We come from Mexico, from communities where our towns are run by gangsters. We thought we were coming to the United States to escape those kinds of structures. Now here we are, and we know you guys are a bunch of mafiosos." He was saying, you're telling me that there's no transparency around how these rates are set and you're taking this much money from my paycheck every month! "Ustedes quieren sacar la tortilla de la boca," is what he said. "You guys want to take the tortilla out of the mouth." Like, how could you possibly be charging us this much?

By 2016, the county was feeling very threatened, obviously, after the round two pandemonium. I've never seen that many lawyers out on the westside. Luckily, this was also after that ridiculous clip of Buddy Mendes was caught and went Fresno viral. There was enough embarrassment after that meeting that Buddy Mendes sent a letter to the federal Bureau of Reclamation, being like, "Can you guys please give us a little bit of extra free water?" That was never going to fly, but he sent it anyway, which was nice. Thanks, Buddy. Westlands was also threatened by having all of these eyes on them.

At Westlands next board meeting, the board unanimously decided to reverse all the overcharges to Fresno County, refunding the county the difference of the water rate from the charges assessed since 2011. I was at this meeting, and the chief counsel made a point to look at me and deliver this information to me in a condescending way, as if to say, "Stop yelling, little girl, all you needed to do was ask." This difference was enough for the county to partially pay back their arrears and at least ensure that residents were not receiving pink slips on their doors warning shut off for inability to pay.

With major assistance from the governor's office, we then arranged for a large drought relief enrollment to take place on a community-wide scale, which dropped resident water rates dramatically by Christmas and paid back individual ratepayer arrears. This was critical for two residents—one extremely elderly man, and the other who was my age, dealing with a debilitating heart illness and a complicated pregnancy and suffering a great deal from the monthly stress of her water being shut off when she couldn't pay her bill.

That's not the end of the story. A couple months after that, magically, the county comes back to me and says, "Turns out that the results of our well studies in these communities looks pretty good. We can reach clean drinking water if we drill down 3,000 feet. We just need to tap the Corcoran clay layer and we can access clean drinking water." Interesting revelation for the county to have after being threatened with a lawsuit multiple times and realizing they have no idea how the rates are being set.

Some residents ended up not being able to continue as advocates. One day, a Westlands representative called up a community member on his personal cell phone and said, "We need the names of all of the people that are activists in your community." After that the resident called me up and said, "I could lose my job from this, and so I'm gonna have to stop talking." This was the person that did most of the organizing, such as collecting the petitions. Others, though, became more involved as activists.

Many of these residents are now heavily a part of all kinds of other climate and land-use related advocacy with Leadership Counsel and Community Water Center. Their political capacity building during that time period was critical to them becoming huge advocates for their community in all kinds of other ways. They started a Green Raiteros program and got a grant to buy a community Tesla. Now they have transport back and forth for medical appointments and to hearings of the board of supervisors. They now have a car that they share and pay one person to provide rides every day. Getting to Fresno has been one of the biggest barriers for people to politically participate. Doing it in a Tesla is pretty sweet. Those things are going to keep happening. Once you step into activism like that, I don't think anybody's going to stop.

I would like to document this story through a litigation perspective. What would've happened had we actually been able to litigate this issue at the time? It's something that I think about every day. What could've happened had we worked with one or two plaintiffs from the community to litigate the voting rights issue.

Can we have this undemocratic voting structure at water districts removed in California? It truly is an injustice, an ecological injustice, regardless of how it's rationalized as an economically sound practice, for administrative streamlining or to make sure that people that use the water most have the most decision-making authority. Regardless of its rationale, fundamentally, to govern a precious resource in that way, it's so spiritually wrong. Anybody who hears about it knows that. I want to figure out, how do we attack that? How do we change that?

In the midst of this whole debacle, I left CRLA. I had made the choice for a number of reasons. First, I had no real legal oversight, which is part of the reason why we didn't end up litigating this issue. There was no lawyer helping me out. Another was that I couldn't represent undocumented people, because CRLA is federally funded.

Agroecology

At this time, I was hired as coordinator of the San Joaquin Valley Sustainable Ag Collaborative by six amazing environmental justice organizations: The Center on Race, Poverty and the Environment; Leadership Counsel for Justice and Accountability; Community Water Center; California for Pesticide Reform; El Quinto Sol de America and Cultiva la Salud.

They were thinking about how to collaborate towards a sustainable agricultural policy agenda, developing a strategy of how to advance greater equity in agriculture. They recruited me to help coordinate that agenda, and to imagine priorities with them. They were unclear about how to frame political movement and grassroots organizing around sustainable agriculture in the Valley.

Later I introduced the concept of agroecology to the group as a movement strategy utilized by landless people and peasants around the world. Agroecology, at its center, is a science, a practice, and a move-ment. That resonated with all of these members, and we renamed our organization "Community Alliance for Agroecology" (CAFA). At first a lot of these groups had no idea that there were small farms, tenant farm-ers, and farmers of color growing fresh fruits and vegetables for the com-munity. For many of them "agriculture" was big landowners that don't think twice about polluting the groundwater or the local air, who set their waste on fire and abuse their workers. That was the long and short of what a farmer was.

Thanks to CAFA, that shifted. These groups came together to see that food is being produced by subsistence growers who speak different languages. We found farms that embody those values. One was a little twenty-three-acre farm that belongs to Visalia Friends Meeting, shared in partnership with the Wukchumni tribe. Quaker Oaks Farm is in Tulare County on native Wukchumni tribal land. The land itself is also the site of the Quaker Meetinghouse in Visalia. The farm serves multiple purposes. There is subsistence agriculture happening there, and the land is organi-cally managed. It's one of the few places where there aren't chemicals being utilized for ag production in the middle of the most intensive, chemically-saturated ag region in the state.

The Community Alliance for Agroecology partnered with Quaker Oaks Farm to do planting days and community education. We held "agroecol-ogy crash courses" there, where local farmers and residents came out and learned basic science. We looked at things like the carbon cycle, hydrogen cycle, nitrogen cycle, to understand how those cycles have been fractured by industrial agriculture. We advanced both local strategies and policies that help heal the local ecosystem.

We also coordinated a series of encuentros or meetups. My close friend Antonio Roman-Alcala and I planned the first of these encuentros in Cali-fornia, and it was held at Quaker Oaks Farm. The term encuentro is derived from agroecology movements in Latin America. The inspiration for agro-ecology, for many of us, comes from the Landless People's Movement or Movimiento Sem Terra in Brazil. We borrowed that language by hosting en-cuentros here in the valley, and later in other parts of the state, where we exchange wisdom and knowledge. This first encuentro brought people from CAFA together with a bunch of folks from Santa Ana and the Bay Area. It

Figure 8.2. Janaki Jagannath, at the Reedley Peace Center's "In the Struggle" speaker series, December 9, 2016. Courtesy of Janaki Jagannath.

was an incredible confluence of people in Tulare County. For example, there were landless Latin American farmers from Santa Ana who had been an organizing anti-gentrification through a network of backyard market gardening. It was amazing.

Preparing my transition, I was a part of hiring a new director, Kassandra Hishida, who's an amazing human being and knows the Valley better than I ever will. She's from Fresno and comes from a Japanese and Mexican family with historical ties in agriculture. The organization is continuing to thrive, working on policy, including helping to pass the Farmer Equity Act in 2017, which created a definition of socially disadvantaged farmer and rancher in California. We're now starting to see set asides in state climate and easement programs for farmers of color.

Kass and the whole CAFA crew continue to participate in encuentros, movement building and exchange of ideas around environmental justice in agriculture. I think it's the future for how policies are going to be built. My intuition says agroecology is the way that representation for farmers and people of color in agriculture is going to be framed. Meanwhile, Kassandra is also partnered now with Quaker Oaks Farm to provide hands-on trainings around ecological agricultural practices.

All this gives me hope, and what gives me hope also gives me a sense of urgency. There's such dramatic change to be made in terms of policy when it is linked to community movements with proper organizing tools.

Agriculture Is Culture

Industrial agribusiness is not an impregnable structure.

As an organizer and a scholar, Jagannath entered the valley and in short order began to deconstruct the mythic strengths of the system's representatives, withstanding dismissal and intimidation. Her lessons also show us that there is work to be done within the interstitial, in-between spaces that appear to be margins and peripheries but can be lifted up and centered.

Jagannath delineated the problems she encountered while positioned to defend farmworkers, residents of rural colonias, and the public's interest. An investigator's inquisitiveness and innate curiosity led her to each succeeding effort, whether looking at service district financing, enforcing existing laws to protect workers, or ensuring that segregated communities have clean, affordable water. When needed, her research focused on structural concerns and aimed to delineate systemic problems.

Going further, she learned to innovate approaches to mobilize community in real time during crisis and with little institutional support. She engaged seemingly unmovable institutions with effective political leverage. She played her role effectively and achieved the goals she set out to accomplish.

The solutions she brought forward solved actual problems for residents. Her example illustrates that the work of politically engaged scholarship is not exclusive to professional experts or credentialed academics.

As we prepared to leave, Janaki tells us:

> Agriculture, like Isao Fujimoto always said, is culture. It's not about the dominant, hegemonic idea of agriculture constructed by white people for the purpose of maintaining a posture of power. We have to collectively reimagine and cultivate true diversity from the microbial level up to the societal level in order reclaim that power.

The Valley Opens

Heading south, back to Fresno, we cross the Yolo Bypass. Its levees retain wetlands, waterfowl habitats, and fisheries, mixed within rice fields.

Years earlier, a thousand farmworkers waved UFW banners from the same embankment. We sense their presence, the continuing demand for justice.

The valley opens before us as the sun sets.

Conclusion

When I entered graduate school, my goal was to find new, practical ways to make political change.

Students a generation before me had protested for "relevant" instruction, and I felt an affinity with their earlier demand. In my dissertation, I distilled a set of axioms describing politically engaged scholarship so that they could be applied to future work. Today, I continue to refer to them:

- Practice supersedes theory.
- Hybridize roles and shift positions as necessary.
- Engage problems directly over extended periods of time.
- Hold, carry, and share truth.
- Expect political reaction.
- Pressure indicates relevance.
- Persevere through adversities.
- Leverage legal precedent and public process.
- Design research to interrogate social problems.
- Produce texts for varied constituencies.
- Enable social movements.

These points are guideposts, not an exhaustive list. We hope that future scholars will sharpen and expand them based upon their own experience and interpretations.

The basic idea is that the role of a scholar in society should not be limited to scientific discovery, publishing in academic journals, and teaching on campus. Nor is scholarship exclusively the work of those with letters after their names.

Strategies conform to the ground upon which they are enacted and put in motion. Similarly, applied social theory needs to correspond to and answer actual lived problems. When crises arise, the need for activism becomes immediate. Applicable theory tends toward conjecture without engagement.

The lessons drawn from the San Joaquin Valley's politically engaged scholars show us that they utilized multiple roles and positions in responding to the needs of community. These were adapted from the realities they experienced, community needs identified, and opportunities to achieve through their engagement. They worked, for example, as labor organizers, policy advocates, government researchers, non-profit directors, community development specialists, project facilitators, journalists, community workers, and coordinators of coalitions and networks. They closed the gap between their intellectual work and the lives of people they wanted to learn from and assist.

In many cases, effective engagement to create social and political change took decades, requiring the work of a succession of scholars. Their extended collaboration bridged shared values and common objectives, spanning social movements and historical epochs. Over time, as their understanding matured, they improved tactics, innovated strategies, and refined theory. Intergenerational engagement became necessary for a sustained assault against systemic and structural problems. In these contests over truth, they were obligated to hold their positions until they were socially accepted or convinced otherwise. Along this vein, we find a number of occasions where older scholars, nearing the end of their lives, pass on their intention and extend invitations to younger scholars to continue the work.

In the valley, when political pressure was exerted on the scholars, it often revealed pertinent vulnerabilities in their adversaries. Some scholars, including Galarza, tactically invited attack by baiting opponents. More often, powerful economic interests weighed in on the scientific process attempting to intimidate scholars and muddle or falsify results. In retrospect, we see that political pressure indicated that the scholars were hitting their mark. If they had identified a meaningful target and there was political reaction, it was because a worthwhile vulnerability had been breached. As a result, politically engaged scholars should expect political pressure and prepare for, in Galarza's words, "some pretty rough treatment." Simply knowing this may offer some solace when the attacks come. Certainly, by that time, relevance will no longer be a concern.

Earlier in the struggle, scholars like Taylor and Galarza appealed to legal precedent and public process as strategic maneuvers. In Taylor's case, the efficacy of his defense of reclamation law was buttressed by the inability of agribusiness to easily violate the law's mandate. Given this circumstance, his tactic of writing law review articles was an obvious leverage point and strategic choice. Galarza's strategy, in the case of the Braceros program, was different—his goal was to overturn an unjust law rather than encourage enforcement of an enacted, democratic one. Public Law 78 undermined wages and working conditions for farmworkers. In effect, it was an agribusiness subsidy where the costs were borne by the most vulnerable and exploited workers in the economy while the benefits accrued to the wealthiest and most privileged in society. The strategy's success shocked the agricultural industry, forcing growers into collective bargaining negotiations. Soon, the first labor contracts with farmworkers were signed in California.

Research, combined with community organizing and pedagogies aimed at empowerment, threaten power structures. Within this potent mix, valley scholars framed their research within adaptable, participatory methods. While scientific research in the valley produced groundbreaking findings, it was the on-the-ground political engagement that contributed most to the base-building work of educational empowerment, organizing workers, and securing community. Some of these innovative approaches occurred as new fields of academic study emerged, such as action research and ethnic studies. For over a decade, Galarza used scholarship combined with direct action—popular education, litigation, and strikes—as methods and tactics to achieve economic justice. Later, Villarejo adapted investigative methods while partnering with social movement groups, while Fujimoto integrated politically engaged research into his classroom pedagogy and incorporated extensive undergraduate fieldwork into his community studies curriculum. Recently, Jagannath organized farmworkers within the context of an extreme drought, negotiating multiple levels of bureaucracy while confronting county officials aligned with agribusiness interests.

The production of texts mirrored the diversity of methods. Valley scholars published in a wide variety of venues and styles, including popular magazines and with visual representations from photographs, films, and maps. They adjusted their voice for different audiences and altered publication venues for strategic opportunities. All told, the publication of books may have been the most durable, long-lasting, and impactful. Academic journal articles and government reports were not easily accessible to community members who needed the information most, sometimes during pitched battles.

These scholars carried forward past lessons for us to remember and learn from, and which they applied as they entered the fight. They often problem-solved with community at moments of upheaval and crisis, building understanding of institutions and structures through shared struggle and engagement. They tapped into their awareness of history, scientific training and personal experience to theorize ways for future generations to move ahead. In some respects, they did our homework for us.

In the past, when movements faded, grew tired or appeared defeated, scholars became holders of memory and keepers of flame. They stored knowledge and taught lessons, keeping a sometimes waning fire alive by gathering new fuels to reignite cooling embers. Their belief in specific values—including justice, equity, and democracy—grounded their findings and rooted their commitment to endure.

Social movements are inseparable from community aspirations. The work of politically engaged scholars is directly linked to these movements for change. Their unique roles, both tactical and strategic, assist in defining complex systems and mapping organizational structures so they may be transformed for the public's benefit.

In the San Joaquin Valley, the discriminatory systems and oppressing structures are characterized by industrial agribusiness.

Agrarian Democracy vs Industrial Agriculture

The history of scholars who worked in the San Joaquin Valley offers an analytical framework for researching the effects of large-scale factory farming on rural communities.

At the center of this book is the Goldschmidt hypothesis and Mac-Cannell retests. Both of these scholars set up conventional scientific studies to answer a researchable problem: Is industrial agriculture detrimental to rural society? The definitive affirmative answer to that problem was first answered through their empirically-supported findings, then substantiated by subsequent research. (It may be argued that an additional layer of validity now resides within the narrative of collusion and corruption that weighed down upon all of the scholars who dared ask questions contrary to the privileged agricultural interests in the valley and state.)

The challenge still before skeptics in the scientific community and proponents of monopolized agribusiness is to disprove these findings. As MacCannell states in his letter to Goldschmidt, *"If they want to hold to their position, they must do research, using essentially the same design, in which they introduce new variables and demonstrate that the farm structure-community conditions relationship we have discovered is spurious. Any lesser response will reveal the criticism to be politically motivated. We have not yet moved to this stage in the debate."*

Law breaking by large landowners and major corporate interests became more blatant over time. This lawlessness combined with callousness to suffering and institutional racialized oppression as concurrent themes in the valley. No more foreboding lesson emerges from this history than the destructive power of the purposeful undermining of democracy and public process. Democracy, expressed in the rule of law and ability to bring forward factually substantiated information into the public arena, was systematically undermined and corrupted. In response we see the valley scholars shift tactics to direct engagement, community organizing, and critical pedagogies. Galarza, Villarejo, and Fujimoto were experts in these educational approaches and methods of organizing. Today numerous other emerging scholars, like Jagannath, are innovating in concert with community members to address immediate crises and structural problems.

We designed this book to be a guide for future work. The earlier methods and approaches described here can now be joined with modern technologies to analyze and engage similar problems in other regions. The Midwestern United States offers such a context today. By the 1980s, the economic foundations of the Midwest were already being restructured and consolidated in similar ways to what occurred in California. As this historic center of American agrarian democracy imploded, family farmers were driven off of the land. Bankruptcies and suicides became indicators of economic restructuring, a real-time experiment perpetrated through government policies and financial institutions at the expense of working people, family farmers, and the public's interest.

Today we reap what was sown. Previously, the Midwest was one of the nation's most progressive regions; today is one of the most reactionary. An entrepreneurial middle class has increasingly disappeared from rural farming communities. Main streets atrophy into empty shells, deserted and slumbering like old ghost towns. Conversely, California's Central Valley is mobilizing in intersectional ways, drawing strength from its traditions of multiracial organizing and the rich diversity of peoples who are coalescing after generations of struggle. Nationally, these differing regional movements and social dynamics may meld together in coming years integrating research analysis, policy solutions, and organizing campaigns.

A simple take-away frames our understanding of industrial agriculture and agrarian democracy—*an equitable economy is both a necessary condition and measurable outcome for a democratic society*. The presence of pollution, hunger, homelessness and poverty are explicit indicators of political corruption at the most basic level. Conversely, without a broadly secure society, the ability of people to meaningfully participate in civil society and democratic government erodes.

The Future Is Now

On June 7th, 2018, just after California's primary election, I posted a message on social media. A previously unattainable seat in local government had been won by a large margin—a surprise early outcome heading into the general election.

After 2016, there was a re-doubled commitment to electoral politics from activists and organizers across the valley. While the demographic make-up of the region had transformed (much of it a result of demand for agricultural labor from agribusiness over the preceding decades), these changes had not yet fully been expressed in local elections.

Now, the numbers were on our side. Each day new voters were being registered, mostly from the Latinx community who worked in the fields and packing houses, or who witnessed their families experience that hardship for a generation or more. They had directly experienced systemic racism and structural barriers barring advancement, no matter how hard they worked.

Elections have consequences, and so we set out to increase voter participation and to identify better candidates. Getting progressive

representatives into local office was a simple, effective, and straightforward strategy of propelling political change.

Here is the message I posted:

Tulare County's First Latino Supervisor

My friend, Eddie Valero, was elected to the Tulare County Board of Supervisors on June 5th 2018.

Sometimes history changes and the world reverberates to the seismic
shift, in this case however, perhaps due to Eddie's extraordinary humility
and sense of service, his victory is being marked by the quiet acknowledge-
ment of his friends and supporters.

All of us, though, awaken today with the thought "Did you feel that?" or,
in other words, "Did this really happen?" Make no doubt about it, young
people from across the valley's broad spectrum of diversity lifted Eddie up
on their shoulders as they walked his district's many working class neighborhoods, week after week, door by door. And along with Eddie himself,
they did this with joyfulness and smiles.

Perhaps because of the harshness of the valley, we tend to take successes in
stride and without fanfare, but do know that an earthquake moved California
two days ago with its epicenter in the farmworker communities of eastern
Tulare County (and especially Me and Martha's restaurant in Dinuba!)

So many of us truly love Eddie with all of our hearts, now we get to
share him with all of you. When you get a chance, stop by and give him a
big hug and hearty thank you.

And the next time you drive through Cutler and East Orosi, know
that these communities are rising, and hopeful, and beautiful—and they
elected one of their own.

What I had not put into that post was that Eddie Valero was also a
fellow doctoral student in my program at Cornell University, the same
one in which Scott is a faculty member and professor.

Eddie began his campaign for county supervisor before finishing his
degree. Prior to his entry into politics, I encouraged him to keep writing, as he was "ABD" (all but dissertation), and so close to completing
his doctorate. Seeing his near total commitment to community service,
I worried that a situation similar to Isao's arrival and overcommitments
at UC Davis could sidetrack Eddie from finishing.

Once he was in the race, however, I quieted my prodding. Eddie was doing just what he needed to be doing. What was the degree for but to prepare someone to make a run for office or assume some other similar responsibility? The times would not wait, the opportunity opened, the need was there. I sensed, however, that Eddie did not calculate like this—he simply followed his heart toward the most meaningful ways to serve his community.

In the general election that followed a few months later, a wave of young progressives, many from communities of color or immigrant backgrounds, swept into office. We won sixteen of our eighteen targeted races. Two congressional seats were flipped. I participated directly in the election mobilizations, which were overwhelmingly positive, even joyous, and community-led. An awakening had occurred.

Now a Tulare County Supervisor, I asked Eddie to describe himself as a scholar. *"I am a hybrid—less of a scholar and more a person who does local community engagement. I am an activist scholar."* His activism is community engagement, and he prioritized those relationships and that service over academic work.

Eddie's approach to scholarship and political engagement follow in valley's tradition yet he shifted the objective—scholars were now becoming elected leaders.

The Next Generation

We have been on a journey.

A storyline of testimony laid out as an exploration of inquiry, a presentation of findings, an affirmation of values. A view into a contest over the structure of rural society.

Succeeding generations of scholars have presented their academic research and personal stories to answer past questions, and the ongoing arc of their collaboration offers hope in our struggle to achieve a just, equitable, and democratic society. Their lessons and findings are before us for the next generation of scholars to apply, build upon and carry forward. We finish this book by highlighting a few outstanding questions—perhaps the seeds of problems yet to be picked up in future years.

In 1991, Trudy Wischemann submitted an interim grant report to the California Council for the Humanities. Titled "Seeing the Invisible:

Mega-Farms and the Rural Communities of California," she concluded her report by quoting Merrill Goodall giving a public lecture on June 13 of that same year. In his address, Goodall rhetorically asks a series of still-pertinent questions:

> California's new political economy is so far not studied extensively by social scientists. We haven't learned to ask: Who benefits from the development of land and water resources? Who pays the costs of development, who is hurt? What economic and political mechanisms facilitate the control of benefits and costs? What are the social effects of large-scale, absentee-owned agriculture? What regional benefits and costs are associated with water transfer systems? Who should vote in a democratic polity—the resident and registered or the non-resident owners of property?[1]

His line of questioning has us recall Jagannath asking, "*Can we have this undemocratic voting structure at water districts removed in California? . . . Anybody who hears about it knows that. I want to figure out, how do we attack that? How do we change that?*"

A straightforward question, an object of inquiry, always opens pathways for engagement and research. The paradoxes associated with institutions like the Westlands Water District offer an invitation and opportunity to investigate. There are so many similar problems to be examined and solved in regions like the San Joaquin Valley, where systemic, institutionalized, and structural oppression is occurring.

We recognize a new generation of scholars and organizers currently moving into frontline advocacy positions and leadership roles across the region today. They join ongoing, campus-based researchers at Fresno State University, UC Merced, UC Davis, and other colleges and universities. All are part of a movement to transform the region's history of racism and its skewed, corrupt power structure.

This groundswell is increasingly led by the sons and daughters of farmworkers. These local leaders—sometimes without formal university training—are naming and analyzing the problems they experienced and have known over their entire lives. Community members are experts in their own sophisticated ways, and their experience is foundational to the work of organizing and mobilizing communities. Everyone has something to offer.

Figure C.1. Janaki Jagannath, with the Ballis map of the Westlands Water District. Courtesy of Janaki Jagannath.

Solutions always reside within problems. Unjust and formidable power structures hold internal contradictions, yet it is necessary to enter them to discover these vulnerabilities. Once inside, we can create dissonance—hemorrhages weakening seemingly impenetrable walls—and find allies to exploit openings.

More powerful still is the opportunity to participate in democratic movements and build alternative structures to realize racial justice and foster a sharing economy. Integrate economic production to achieve equity and justice. Regulate capital to serve local community. Create land trusts, build food commons.

We know that monocultures threaten complex, self-regulating natural systems, yet are also troubled when narrow, didactic problem-solving approaches stifle social movements before they become dynamic.

Diversity, within human, agroecological, and natural communities, offers a way forward where communities can learn and build together.

As you get started, know that the struggle is won by refusing to surrender.

ACKNOWLEDGMENTS

In the Struggle has been a collaborative endeavor.

A story told through many voices, the book's subjects are also its narrators who offer testimony of their shared experiences, lessons, and commitments. In this sense, and many others, we acknowledge the scholars whose lives and work we lift up and center—Paul Taylor, Ernesto Galarza, Walter Goldschmidt, Isao Fujimoto, Dean MacCannell, Don Villarejo, Trudy Wischemann, and Janaki Jagannath. In chronicling their collective journey, we learn from each of them in unique ways and join them in common cause.

Well aware of the history of censorship around the book's subject matter and previous scientific findings, we were attuned to the values and principles of its publisher. In New Village Press (NVP), and especially Lynne Elizabeth, we found a publisher that we trusted with the book's stories. NVP also bridged our desire to be in conversation across transdisciplinary arenas and multiple audiences, including scholars, practitioners, organizers, and activists. The birthing of this book arrived after a very long gestation, and its publication starts another life entirely with our hope that it grows and thrives. Subsequently, our developmental editor, Layla Forrest-White, helped us to wrestle the book's unwieldy set of voices and cast of characters into a stronger storyline. Her background, training, and activism enabled her to understand and advise us on how to frame a complex multi-generational narrative involving numerous settings, speakers, positions, and objectives.

The work of scholars is embedded into every aspect of *In the Struggle*, which evolved from a doctoral dissertation. Sofia Villenas and Gil Gillespie were the other two faculty members on that dissertation committee, and both of them were involved in crafting the early ideas that coalesced into the book. Colleagues at both UC Davis and Cornell contributed weightily to the book in a myriad of ways. Karen Watson

Gegeo at Davis and Tom Lyson at Cornell were especially helpful at illustrating how to stir up "good trouble" within sometimes staid institutions.

We thank the staff at the UC Berkeley's Bancroft Library and Stanford's Cecil H. Green Library who assisted us in orienting and navigating the archives of Paul Taylor and Ernesto Galarza. Also, Dr. Julie Zimmerman, a Rural Sociology professor in the Department of Community and Leadership Development at the University of Kentucky and historian for the Rural Sociological Society, was especially helpful in navigating historic RSS conferences and papers. And a special note of thanks to the Office of Engagement Initiatives at Cornell University for providing funding for travel, interviews, and archival research for the book.

As this book goes to print, a new generation of politically engaged scholars is at work, in the San Joaquin Valley and many other areas of the world. We are with you in the struggle to improve the lives of rural peoples—farmworkers, farming families, and agrarian communities.

Finally, we acknowledge the love and support of our wives and partners, Dawna O'Connell and Donna Lupardo, for the time our work has taken us away from home, your counsel and advice, the assistance in matters large and small.

NOTES

INTRODUCTION

1 *As You Sow* was originally published in 1947 by The Free Press of Glencoe, Illinois. It was also published in the same year by Harcourt, Brace and Company of New York. A positive review listing Harcourt, Brace and Company as the publisher appeared in *The New York Times* on July 6, 1947, under the evocative headline, "The Earth and the Fullness Thereof." The Harcourt, Brace and Company version features a powerful blurbs by Carey McWilliams and Alice Tisdale Hobart. Despite the positive review in *The New York Times* and these high-profile jacket blurbs, the 1947 edition was not popularly known. Goldschmidt's studies were effectively buried until a new, expanded version of the book was published in 1978. It is that later edition that we use and quote from in this book.

1. BAPTISM BY FIRE

1 Trudy later told me the person Goldschmidt couldn't remember is Merrill Goodall. On his research about California water policy, see especially Merrill Goodall, Timothy De Young, and John D. Sullivan, *California Water: A New Political Economy* (Montclair, NJ: Allanheld, Osmun, and Co., 1978).

2 Walter Goldschmidt to Paul Taylor, May 14, 1940, Box 7, Folder 7: Goldschmidt, Walter Rochs, 1913–, Paul Schuster Taylor papers, BANC MSS 84/38 c, The Bancroft Library, University of California, Berkeley.

3 Draft "Statement for the Committee on Small Business" sent to Paul Taylor by Walter Goldschmidt, Box 7, Folder 7: Goldschmidt, Walter Rochs, 1913–, Paul Schuster Taylor papers, BANC MSS 84/38 c, The Bancroft Library, University of California, Berkeley.

4 The two problems and their related questions Goldschmidt was asked to take up in his research were: Problem 19: "What modifications, if any, of the existing statutory limit to the size of land holdings that can receive water from irrigation works constructed by the Bureau of Reclamation should be recommended with respect to the Central Valley Project?" Problem 24: "What effect will the project have on agricultural economy and rural life in the Central Valley? . . . What effects on urban and industrial patterns and functions? Which prospective effects will tend to promote the public welfare? Which will tend to impair the public welfare? . . . How, in short, can the project be made to serve the best interests of the public, in the Valley, the State as a whole, and the Nation at Large?" Quoted in Emmett Preston Fiske, *The College and Its Constituency: Rural and Community*

Development at the University of California 1875–1978 (Ph.D. diss., University of California, Davis, 1979), 261.

5 Draft "Statement for the Committee on Small Business" sent to Paul Taylor by Walter Goldschmidt, Box 7, Folder 7: Goldschmidt, Walter Rochs, 1913–, Paul Schuster Taylor papers, BANC MSS 84/38 c, The Bancroft Library, University of California, Berkeley.

6 Ibid. See Fiske, *The College and Its Constituency*, 261–264 for more detail on the formulation and analysis of Goldschmidt's research.

7 See Mary Montgomery and Marion Clawson, *History of Legislation and Policy Formation of the Central Valley Project* (Berkeley, CA: USDA, Bureau of Agricultural Economics, 1946).

8 Draft "Statement for the Committee on Small Business" sent to Paul Taylor by Walter Goldschmidt, Box 7, Folder 7: Goldschmidt, Walter Rochs, 1913—, Paul Schuster Taylor papers, BANC MSS 84/38 c, The Bancroft Library, University of California, Berkeley. The article Goldschmidt is referring to at the end of this passage is Richard S. Kirkendall, "Social Science in the Central Valley of California: An Episode," *California Historical Society Quarterly* 43, no. 3 (Sept 1964): 195–218.

9 Quoted in Kirkendall, "Social Science in the Central Valley," 198.

10 Walter Goldschmidt, *As You Sow: Three Studies in the Social Consequences of Agribusiness* (Montclair, NJ: Allanheld, Osmun, & Co., 1978), 416.

11 Ibid.

12 Draft "Statement for the Committee on Small Business" sent to Paul Taylor by Walter Goldschmidt, Box 7, Folder 7: Goldschmidt, Walter Rochs, 1913–, Paul Schuster Taylor papers, BANC MSS 84/38 c, The Bancroft Library, University of California, Berkeley. Also see "Summary of Findings" in Goldschmidt, *As You Sow*, 282–284.

13 Goldschmidt, *As You Sow*, 420.

14 Ibid., 421.

15 See C. Wright Mills and Melville J. Ulmer, *Small Business and Civic Welfare: Report of the Smaller War Plants Corporation to the Special Senate Committee to Study Problems of American Small Business, United States Senate* (Washington, DC: U.S. Government Printing Office, 1946).

16 Paul Wallace Gates, "The Role of the Land Speculator in Western Development," *The Pennsylvania Magazine of History and Biography* 66, no. 3 (July 1942): 314.

17 Small Farm Viability Project, "The Family Farm in California: Report of the Small Farm Viability Project" (Sacramento: The Governor's Office of Planning and Research [Employment Development], Department of Food and Agriculture and Department of Housing and Community Development, 1977).

18 William D. Heffernan, "Structure of Agriculture and Quality of Life in Rural Communities." In *Rural Society in the U.S.: Issues for the 1980s*, eds. Don A. Dillman and Daryl J. Hobbs (Boulder, CO: Westview Press, 1982), 340.

19 Wendell Berry, *The Unsettling of America: Culture & Agriculture* (San Francisco: Sierra Club Books, 1977), 172.

20 Numerous studies and academic papers have validated and supported Gold-schmidt's original case study's findings. They include the following (full citations are listed in the references section of this book): Buttel (1980, 1983; Crowley and Roseigno (2004); Deller (2003); Durrenberger and Thu (1996); Flora and Flora (1988); Fujimoto (1977); Goldman et al. (1977); Heady and Sonka (1974); Heffernan (1972, 1982); LaRose (1972); Lobao (1990); Lyson et al. (2001); MacCannell (1983, 1986, 1988); MacCannell and Dolber-Smith (1988); MacCannell and White (1981, 1984); Martinson et al. (1976); Poole (1981); Rodefeld (1974); Smithers et al. (2004); Theodoropoulou (1990); Thu and Durrenberger (1998). Buttel in testimony before the U.S. Congress stated that a body of scholarship is "sufficiently solid and consistent so as to justify a most crucial conclusion: Larger-than-family tends to be associated with adverse social and economic conditions in agricultural communities" ("Farm Structure," 151).

21 Kirkendall, "Social Science in the Central Valley," 208.

22 Paul S. Taylor, "Walter Goldschmidt's Baptism by Fire: Central Valley Water Politics." In *Paths to the Symbolic Self. Essays in Honor of Walter Goldschmidt. Anthropology UCLA*, Vol. 8, eds. James Loucky and Jeffery R. Jones (Los Angeles: University of California, 1976), 136, 137.

23 Montgomery and Clawson, *History of Legislation and Policy Formation of the Central Valley Project.*

24 Ibid., 166.

25 Draft "Statement for the Committee on Small Business" sent to Paul Taylor by Walter Goldschmidt, Box 7, Folder 7: Goldschmidt, Walter Rochs, 1913–, Paul Schuster Taylor papers, BANC MSS 84/38 c, The Bancroft Library, University of California, Berkeley.

26 Ibid.

27 Ibid.

28 Goldschmidt, *As You Sow*, 455.

29 Ibid., 487. Italics in original.

30 Article attached to 11/27/78 letter in Box 7, Folder 7: Goldschmidt, Walter Rochs, 1913–, Paul Schuster Taylor papers, BANC MSS 84/38 c, The Bancroft Library, University of California, Berkeley. The article is a printed version of Goldschmidt's panel presentation to the September 1978 Rural Sociological Society, published as W. Goldschmidt, "Reflection on Arvin and Dinuba," *Rural Sociological Society* 6, no. 5 (Sept. 1978).

31 Kirkendall, "Social Science in the Central Valley," 206. For an excellent account of the BAE's work, see Jess Gilbert, *Planning Democracy: Agrarian Intellectuals and the Intended New Deal* (New Haven, CT: Yale University Press, 2015).

32 Article attached to 11/27/78 letter in Box 7, Folder 7: Goldschmidt, Walter Rochs, 1913—, Paul Schuster Taylor papers, BANC MSS 84/38 c, The Bancroft Library, University of California, Berkeley. The article is a printed version of Goldschmidt's panel presentation to the September 1978 Rural Sociological Society, published as W. Goldschmidt, "Reflection on Arvin and Dinuba," *Rural Sociological Society* 6,

no. 5 (Sept. 1978). Sheridan Downey's book, *They Would Rule the Valley*, was privately published in 1947 in San Francisco.

33 Ibid.

34 Taylor, "Walter Goldschmidt's Baptism by Fire," 138

35 Goldschmidt testimony is quoted in Goldschmidt, *As You Sow*, 487.

36 *Los Angeles Times*, "Debts Could End Family Farm Era" (Feb. 24, 1985), 10.

37 The blog was waltergoldschmidt.wordpress.com.

2. STUDY YOUR TARGETS

1 *Paul Schuster Taylor, California Social Scientist*, vol. 1, *Education, Field Research, and Family*, 329–330, 332–333. Interviews conducted in 1970 by Suzanne Reiss (Regional Oral History Office, The Bancroft Library, University of California, Berkeley, 1973. Vols. 2 and 3, *California Water and Agricultural Labor*, for which interviews were conducted by Malca Chall, were published in 1975). This oral history is hereafter cited as follows: "Taylor Oral History," with volume and page numbers.

2 Taylor Oral History, I: 334. The Marines in Taylor's regiment suffered 4,000 casualties in the Battle of Belleau Wood, including about 1,000 killed—the "largest number of casualties suffered by a single American brigade during the war." For their actions and bravery, they were awarded the French Croix de Guerre. Historians have viewed the battle as a turning point moment in military history. As they fought, the Marines "left behind fourteen decades of small-scale skirmishes with insurgents [and] pirates . . . and entered the industrialized world of massive fire power and wholesale slaughter." Michael E. Ruane, "The Battle of Belleau Wood Was Brutal, Deadly and Forgotten. But It Forged a New Marine Corps," *Washington Post*, May 31, 2018, https://www.washingtonpost.com.

3 Taylor Oral History, I: 77.

4 On the life and work of John Commons, see John Dennis Chase, *A Worker's Economist: John R. Commons and His Legacy from Progressivism to the War on Poverty* (New York: Transaction Publishers, 2017).

5 Taylor Oral History, I: 43, 44, 97–98, 97, 58, 97, 58–59.

6 On the cotton strike, see Cletus E. Daniel, *Bitter Harvest: A History of California Farmworkers, 1870–1941* (Berkeley: University of California Press, 1981); Devra Weber, *Dark Sweat, White Gold: California Farm Workers, Cotton, and the New Deal* (Berkeley: University of California Press, 1994); and Anne Loftis, *Witnesses to the Struggle: Imaging the 1930s California Labor Movement* (Reno: University of Nevada Press, 1998).

7 Taylor Oral History, II: 1–4.

8 Clark Kerr, "Preface," in Paul Taylor, *On the Ground in the Thirties* (Salt Lake City, UT: Peregrine Smith, 1983), vii–viii.

9 Paul S. Taylor, "Nonstatistical Notes from the Field," *Land Policy Review* V, no. 1 (U.S. Department of Agriculture, Bureau of Agricultural Economics, January 1942). Quoted here from *On the Ground in the Thirties*, 233. The entire article is republished in that book.

10   Taylor Oral History, I: 98–99.

11   Taylor Oral History, II: 102–103, 106–107, 103.

12   Taylor Oral History, I: 99; Taylor Oral History, II: 111, 110, 111, 110; Taylor Oral History, I: 99–100, 101, 103, 104, 105.

13   Taylor, *On the Ground in the Thirties*, ix.

14   Ibid.

15   On Lange's and Taylor's work, see Jan Goggans, *California on the Breadlines: Dorothea Lange, Paul Taylor, and the Making of a New Deal Narrative* (Berkeley: University of California Press, 2010) and Richard Steven Street, *Everyone Had Cameras: Photography and Farmworkers in California, 1850–2000* (Minneapolis: University of Minnesota Press, 2008). On Lange's life and work, see Linda Gordon, *Dorothea Lange: A Life Beyond Limits* (New York: W.W. Norton & Company, 2009).

16   Taylor Oral History, I: 126–127.

17   Ibid., 139, 142.

18   Ibid., 155.

19   Taylor Oral History, II: 13.

20   Paul S. Taylor, "The 160-Acre Water Limitation and the Water Resources Commission," *Western Political Quarterly* 3, no. 3 (Sept. 1950): 435.

21   Quoted in Paul S. Taylor, "Central Valley Project: Water and Land," *Western Political Quarterly* 2, no. 2 (June 1949), 239.

22   Quoted in Ibid., 240. Italics added by Taylor.

23   James B. Jamieson, Sidney Sonenblum, Werner Z. Hirsch, Merrill R. Goodall, and Harold Jaffe, *Some Political and Economic Aspects of Managing California Water Districts* (Los Angeles: Institute of Government and Public Affairs, UCLA, 1974), 211.

24   See D. David P. Billington, Donald C. Jackson, and Martin V. Melosi, *The History of Large Federal Dams: Planning, Design, and Construction* (Denver, CO: U.S. Department of Interior, 2005).

25   Taylor Oral History, I: 172–173, 312, 172–173, 171, 178.

26   Ibid., 181–183, 183–187.

27   Taylor Oral History, II: 158–160, 149–150.

28   Taylor Oral History, I: 170, 53, 170, 53; Taylor Oral History, II: 240–241, 252; Taylor Oral History, I: 189–190.

29   Taylor Oral History, III: 319, 323a–324, 325; Taylor Oral History, I: 190.

30   Taylor Oral History, III: 306, 308, 309–310, 311.

31   Paul S. Taylor, "The Excess Land Law: Execution of a Public Policy," *Yale Law Journal* 64, no. 4 (Feb. 1955), 484.

32   Paul S. Taylor, "Destruction of Federal Reclamation Policy? The Ivanhoe Case," *Stanford Law Review* 10, no. 1 (Dec. 1957), 92.

33   Ibid., 82. Italics in original.

34   Quoted in ibid. Emphasis added by Taylor.

35   Paul S. Taylor, "The Excess Land Law: Pressure vs. Principle." *California Law Review*, Vol. 47, no. 3 (Aug., 1959), 500.

36 Taylor, "Destruction of Federal Reclamation Policy? The Ivanhoe Case," 94–95.
37 Ibid., 95.
38 Paul S. Taylor, "Excess Land Law: Calculated Circumvention," *California Law Review*, 52, no. 5 (December 1964), 986.
39 Ibid., 1007.
40 Ibid., 982.
41 Paul W. Gates, "Foreword," in Paul S. Taylor, *Essays on Land, Water and the Law in California* (New York: Arno Press, 1979), iv.
42 Taylor Oral History, I: 179–180.
43 Ibid., 191–192.
44 Ibid., 319–320, 315.
45 Ibid., 302–303, 314, 313, 314, 317, 317–318.
46 Ibid., 315.
47 Ibid., 313, 316, 303, 312, 313, 303, 304, 313, 304, 305, 311–312, 319.
48 Taylor Oral History, II: 67–68, 70; Taylor Oral History, III: 383–385, 391.
49 Paul S. Taylor, "The Relation of Research to Legislative and Administrative Decisions," *Journal of Social Issues* (Fall 1947), 52.
50 Taylor Oral History, III: 500–502, 504.

3. TERROR AS EDUCATION

1 Galarza tells the story of his youth in *Barrio Boy* (Notre Dame, IN: University of Notre Dame Press, 2011). For a brief biography and selection of Galarza's writings, see *Man of Fire: Selected Writings*, eds. Armando Ibarra and Rodolfo D. Torres (Urbana: University of Illinois Press, 2017).
2 Ernesto Galarza, "The Burning Light: Action and Organizing in the Mexican Community in California," an oral history conducted in 1977, 1978, and 1981 by Gabrielle Morris and Timothy Beard, Regional Oral History Office, The Bancroft Library, University of California, Berkeley, 1982, 1.
3 *Common Ground*, 28–29, Box 1, Folder 8: Articles 1944–1959, Ernesto Galarza Papers, M0224, Dept. of Special Collections, Stanford University Libraries, Stanford, CA.
4 Galarza, "The Burning Light," 16.
5 Joan London and Henry Anderson, *So Shall Ye Reap: The Story of Cesar Chavez & the Farm Workers' Movement* (New York: Thomas Y. Crowell Company, 1970), 123.
6 Ibid.
7 Galarza, "The Burning Light," 4–5.
8 Ibid., 19–20.
9 For extensive resources related to the Bracero program, see The Bracero History Archive: http://braceroarchive.org/.
10 Box 1, Folder 8: Articles 1944–1959, 1–2. Ernesto Galarza Papers, M0224, Dept. of Special Collections, Stanford University Libraries, Stanford, CA.
11 Ernesto Galarza, *Farm Workers and Agri-business in California, 1947–1960* (Notre Dame, IN: University of Notre Dame Press, 1977), 251.

12 Box 2, Folder 8: *Strangers in Our Fields*, Correspondence 1955–1956. Ernesto Galarza Papers, M0224, Dept. of Special Collections, Stanford University Libraries, Stanford, CA.

13 Ibid.

14 Ernesto Galarza, *Strangers in Our Fields* (Washington, DC: Joint United States-Mexico Trade Union Committee, 1957), iv.

15 Ibid., 75.

16 Ibid., 1.

17 Ernesto Galarza, *Merchants of Labor: The Mexican Bracero Story* (Charlotte, NC: McNally & Loftin, 1964), 16.

18 Ibid., 107. Here, Galarza is citing the California Census of Agriculture.

19 Ibid., 232.

20 Box 1, Folder 3: Correspondence 1938–1980. Ernesto Galarza Papers, M0224, Dept. of Special Collections, Stanford University Libraries, Stanford, CA.

21 Ibid.

22 Ernesto Galarza, *Spiders in the House and Workers in the Field* (Notre Dame, IN: University of Notre Dame Press, 1970), 243.

23 In *Spiders in the House and Workers in the Field*, Galarza refers to himself in the third person, as "Galarza."

24 Galarza, *Spiders in the House and Workers in the Field*, 51.

25 Ibid., 53.

26 Ibid., 57–58. Italics in original.

27 Ibid., 143.

28 Ibid., 59.

29 Ibid., 66, 69.

30 Ibid., 149–150.

31 Ibid., 273.

32 Galarza, *Farm Workers and Agri-business in California*, xiii.

33 Ibid., xii–xiii.

34 Ibid., 352.

35 Galarza, *Spiders in the House*, 75.

36 Ibid., 74.

37 Galarza, *Farm Workers and Agri-business in California*, 355.

38 For details on Galarza's team's action research methods, see Mario Barrera and Geralda Vialpando, *Action Research in Defense of the Barrio: Interviews with Ernesto Galarza, Guillermo Flores and Rosalio Muñoz* (Los Angeles: Aztlán Publications Pamphlet, 1974).

39 Galarza, *Farm Workers and Agri-business in California*, 20.

40 Ibid., 350.

41 Galarza, "The Burning Light," 28.

42 Ibid., 34.

43 Ibid., 36–37.

44 Ibid., 38–48.

45 Ibid., 46–48.

46 Ibid., 107–108.

47 On Fred Ross, a key organizer in the California farmworker struggles, see Gabriel Thompson, *America's Social Arsonist: Fred Ross and Grassroots Organizing in the Twentieth Century* (Berkeley: University of California Press, 2016).

48 Galarza, "The Burning Light," 11–12.

4. IN FRONT OF THE BAYONET

1 See Frank Young, "Macrosocial Accounting for Developing Countries," *Sociologia Ruralis* 12, nos. 3–4 (1972): 288–301, and Dean MacCannell, "The Elementary Structures of Community: Macrosocial Accounting as a Method for Community Analysis and Policy Formation," in *Community Development Research: Concepts, Issues, and Strategies*, edited by Edward J. Blakeley (New York: Behavioral Sciences Press, 1979).

2 Dean MacCannell, "Industrial Agriculture and Rural Community Degradation," in *Agriculture and Community Change in the U.S.: The Congressional Research Reports*, edited by Lou Swanson (Boulder, CO: Westview Press, 1988), 15–16.

3 Frank Young, "Location and Reputation in a Mexican Village Network," *Human Organization* 23, no. 1 (1964): 40.

4 Ibid., 36.

5 Frank Young and Isao Fujimoto, "Social Differentiation in Latin American Communities," *Economic Development and Cultural Change* 13, no. 3 (1965), 344–346.

6 MacCannell, "The Elementary Structures of Community," 43. Italics in original.

7 Ibid., 34.

8 MacCannell's book, *The Tourist: A New Theory of the Leisure Class*, was originally published in 1976 by Schocken Books. A fourth edition of this groundbreaking, influential book was published in 2013 by the University of California Press.

9 Dean MacCannell and Jerry White, "On the Relationship of Agriculture to Rural Community Conditions in California" (Davis: University of California, Department of Applied Behavioral Economics, 1981), 1. This report is cited in Fred Buttel, "Farm Structure and the Quality of Life in Agricultural Communities: A Review of Literature and a Look Toward the Future," in *Agricultural Communities: The Interrelationship of Agriculture, Business, Industry, and Government in the Rural Economy, A Symposium*, prepared by the Congressional Research Service Library of Congress for the Committee on Agriculture U.S. House of Representatives (Washington, DC: U.S. Government Printing Office, 1983).

10 Dean MacCannell and Jerry White, *The Relationship of Agriculture to Rural Community Conditions in California* (Davis: University of California, Department of Applied Behavior Sciences, 1981), 32–33.

11 Ibid., 34.

12 Ibid., 35.

13 Dean MacCannell and Jerry White, "The Social Costs of Large-Scale Agriculture and the Prospects for Land Reform in California," in *Land Reform, American*

Style, edited by Charles C. Geisler and Frank J. Popper (Totowa, NJ: Rowman and Allanheld, 1984).

14 Paul Taylor had recommended the Westlands towns of Mendota or Firebaugh over Arvin for Walter Goldschmidt's original study.

15 MacCannell and White, "The Social Costs of Large-Scale Agriculture," 39.

16 Ibid., 35.

17 Ibid., 43.

18 Ibid., 45.

19 Ibid., 46.

20 Quoted in Ibid., 38.

21 Ibid., 37.

22 Ibid., 52.

23 Ibid., 38.

24 Ibid., 53.

25 Dean MacCannell and Edward Dolber-Smith, "Report on Social Conditions in the Rural Communities of the Most Agricultural Regions of the Sun Belt," Background Papers for the United States Congress, Office of Technology Assessment, Technology Public Policy and the Changing Structure of American Agriculture (Washington, DC: U.S. Government Printing Office, 1986), and Dean MacCannell, "The CATF Region," in the United States Congress, Office of Technology Assessment, *Technology, Public Policy and the Changing Structure of American Agriculture*, OTA-F-285 (Washington, DC: U.S. Government Printing Office, March, 1986), 223–227 and 247.

26 MacCannell, "Industrial Agriculture and Rural Community Degradation," 44.

27 Ibid., 55.

28 Ibid., 45.

29 Ibid., 42.

30 Ibid., 35.

31 Ibid., 26.

32 Ibid., 45.

33 Ibid., 62–63.

34 Ibid., 42.

35 Ibid., 15.

36 Luther Tweeten, "The Economics of Small Farms," *Science* 219, no. 4588 (March 4, 1983), 1037–1041.

37 See Michael N. Hayes and Alan L. Olmstead "Farm Size and Community Quality: Arvin and Dinuba Revisited," *American Journal of Agricultural Economics* 66 (1984): 430–436. (On May 19, 2014, Alan Olmstead presented at a Giannini Foundation conference titled, "Climate Change: Challenges to California's Agriculture and Natural Resources," in Sacramento, California. During a break after his panel, I introduced myself and described my doctoral research, then I asked him, "Do you have any regrets about contradicting Goldschmidt's hypothesis given what transpired in the valley since then, the region's devastating poverty

and pollution?" Olmstead paused, and answered, "In principle he [Goldschmidt] is right, he just couldn't draw those conclusions from the data he had.")

38 In practice 160 was expanded to 320 acres, for a husband and wife farming together.

39 Congressman Vic Fazio, Democrat, was Representative of the district in the U.S. House of Representatives.

40 In *California Water: A New Political Economy* (Montclair, NJ: Allanheld, Osmun, and Co., 1978), Merrill Goodall, Timothy De Young, and John D. Sullivan described special districts as "legally constituted government entities" (5). In *The Water Districts of California* (Sacramento, CA: Association of California Water Agencies, 1979), Charles D. Hobbs later called them "invisible governments" (48). Special districts are endowed with public sanction and responsibilities including the right to sue and be sued, acquire real and personal property, hire employees, enter into contracts, use eminent domain, levy user fees, and tax. See Charles E. Phelps, Nancy Young Moore, and Morlie Hammer Graubard, *Efficient Water Use in California: Water Rights, Water Districts, and Water Transfers* (Santa Monica, CA: Rand Corp., 1978). Essentially, special districts have the same powers as city or county governments. As a special district, California Water Districts stand out with their undemocratic, property-based system of representation as they are formed through a petition of landowners representing the majority of the area of the proposed district followed by a vote of landowners in an election. Voting landowners are given one vote for each $100 of assessed land value (James B. Jamieson, Sidney Sonenblum, Werner Z. Hirsch, Merrill R. Goodall, and Harold Jaffe, *Some Political and Economic Aspects of Managing California Water Districts* [Los Angeles, CA: Institute of Government and Public Affairs, UCLA, 1974, Report No. 190], 41). Due to this system, it is possible for a few large landowners to propose, elect, and then control a California Water District. Since California Water Districts were enabled under statutes that restricted voting by requiring a property qualification, they appear to be unconstitutional. The Fourteenth Amendment to the Constitution states, "No State shall make or enforce any law which shall abridge the privileges or immunities of citizens of the United States . . . nor deny to any person within its jurisdiction the equal protection of the laws." Even more explicit, the California Constitution ensures, "No property qualifications shall ever be required for any person to vote or hold office." State and federal courts have, however, supported the undemocratic nature of special districts. In 1972, the California Supreme Court ruled in *Salyer Land Co. et al. v. Tulare Lake Basin Water Storage District* that a limited franchise was permissible to only landlords who had "a direct, primary and substantial interest in its governance" (Jamieson et al., 165). This case was appealed to the United States Supreme Court, which found, using circular logic, that "the voter qualification statutes for California water storage district elections are rationally based, and therefore do not violate the Equal Protection Clause." Justice Douglas, in his

dissent, said the abuses of corporate voting were "unthinkable in terms of the American traditions that corporations should be admitted to the franchise .... The result is a corporate political Kingdom undreamed of by those who wrote our Constitution" (Jamieson et al., 166).

5. TAKE A BATH AMONG THE PEOPLE

1 "Labor's Dwindling Harvest: The Impact of Mechanization on California Fruit and Vegetable Workers," by Paul Barnett, Katherine Bertolucci, Don Villarejo, Regan Weaver and Cindy McNally, California Institute for Rural Studies, Davis, CA, 1978. The first report published by CIRS was "Imperial Valley: Land of Sunshine and Subsidies," by Paul Barnett.

2 The California Institute for Rural Studies website is www.cirsinc.org.

3 These studies can be found on the CIRS website www.cirsinc.org.

4 Don Villarejo, *Getting Bigger: Large Scale Farming in California* (Davis, CA: California Institute for Rural Studies, 1980). Available at https://donvillarejo.github. io. Villarejo was also sole or first author of three leading annual review journals: *Annual Review of Public Health, Occupational Medicine: State of the Art Reviews,* and *Maxcy-Rosenau-Last Public Health and Preventive Medicine,* 15th Edition. The latter is the distinguished "encyclopedia" of public health. He also offered expert witness testimony in both congressional committees and court trials.

5 CIRS website, http://www.cirsinc.org, retrieved on 11/6/10. As of the time of this writing (7/18/20), the mission has been slightly revised.

6 Don Villarejo, *Research for Action: A Guidebook to Public Records Investigation* (Davis, CA: California Institute for Rural Studies, 1980), iii.

7 Ibid.

8 Ibid., iv.

9 Public records investigations continue to be necessary in certain circumstances, and internet searches have their own limitations. Three examples, among many, illustrate this point. First, Yolo County does not make available the important Assessor's Roll of Secured Property, precluding searches of owners of record of real property by name. The reason given is to protect individual privacy. Second, the change of state law that formerly required public disclosure of all members of the Board of Directors of businesses incorporated under California law. Now, only the CEO and CFO must be disclosed. Finally, the growing and widespread use of "shell companies" set up outside U.S. jurisdiction had made it virtually impossible to track ownership of a portion of real property, especially of high-valued property. Some vital information is not available via the internet, despite widespread belief to the contrary.

10 Don Villarejo, Jude Crisfield, and Phyllis White, *New Lands for Agriculture: The California State Water Project* (Davis, CA: California Institute for Rural Studies, 1981).

11 Villarejo, Crisfield, and White, *New Lands for Agriculture,* 12.

12 Ibid., 10.

13 Ibid., 12.
14 Don Villarejo, *How Much Is Enough? Federal Water Subsidies and Agriculture in California's Central Valley* (Davis, CA: California Institute for Rural Studies, 1986); and Don Villarejo and Judith Redmond, *Missed Opportunities: Squandered Resources. Why Prosperity Brought by Water Doesn't Trickle Down in California's Central Valley* (Davis: California Institute for Rural Studies, 1988).
15 Mark Arax and Rick Wartzman, *The King of California: J. G. Boswell and the Making of a Secret American Empire* (New York: Public Affairs, 2003).
16 This request likely instigated the OTA studies that Harbridge House conducted and on which Dean MacCannell was hired as a research consultant.
17 Villarejo, *How Much Is Enough?*, ii.
18 Ibid., 1–3.
19 Ibid., 7.
20 These districts were: Arvin-Edison Water Storage District (Kern County), Delano-Earlimart Irrigation District (Kern & Tulare Counties), Feather Water District (Sutter County), Glenn-Colusa Irrigation District (Glenn & Colusa Counties), Kern-Tulare Water District (Kern & Tulare Counties), Lower Tule River Irrigation District (Tulare County), Orland-Artois Water District (Glenn County), Reclamation District No. 108 (Colusa & Yolo Counties), San Luis Water District (Fresno & Merced Counties), and Westlands Water District (Fresno & Kings Counties).
21 Villarejo, *How Much Is Enough?*, 19.
22 Ibid., 71.
23 Ibid., 72.
24 Ibid., 101.
25 Villarejo and Redmond, *Missed Opportunities: Squandered Resources*, iii.
26 Ibid., 44.
27 Ibid., 12.
28 Ibid., 48. Bold in the original.
29 Emmett P. Fiske, *The College and Its Constituency: Rural and Community Development at the University of California 1875–1978* (Ph.D. diss., University of California, Davis, 1979). Also see Jim Hightower, *Hard Tomatoes, Hard Times: The Failure of the Land Grant College Complex* (Washington, DC: Agribusiness Accountability Project, 1973).
30 Villarejo's Kellogg story was similar to one that arose from a profile O'Connell edited of Tom Lyson at Cornell University, published in Scott J. Peters, *Democracy and Higher Education: Traditions and Stories of Civic Engagement* (East Lansing, MI: Michigan State University Press, 2010). In that case, Dean David Call nixed a $750,000 Kellogg grant to fund a collaborative sustainable agriculture initiative that involved sustainable ag groups from around the state through that university's Farming Alternatives Program (FAP). Within a few years, the FAP program was discontinued under the ostensible

justification of a lack of funding. While framed as neutral institutions, there were and are political interests at play in public universities.

31 The website is https://donvillarejo.github.io.

6. WAR STORIES

1 Isao Fujimoto, *The People and the University: A Conference to Initiate the Redirection of Priorities for University Research* (Davis, CA: Department of Applied Behavioral Sciences, 1973), 37.

2 Emmett P. Fiske, *The College and Its Constituency: Rural and Community Development at the University of California 1875–1978* (Ph.D. diss., University of California, Davis, 1979), 433.

3 Quoted in Fiske, *The College and Its Constituency*, 434.

4 This lecture was filmed by the Human and Community Development Department at UC Davis.

5 For a detailed account of Isao's life story, see his memoir: Isao Fujimoto, *Bouncing Back: Community, Resilience & Curiosity* (Sacramento, CA: I Street Press, 2017).

6 On Ella Baker, see Charles M. Payne, *I've Got the Light of Freedom: The Organizing Tradition and the Mississippi Freedom Struggle* (Berkeley: University of California Press, 1995/2007), and Barbara Ransby, *Ella Baker and the Black Freedom Movement: A Radical Democratic Vision* (Chapel Hill, NC: University of North Carolina Press, 2003).

7 Richard S. Kirkendall, "Social Science in the Central Valley of California: An Episode." *California Historical Society Quarterly* 43, no. 3 (Sept. 1964), 195–218.

8 Alex McCalla was Dean and Associate Director of the California Agricultural Experiment Station from 1970 to 1975.

9 Isao Fujimoto and David Benaroya Helfant, eds., *Perspectives on Community* (Berkeley, CA: Citizen Action Press, 1978) iv.

10 Isao Fujimoto, "How Do We Relate Our Research to the Community?," in Fujimoto and Helfant, *Perspectives on Community*, 28.

11 Ibid.

12 Anonymous, "Journal Critique of ABS 151," in Fujimoto and Helfant, *Perspectives on Community*, 29–31.

13 Ibid., 31.

14 Davis Motion of the Ocean Super Collective, *Getting the Straight Dope: A Handbook for Action-Research in the Community* (Davis, CA: 1973), i.

15 Isao Fujimoto, "Some Guiding Assumptions," in Ibid., ii.

16 Ibid.

17 Laura Nadar, "Up the Anthropologist—Perspectives Gained from Studying Up," In *Reinventing Anthropology*, edited by Dell Hymes (New York: Pantheon Books, 1972), 284–310.

18 Fujimoto, "Some Guiding Assumptions", ii.

19 Ibid.

CONCLUSION

1 Merrill Goodall, "Water in California Agriculture," *Sustainable Agriculture* 5, no. 1 (Fall 1992). Goodall was a professor at Claremont Graduate University in its School of Politics and Economics. His book *California Water: A New Political Economy*, co-authored with John D. Sullivan and Timothy De Young and published in 1978, is an important resource to understanding the institutional structure of California's water districts.

BIBLIOGRAPHY

ARCHIVES AND ORAL HISTORIES

Ernesto Galarza Papers. M0224. Dept. of Special Collections. Stanford University Libraries, Stanford, CA.

Ernesto Galarza, "The Burning Light: Action and Organizing in the Mexican Community in California," an oral history conducted in 1977, 1978, and 1981 by Gabrielle Morris and Timothy Beard. Regional Oral History Office. The Bancroft Library. University of California, Berkeley, 1982.

Paul Schuster Taylor Papers. BANC MSS 84/38 c. The Bancroft Library. University of California, Berkeley.

Paul Schuster Taylor, California Social Scientist, Vol. 1, *Education, Field Research, and Family*, interviews conducted in 1970 by Suzanne Reiss (Regional Oral History Office, The Bancroft Library, University of California, Berkeley, 1973, Vols. 2 and 3, *California Water and Agricultural Labor*, interviews conducted in 1971 and 1972 by Malca Chall) (Regional Oral History Office, The Bancroft Library, University of California, Berkeley, 1975)

BOOKS AND ARTICLES

Anonymous. "Journal Critique of ABS 151." In *Perspectives on Community, edited by* Isao Fujimoto and David Benaroya Helfant. Berkeley, CA: Citizen Action Press, 1978.

Arax, Mark and Rick Wartzman. *The King of California: J. G. Boswell and the Making of a Secret American Empire*. New York: Public Affairs, 2003.

Barnett, Paul, "Imperial Valley: Land of Sunshine and Subsidies." California Institute For Rural Studies (available to download at www.cirsinc.org/publications/major-studies#), 1978.

Barnett, Paul, Katherine Bertolucci, Don Villarejo, Regan Weaver, and Cindy McNally, "Labor's Dwindling Harvest: The Impact of Mechanization on California Fruit and Vegetable Workers." Davis, CA: California Institute for Rural Studies, 1978 (available to download at www.cirsinc.org/publications/major-studies# http://cirsportal.org/wp-content/uploads/2019/10/Labors-Dwindling-Harvest.pdf).

Barrera, Mario and Geralda Vialpando, *Action Research in Defense of the Barrio: Interviews with Ernesto Galarza, Guillermo Flores, and Rosalio Muñoz*. Los Angeles: Aztlán Publications Pamphlet, 1974.

Berry, Wendell. *The Unsettling of America: Culture & Agriculture*. San Francisco: Sierra Club Books, 1977.

Billington, David P., Donald C. Jackson, and Martin V. Melosi. *The History of Large Federal Dams: Planning, Design, and Construction.* Denver, CO: U.S. Department of Interior, 2005.

Buttel, Fred. "Agricultural Structure and Rural Ecology: Towards a Political Economy of Rural Development." *Sociologia Ruralis* 20, no. 1/2 (1980): 44–62.

Buttel, Fred. "Farm Structure and the Quality of Life in Agricultural Communities: A Review of Literature and a Look Toward the Future." In *Agricultural Communities: The Interrelationship of Agriculture, Business, Industry, and Government in the Rural Economy, A Symposium.* Prepared by the Congressional Research Service Library of Congress for the Committee on Agriculture U.S. House of Representatives. Washington, D.C.: U.S. Government Printing Office, 1983.

Chase, John Dennis. *A Worker's Economist: John R. Commons and His Legacy from Progressivism to the War on Poverty.* New York: Transaction Publishers, 2017.

Commons, John R. *Institutional Economics: Its Place in Political Economy.* New York: Macmillan Company, 1934.

Crowley, Martha and Vincent J. Roscigno. "Farm Concentration, Political Economic Process and Stratification: The Case of the North Central U.S." *Journal of Political and Military Sociology* 32 (2004): 133–155.

Daniel, Cletus E. *Bitter Harvest: A History of California Farmworkers, 1870–1941.* Berkeley: University of California Press, 1981.

Davis Motion of the Ocean Super Collective. *Getting the Straight Dope: A Handbook for Action-Research in the Community.* Davis, CA: 1973.

Deller, Steven C., Brian W. Gould, and Bruce Jones. "Agriculture and Rural Economic Growth." *Journal of Agricultural and Applied Economics* 35, no. 3 (2003): 517–527.

Downey, Sheridan. *They Would Rule the Valley.* San Francisco: Published Privately, 1947.

Durrenberger, E. Paul and Kendall M. Thu. "The Expansion of Large Scale Hog Farming in Iowa: The Applicability of Goldschmidt's Findings Fifty Years Later." *Human Organization* 55, no. 4 (1996): 409–415.

Fiske, Emmett Preston. *The College and Its Constituency: Rural and Community Development at the University of California 1875–1978.* Ph.D. diss., University of California, Davis, 1979.

Fitzgerald, Deborah. *Every Farm a Factory: The Industrial Ideal in American Agriculture.* New Haven, CT: Yale University Press, 2003.

Flora, Cornelia Butler and Jan L. Flora. "Public Policy, Farm Size, and Community Well-Being in Farming Dependent Counties of the Plains." In *Agriculture and Community Change in the U.S.: The Congressional Research Reports,* edited by Louis E. Swanson. Boulder, CO: Westview Press, 1988.

Fujimoto, Isao. *The People and the University: A Conference to Initiate the Redirection of Priorities for University Research.* Davis, CA: Department of Applied Behavioral Sciences, 1973.

Fujimoto, Isao. "The Communities of the San Joaquin Valley: The Relation Between Scale of Farming, Water Use, and Quality of Life." Hearings before the

Subcommittee on Family Farms, Rural Development and Special Studies of the Committee on Agriculture, 95th Congress, first session. Washington, DC: U.S. Government Printing Office, 1977.

Fujimoto, Isao. "How Do We Relate Our Research to the Community?" In *Perspectives on Community*, edited by Isao Fujimoto and David Benaroya Helfant. Berkeley, CA: Citizen Action Press, 1978.

Fujimoto, Isao. *Dynamic Mosaic: California Central Valley Partnership's Collaborative Multiethnic Approach to Organizing Immigrant Communities*. Ph.D. diss., Cornell University, 2010.

Fujimoto, Isao. *Bouncing Back: Community, Resilience & Curiosity*. Sacramento, CA: I Street Press, 2017.

Fujimoto, Isao and David Benaroya Helfant, eds. *Perspectives on Community*. Berkeley, CA: Citizen Action Press, 1978.

Galarza, Ernesto. *Strangers in Our Fields*. Washington, DC: Joint United States-Mexico Trade Union Committee, 1957.

Galarza, Ernesto. *Merchants of Labor: The Mexican Bracero Story*. Charlotte, NC: Mc-Nally & Loftin, 1964.

Galarza, Ernesto. *Spiders in the House and Workers in the Field*. Notre Dame, IN: University of Notre Dame Press, 1970.

Galarza, Ernesto. *Farm Workers and Agri-business in California, 1947–1960*. Notre Dame, IN: University of Notre Dame Press, 1977.

Galarza, Ernesto. *Barrio Boy*. Notre Dame, IN: University of Notre Dame Press, 2011.

Galarza, Ernesto. *Man of Fire: Selected Writings*. Edited by Armando Ibarra and Rodolfo D. Torres. Urbana: University of Illinois Press, 2017.

Gates, Paul Wallace. "The Role of the Land Speculator in Western Development." *Pennsylvania Magazine of History and Biography* 66, no. 3 (1942).

Gates, Paul Wallace. "Foreword." In *Essays on Land, Water and the Law in California* by Paul S. Taylor. New York: Arno Press, 1979.

Geisler, Charles C. and Frank J. Popper, eds. *Land Reform, American Style*. Totowa, NJ: Rowman & Allanheld, 1984.

Gilbert, Jess. *Planning Democracy: Agrarian Intellectuals and the Intended New Deal*. New Haven, CT: Yale University Press, 2015.

Goggans, Jan. *California on the Breadlines: Dorothea Lange, Paul Taylor, and the Making of a New Deal Narrative*. Berkeley: University of California Press, 2010.

Goldman, G., D. McLeod, T. Nakazawa, and D. Strong. *Economic Effects of Excess Land Sales in the Westlands Water District*. Berkeley: University of California Special Publication No. 3214, 1977.

Goldschmidt, Walter. *As You Sow: Three Studies in the Social Consequences of Agribusiness*. Montclair, NJ: Allanheld, Osmun, & Co., 1978.

Goldschmidt, Walter. "Reflection on Arvin and Dinuba." *Rural Sociological Society* 6, no. 5 (Sept. 1978): 11-20.

Goodall, Merrill. "Water in California Agriculture." *Sustainable Agriculture* 5, no. 1 (Fall 1992).

Goodall, Merrill, Timothy De Young, and John D. Sullivan. *California Water: A New Political Economy*. Montclair, NJ: Allanheld, Osmun, and Co., 1978.

Gordon, Linda. *Dorothea Lange: A Life Beyond Limits*. New York: W.W. Norton & Company, 2009.

Gramsci, Antonio. *Selections from the Prison Notebooks*. New York: International Publishers, 1971.

Hayes, Michael N. and Alan L. Olmstead. "Farm Size and Community Quality: Arvin and Dinuba Revisited." *American Journal of Agricultural Economics* 66 (1984): 430–436.

Heady, Earl O. and Steven T. Sonka. "Farm Size, Rural Community Income and Consumer Welfare." *American Journal of Agricultural Economics* 56 (1974): 534–542.

Heffernan, William D. "Sociological Dimensions of Agricultural Structures in the United States." *Sociologia Ruralis* 12 (1972): 481–499.

Heffernan, William D. "Structure of Agriculture and Quality of Life in Rural Communities." In *Rural Society in the U.S.: Issues for the 1980s*, edited by Don A. Dillman and Daryl J. Hobbs. Boulder, CO: Westview Press, 1982.

Hightower, Jim. *Hard Tomatoes, Hard Times: The Failure of the Land Grant College Complex*. Washington, DC: Agribusiness Accountability Project, 1973.

Hobbs, Charles D. *The Water Districts of California*. Sacramento, CA: Association of California Water Agencies, 1979.

Igler, David. *Industrial Cowboys: Miller & Lux and the Transformation of the Far West, 1850–1920*. Berkeley: University of California Press, 2001.

Jamieson, James B., Sidney Sonenblum, Werner Z. Hirsch, Merrill R. Goodall, and Harold Jaffe. *Some Political and Economic Aspects of Managing California Water Districts*. Los Angeles, CA: Institute of Government and Public Affairs, UCLA, Report No. 190, 1974.

Kerr, Clark. "Preface." In *On the Ground in the Thirties* by Paul S. Taylor. Salt Lake City, UT: Peregrine Smith, 1983.

Kirkendall, Richard S. "Social Science in the Central Valley of California: An Episode." *California Historical Society Quarterly* 43, no. 3 (Sept. 1964): 195–218.

Lange, Dorothea and Paul S. Taylor. *American Exodus: A Record of Human Erosion*. New York: Reynal & Hitchcock, 1939.

LaRose, Bruce. "Arvin and Dinuba Revisited: A New Look at Community Structure and the Effects of Scale on Farm Operations." Hearings before the Subcommittee on Migratory Labor of the Committee on Labor and Public Welfare, United States Senate, 92nd Congress, First and Second Sessions, Farm Workers in Rural America, 1971–1972, Appendix, Part 5A, pp. 3355–3362. Washington: United States Government Printing Office, 1972.

Lobao, Linda M. *Locality and Inequality: Farm and Industry Structure and Socioeconomic Conditions*. Albany: The State University of New York Press, 1990.

Loftis, Anne. *Witnesses to the Struggle: Imaging the 1930s California Labor Movement*. Reno: University of Nevada Press, 1998.

London, Joan and Henry Anderson. *So Shall Ye Reap: The Story of Cesar Chavez & the Farm Workers' Movement*. New York: Thomas Y. Crowell Company, 1970.

Los Angeles Times. "Debts Could End Family Farm Era." Feb. 24, 1985.

Lynd, Robert Staughton, and Helen Merrell Lynd. *Middletown: A Study in American Culture*. New York: Harcourt, Brace, Jovanovich, 1929.

Lynd, Robert Staughton, and Helen Merrell Lynd. *Middletown in Transition: A Study in Cultural Conflicts*. New York: Harcourt, Brace, Jovanovich, 1937.

Lyson, Thomas A., Robert J. Torres, and Rick Welsh. "Scale of Agricultural Production, Civic Engagement, and Community Welfare." *Social Forces* 80, no. 1 (2001): 311–327.

MacCannell, Dean. "The Elementary Structures of Community: Macrosocial Accounting as a Method for Community Analysis and Policy Formation." In *Community Development Research: Concepts, Issues, and Strategies*, edited by Edward J. Blakeley. New York: Behavioral Sciences Press, 1979.

MacCannell, Dean. "The CATF Region." United States Congress, Office of Technology Assessment. *Technology, Public Policy and the Changing Structure of American Agriculture*, OTA-F-285. Washington, DC: U.S. Government Printing Office, March, 1986.

MacCannell, Dean. "Industrial Agriculture and Rural Community Degradation." In *Agriculture and Community Change in the U.S.: The Congressional Research Reports*, edited by Louis E. Swanson. Boulder, CO: Westview Press, 1988.

MacCannell, Dean. *The Tourist: A New Theory of the Leisure Class*. Berkeley: University of California Press, 2013.

MacCannell, Dean and Jerry White. *The Relationship of Agriculture to Rural Community Conditions in California*. Davis, CA: University of California, Department of Applied Behavior Sciences, 1981.

MacCannell, Dean and Jerry White. "The Social Costs of Large-Scale Agriculture and the Prospects for Land Reform in California." In *Land Reform, American Style*, edited by Charles C. Geisler and Frank J. Popper. Totowa, NJ: Rowman and Allanheld, 1984.

MacCannell, Dean and Edward Dolber-Smith. "Report on Social Conditions in the Rural Communities of the Most Agricultural Regions of the Sun Belt." *Background Papers for the United States Congress, Office of Technology Assessment, Technology Public Policy and the Changing Structure of American Agriculture*. Washington, DC: U.S. Government Printing Office, 1986.

McWilliams, Carey. *Factories in the Fields: The Story of Migratory Labor in California*. Boston, MA: Little, Brown and Company, 1939.

Martinson, Oscar B., Eugene A. Wilkening, and Richard D. Rodefeld. "Feelings of Powerlessness and Social Isolation among 'Large-Scale' Farm Personnel." *Rural Sociology* 41, no. 4 (1976): 452–472.

Mills, C. Wright and Melville J. Ulmer. *Small Business and Civic Welfare: Report of the Smaller War Plants Corporation to the Special Senate Committee to Study Problems of American Small Business, United States Senate*. Washington, DC: U.S. Government Printing Office, 1946.

Montgomery, Mary and Marion Clawson. *History of Legislation and Policy Formation of the Central Valley Project*. Berkeley, CA: USDA, Bureau of Agricultural Economics, 1946.

Nadar, Laura. "Up the Anthropologist—Perspectives Gained from Studying Up." In *Reinventing Anthropology*, edited by Dell Hymes. New York: Pantheon Books, 1972.

New York Times. "The Earth and the Fullness Thereof." July 6, 1947.

O'Connell, Daniel Joseph. *In the Struggle: Pedagogies of Politically Engaged Scholarship in the San Joaquin Valley of California*. Ph.D. diss., Cornell University, 2011.

Payne, Charles M. *I've Got the Light of Freedom: The Organizing Tradition and the Mississippi Freedom Struggle*. Berkeley: University of California Press, 1995/2007.

Peters, Scott J. *Democracy and Higher Education: Traditions and Stories of Civic Engagement*. East Lansing, MI: Michigan State University Press, 2010.

Phelps, Charles E., Nancy Young Moore, and Morlie Hammer Graubard. *Efficient Water Use in California: Water Rights, Water Districts, and Water Transfers*. Santa Monica, CA: Rand Corp., 1978.

Poole, Dennis L. "Farm Scale, Family Life and Community Participation." *Rural Sociology* 46, no. 1 (1981): 112–127.

Ransby, Barbara. *Ella Baker and the Black Freedom Movement: A Radical Democratic Vision*. Chapel Hill, NC: University of North Carolina Press, 2003.

Redmond, Judith and Don Villarejo. *Economic Conditions in the Farming and Food Processing Industries, West San Joaquin Valley*. Final Report Submitted to the San Joaquin Valley Drainage Program, Bureau of Reclamation, U.S. Department of Interior, 1987. https://cirsinc.org/.

Reisner, Marc. *Cadillac Desert: The American West and Its Disappearing Water*. New York: Penguin Books, 1986.

Rodefeld, Richard D. *The Changing Organization and Occupational Structure of Farming and the Implications for Farm Work Force Individuals, Families, and Communities*. Ph.D. diss., University of Wisconsin, Madison, 1974.

Ruane, Michael E. "The Battle of Belleau Wood Was Brutal, Deadly and Forgotten. But It Forged a New Marine Corps." *Washington Post*, May 31, 2018. www.washingtonpost.com.

Scheuring, Ann Foley. *Science and Service: A History of the Land-Grant University and Agriculture in California*. Oakland, CA: The Regents of the University of California, Division of Agriculture and Natural Resources, 1995.

Small Farm Viability Project. "The Family Farm in California: Report of the Small Farm Viability Project." Sacramento: The Governor's Office of Planning and Research (Employment Development), Department of Food and Agriculture and Department of Housing and Community Development, 1977.

Smithers, John, Paul Johnson, and Alun Joseph. "The Dynamics of Family Farming in North Huron County, Ontario. Part II: Farm-Community Interactions." *The Canadian Geographer* 48, no. 2 (2004): 209–224.

Steinbeck, John. *The Grapes of Wrath*. New York: The Viking Press, 1939.

Street, Richard Steven. *Everyone Had Cameras: Photography and Farmworkers in California, 1850–2000*. Minneapolis: University of Minnesota Press, 2008.

Taylor, Paul S. "Nonstatistical Notes from the Field." *Land Policy Review* V, no. 1 (January 1942).

Taylor, Paul S. "The Relation of Research to Legislative and Administrative Decisions." *Journal of Social Issues* (Fall 1947).

Taylor, Paul S. "Central Valley Project: Water and Land." *Western Political Quarterly* 2, no. 2 (June 1949).

Taylor, Paul S. "The 160-Acre Water Limitation and the Water Resources Commission." *Western Political Quarterly* 3, no. 3 (Sept. 1950).

Taylor, Paul S. "The Excess Land Law: Execution of a Public Policy." *Yale Law Journal* 64, no. 4 (Feb. 1955).

Taylor, Paul S. "Destruction of Federal Reclamation Policy? The Ivanhoe Case." *Stanford Law Review* 10, no. 1 (Dec. 1957).

Taylor, Paul S. "The Excess Land Law: Pressure vs. Principle." *California Law Review* 47, no. 3 (Aug. 1959).

Taylor, Paul S. "Excess Land Law: Calculated Circumvention." *California Law Review* 52, no. 5 (Dec. 1964).

Taylor, Paul S. "Walter Goldschmidt's Baptism by Fire: Central Valley Water Politics." In *Paths to the Symbolic Self: Essays in Honor of Walter Goldschmidt. Anthropology UCLA*, Vol. 8, edited by James Loucky and Jeffery R. Jones. Los Angeles: University of California, 1976.

Taylor, Paul S. *Essays on Land, Water and the Law in California*. New York: Arno Press, 1979.

Taylor, Paul S. *On the Ground in the Thirties*. Salt Lake City, UT: Peregrine Smith Books, 1983.

Theodoropoulos, Helen. *The Effects of Agriculture and Ethnicity of Residents on the Social Conditions of Rural Communities in San Joaquin Valley, California*. Ph.D. diss., University of California, Davis, 1990.

Thompson, Gabriel. *America's Social Arsonist: Fred Ross and Grassroots Organizing in the Twentieth Century*. Berkeley: University of California Press, 2016.

Thu, Kendall M. and E. Paul Durrenberger, eds. *Pigs, Profits and Rural Communities*. Albany: State University of New York Press, 1998.

Tweeten, Luther. "The Economics of Small Farms." *Science* 219, no. 4588 (March 1983): 1037–1041.

Villarejo, Don. *Getting Bigger: Large Scale Farming in California*. Davis, CA: California Institute for Rural Studies, 1980. Available at https://donvillarejo .github.io/.

Villarejo, Don. *Research for Action: A Guidebook to Public Records Investigation*. Davis, CA: California Institute for Rural Studies, 1980. Available at https://donvillarejo .github.io/.

Villarejo, Don. *How Much is Enough? Federal Water Subsidies and Agriculture in California's Central Valley*. Davis, CA: California Institute for Rural Studies, 1986. Available at https://donvillarejo.github.io/.

Villarejo, Don, Jude Crisfield, and Phyllis White. *New Lands for Agriculture: The California State Water Project*. Davis, CA: California Institute for Rural Studies, 1981. Available at https://donvillarejo.github.io/.

Villarejo, Don and Stephanie Mandel. *Some Factors Influencing Agricultural Water Demand in California's Central Valley*. Final Report Submitted to the San Joaquin Water Drainage Program, Bureau of Reclamation, U.S. Department of Interior, 1986.

Villarejo, Don and Judith Redmond. *Missed Opportunities: Squandered Resources. Why Prosperity Brought by Water Doesn't Trickle Down in California's Central Valley*. Davis, CA: California Institute for Rural Studies, 1988. Available at https://donvillarejo.github.io/.

Villarejo, Don and Dave Runsten. *California's Agricultural Dilemma: Higher Production and Lower Wages*. Davis, CA: California Institute for Rural Studies, 1993. Available at https://donvillarejo.github.io/publications.html.

Walker, Richard A. *The Conquest of Bread: 150 Years of Agribusiness in California*. New York: New Press, 2004.

Wartzman, Rick. *Obscene in the Extreme: The Burning and Banning of John Steinbeck's The Grapes of Wrath*. New York: PublicAffairs, 2008.

Weber, Devra. *Dark Sweat, White Gold: California Farm Workers, Cotton, and the New Deal*. Berkeley: University of California Press, 1994.

Wilson, Edwin E., Marion Clawson, and United States Bureau of Agricultural Economics. *Agricultural Land Ownership and Operation in the Southern San Joaquin Valley*. Berkeley, CA, 1945.

Wischemann, Trudy. "The Role of Land Tenure in Regional Development: Arvin and Dinuba Revisited." *California Geographical Society* XXX (1990): 25–51.

Wischemann, Trudy. "Seeing the Invisible: Mega-Farms and the Rural Communities of California. Interim Report to the California Council for the Humanities." Davis, CA: California Institute for Rural Studies, 1991.

Young, Frank W. "Location and Reputation in a Mexican Village Network." *Human Organization* 23, no. 1 (1964): 36–41.

Young, Frank W. "Macrosocial Accounting for Developing Countries." *Sociologia Ruralis* 12, nos. 3–4 (1972): 288–301.

Young, Frank W. and Isao Fujimoto. "Social Differentiation in Latin American communities." *Economic Development and Cultural Change* 13, no. 3 (1965): 344–346.

Young, Frank W. and Dean MacCannell. "Structural Differentiation of Communities: An Aerial Photographic Analysis." *Rural Sociology* 32, no. 2 (1967): 334–345.

INDEX

Page numbers in *italics* indicate Figures and Photos.

ABOUT THE AUTHORS

DANIEL J. O'CONNELL is executive director of the Central Valley Partnership, a regional nonprofit organization and progressive network of labor unions, environmental organizations, and community groups spanning the San Joaquin Valley. Trained as a multidisciplinary ethnographer, he holds an M.S. in International Agricultural Development from University of California, Davis, and a Ph.D. in Education from Cornell University. As a politically engaged scholar, his work is dedicated to achieving social, racial, environmental, and economic justice in California.

SCOTT J. PETERS is a professor in the Department of Global Development at Cornell University and a historian of American higher education's public purposes and work. He has spent the past twenty years as a leader in the civic engagement movement in American higher education, most recently serving as faculty co-director of Imagining America: Artists and Scholars in Public Life (IA). He is the lead author of *Democracy and Higher Education: Traditions and Stories of Civic Engagement.* He is also co-editor of the Cornell University Press book series Publicly Engaged Scholars: Identities, Purposes, and Practices.

Lightning Source UK Ltd.
Milton Keynes UK
UKHW020625110621
385328UK00005B/183

9 781613 321225